Oneness with Shiva

Meditate on the Self as the Self

(a supplement to the book Return to Oneness with Shiva)

By Acharya Ricardo B Serrano, R.Ac.

Oneness with Shiva

Meditate on the Self as the Self

(a supplement to the book Return to Oneness with Shiva)

By Acharya Ricardo B Serrano, R.Ac.

ISBN: 978-0-9880502-2-8

©All Rights Reserved

December 31, 2012

Holisticwebs.com

Disclaimer: The Siddha meditations, Hanuman Qigong, Meditation on Three Hearts, and Eight Extraordinary Meridians Qigong are not intended to replace expert medical care. Consult with your physician or licensed health care practitioner regarding the treatment of any medical condition. The author is not held responsible for any negative effects of the meditation practices.

Buenavista, Marinduque, Philippines

DEDICATION

This supplementary book to Return to Oneness with Shiva is dedicated to all the people whose life challenge is quieting the monkey mind (ego) to experience Self-realization which I believe can be attained by the grace of my Sadguru Nityananda and the application of Hanuman Qigong, Meditation on Three Hearts, Eight Extraordinary Meridians Qigong and Siddha meditation, repetition of the mantra *So'ham*, chanting OM NAMAH SHIVAYA and *Namo Kuan Shi Yin Pu Sa* mantra, *Da Bei Zhou*, study of scriptures, discipline, satsang, and service based on the Self-realization teachings of Kashmir Shaivism and Buddhism that are contained in this book.

Meditate on the Self as the Self. To become aware of So'ham, "I am That," is to attain oneness with the Higher Self. My Ishta Devata (chosen deity) is Goddess Saraswati. See Saraswati and Her Mantra, page 27-28

By opening your heart to universal unconditional love via the Shakti (Qi) of kundalini meditation, Qi-healing, shaktipat and Qigong, you become an angel of compassion. You experience the blissful heart opening through the back heart chakra like an angelic being spreading its wings and the universal light pouring and opening the chakras in the spine. - Acharya Ricardo B Serrano See *Sri Vidya Upasana*, p. 13 and *Hanuman Qigong*, p. 53
Chant *Namo Kuan Shi Yin Pu Sa* to cultivate the same compassion embodied by Kuan Yin Bodhisattva
"If there is anything that keeps the mind open to angel visits, and repels the ministry of ill, it is human love." - Nathaniel Parker Willis

Baha'i teachings state that there is no such physical place as heaven or hell, and emphasize the eternal journey of the soul towards oneness with God. They explain that references to "heaven" and "hell" in the Holy Scriptures of other religions are to be understood symbolically, describing states of nearness to and distance from God in this world and in the realms beyond. When we die, the condition of our souls determines our experience of the afterlife.

Heaven and hell are conditions within our own being. - Shoghi Effendi, Lights of Guidance, p.209

The essence of all the prophets of God is one and the same. - Baha'ulla

Meditation is the key for opening the doors of mysteries. - Abdul'Baha

Man, in reality, is a spiritual being, and only when he lives in the spirit is he truly happy. - Baha'i Writings

And with Thy love in my heart all the world's afflictions can in no wise alarm me. – Baha'ullah
Armed with the power of Thy name nothing can ever hurt me. - Baha'ullah

Thy name is my healing, O my God, and remembrance of Thee is my remedy. – Baha'ullah

We are connected to God through the Holy Spirit and the Manifestation of God (Christ, Krishna, Buddha, Baha'ullah, etc). See Baha'is *The Greatest Name* below and ringstone symbol, page 112

Baha'ullah, Divine Teacher of Ricardo B Serrano

Hamsa-So'ham Greatest Name - "Ya Baha'u'l-Abha" (*O Glory of the All-Glorious*)

In the beginning was the Word, and the Word was with God, and the Word was God. - John 1:1

Table of Contents

An Introduction to the Siddha Path 5

What is Kundalini (Shakti) Awakening? 9

What is the Self? 15 Swastika, seal of Buddha's Heart 19

How to Quiet the Mind 20

The Guru is the Means 23 Way of Qi 26

The Nectar of the Inner Self 29

Drugs and Self-Awareness 33 How to Experience Love Now 37

Who am I? 39 Experience Heaven Now 41

Theme of the Song Imagine 45

How to Conquer Death Now 49

Origin of the Heart (Hanuman Qigong) 53

Conclusion 57

Wei Qi Field in Qigong 62 Eight Extraordinary Meridians Qigong 65

A Diamond in the Rough 78 What is Sheng Zhen? 79 Sheng Zhen Gong 81

The Virgin and the Unicorn 82 The Great Invocation & Golden Elixir 83

Bhagawan Nityananda 84 Sri Devi Stotram 92 Mahashivaratri and Cannabis 96

To feel the Love of one's Soul 100 Let go our Ego 102

Atma (Soul) Yoga 103 Acknowledgements & Book References 104

Photos 105 Da Bei Zhou 109 Fanatical Attachment 110

Shiva Sutras & *So'ham* 111 Glossary 124 Yuan Shen 130

Psychic Self-defense 132 Enlightenment Qigong Forms 133

Jesus and Cannabis 136 Earth needs Love after Yolanda 137

Meditation on Three Hearts 139 About the Author 141

An Introduction to the Siddha Path

"Ignorance is the root cause of all suffering. It is also the forgetfulness of one's own Self." – Shankaracharya, Aparokshanubhuti, 17

"The supreme state, which may be attained on some paths after extreme hardship, can be attained without great difficulty on the Siddha path." – Yogashikha Upanishad 1.3

"No one saves us but ourselves. No one can and no one may. We ourselves must walk the path." – Buddha

"Buddhists believe that everyone can become a Buddha. Being a Buddha means being Awakened, free from delusions and sufferings, and perfect in wisdom and compassion." – Ven. Jian Hu, Introduction to Buddhism

"When one attains oneness with the higher soul you lose anger, insecurity, depression, anxiety, fear of old age and death. I am Spirit Soul. Aham Brahmasmi." – Acharya Ricardo B Serrano

The human soul fundamentally yearns to be happy. Moreover, it is apparent that attributes of health and happiness are very similar; both imply wholeness and balance.

Aristotle, the Greek philosopher, reflected on happiness over 2300 years ago. Aristotle described four levels of happiness: instant gratification, gratification through achievement, gratification through the contribution to others, and transcendent gratification. It is in this highest level of happiness that we live more consistently from a place of purpose and truth, using our signature strengths to serve others, and working in various creative ways for the good of the world.

Research shows that only 10% of our happiness is determined by circumstances. 40% is determined by our internal state of mind, and 50% is related to our genetics. So we have the opportunity to improve our happiness based on choices we make, thought patterns, and behaviours. We can also choose to be happy and healthy by being in the Qi flow via the practice of meditation and Qigong to quiet the reptilian part of the brain achieving the third and fourth levels of happiness - gratification through the contribution to others and transcendent gratification, respectively. How you feel is how you heal.

Bahá'u'lláh described God's purpose for man in the following way: "The purpose of God in creating man hath been, and will ever be, to enable him to know his Creator and to attain His Presence."

That aspect of Siddha Guru Swami Muktananda's teachings as shown from excerpts from his books: I AM THAT, The Mystery of the Mind, I Have Become Alive, Perfect Relationship, Kundalini: the Secret of Life, Does Death Really Exist?, Getting Rid of What You Haven't Got, and Guru Gita; is the philosophy of Kashmir Shaivism that is devoted to presenting a practical psychology of liberation. These teachings were revealed by Shiva and kept highly secret until the great Siddha Vasugupta disseminated them throughout the world. Many Siddhas in Vasugupta's lineage wrote works based on the Shiva Sutras.

Supreme Shiva Himself gave birth to the Shiva philosophy, and Vasuguptacharya, a great Siddha being and the head of a distinguished lineage, elaborated it. Shaivism teaches that Shiva and Shakti are the cause of the universe. They are not two but one. Shaivism tells us that Shiva is static, attributeless, and formless and Shakti is His dynamic aspect. Shiva is the seeker's ultimate goal.

This Shiva, who is also called Srikantha, is the Primordial Being of Shaivism. From Shiva came Vasugupta, Somananda, Uptalacharya, Lakshmanagupta, Ramakantha, Abhinavagupta, Kshemaraja, Yogaraja, Kallata, Pradyumna Bhatta, Prajnarjuna, Mahadeva Bhatta, Shrikantha Bhatta, Bhaskra, and other Siddhas. This lineage originating from Shiva has existed since time immemorial.

Why should we know the origin of rivers? Our duty is to bathe in them, to wash away our impurities, and to cool the heat of our bodies. In the same way, it is our duty to understand the sages, to contemplate their teachings, and to practice the sadhana (spiritual practices) which they have shown us. It is our duty to attain our own divinity, to become happy in the bliss of reunion with the Self, and to lead our lives with great freedom and joy. Above all, our task is to complete our journey to the Self. Harboring unnecessary doubts makes a person fall from the path.

The principal texts of Kashmir Shaivism such as Shiva Sutras, Spanda Karikas, and Pratyabhijnahridayam offer a practical and sure-fire roadmap of the divine leading to Self-realization. At the heart of the process of self-awareness is the presence of the Guru, a paramahamsa or self-realized master who, as the Shiva Sutras state, is the means to liberation. Kashmir Shaivism, as Swami Muktananda describes it in his books, revels in the play of consciousness and oneness as the reality of everything. God is everywhere; He is everything. Baba Muktananda writes, "The universe is a garden for us to roam in with love. It is not intended as a source of attachment, jealousy, hatred, or anxiety. These only destroy our equanimity. Give up all desires. If something comes, let it come; if something goes, let it go. It is all Shiva's play. This is not a mere universe; it is the image of Him. Knowing it as Shiva, love it. Meditate on the awareness that all conscious beings as well as inert matter are Shiva. Having the knowledge of Shiva, understand that the world is the embodiment of Him."

A Story: Mohini's forgetfulness and Lord Vishnu's mistaken identification

Once upon a time, two demons were terrorizing heaven. Even the greatest of the devas were powerless against them. In panic, the gods fled, taking refuge at the feet of Lord Vishnu. They appealed to Lord Vishnu for relief and shelter.

Vishnu appraised the situation and, through his power of yoga, saw that the demons had been granted a boon by Lord Shiva whereby they could be slain only by each other. Since they were brothers and fond of each other, this was unlikely. So Vishnu transformed himself into a beautiful woman named Mohini. This alluring creature then appeared before the two devils and batted her eyes.

The first demon said, "Marry me!"

The second demon said, No, marry me!"

Mohini looked at the two loathesome creatures, whose mouths were smeared and caked with blood, and said, "Hey, what kind of girl do you think I am? I can't marry both of you. I'll marry the one who's the strongest and most powerful."

Instantly the two demons set upon each other to see who would win Mohini's hand. The reverberations of their contest shook the universe; the sea sloshed from its bed, the sun fled into the netherworld, and the moon, which had always been romantically pale, turned a shade paler. For days and nights the battle raged. The devils clawed each other's faces and gouged each other's necks. Whenever one of them began to tire, Mohini would simply wink at him, and the battle would resume. At last both devils exhausted themselves and collapsed, dead at her feet.

Mohini, having accomplished her task, now made a fatal mistake. She looked at herself in a pool of water and thought, "My, what a beautiful woman I am. No wonder those monsters wanted my hand." And intoxicated with her own beauty, she sauntered off, regarding her reflection in every stream and pool. In fact, she soon forgot she had ever been Vishnu. She believed she was Mohini and she felt that such a beautiful woman was deserving of a husband. And so she approached the great Lord Shiva and offered to be his wife.

Shiva agreed to marry her, proposing they have Brahma, the Creator, wed them.

But when they approached Brahma to perform the ceremony, the hoary deity looked aghast. He said to Mohini, "You can't marry Shiva!"

"And why not?" Mohini asked.

"Because – you're Vishnu!"

The above humorous fable served a higher end. Baba Muktananda would always conclude by saying Mohini's forgetfulness and predicament are our own. Like Mohini, we are God, but we believe that we are not. Like Vishnu, we are the Self, the Lord of the universe, yet because of our mistaken identification with our body and mind, we think we are a beautiful woman – a doctor, a nurse, or a father or mother.

How did this backward transformation come about? God, by limiting his powers, becomes you and me. According to the Siddhas, all creatures of this world are different characters played by a single actor, God. As the Shiva Sutra 3.9 say, "The Self is an actor."

Additional meditation and Qigong practices included in the book:

Grounding and rooting to mother earth through the practice of Enlightenment Qigong forms especially *Meditation on Three Hearts*, Hanuman Qigong, Eight Extraordinary Meridians Qigong, and Drawing in Heaven and Earth via Wei Qi field activation are added to Siddha spiritual practices to balance the Shakti Qi flow in the body to be happy, build the Lightbody, psychic self-defense, samadhi and avoid post-kundalini syndromes often seen in yoga practitioners.

The "home of happiness" in the brain is our limbic system - or emotional brain. This is what determines feelings, motivation, drive, and affects our immune system. Studies have shown that how you feel is how you heal. The limbic system is a little bit like a young child who listens to everything going on - and then acts accordingly. So how we speak to others and to ourselves affects our limbic system - and therefore our emotions and our health. This is why positive self-talk and behaviours are so important. Are there actual specific health benefits of happiness?

Absolutely! We know people who are content in their work and relationships - especially those who are happy in marriage - also live longer, have lower blood pressure, sleep better, have more energy, heal faster, take fewer medications and have less stress-related and chronic illnesses than those who are not.

The story of Buddha Sakyamuni shows that no one saves us but ourselves, no one can and no one may, and that we ourselves must walk the path to awakening. I believe that his Self-realization or enlightenment (anuttara-samyak-sambodhi – supreme perfect wisdom) is the result of the union or oneness of his incarnated soul (Nirmanakaya) with the higher soul (Sambhogakaya) that is connected to the Divine Spark (Dharmakaya) within all of us.

The classical iconographic representation of the Buddha's realization shows him touching the earth with his right hand, and calling the earth to witness his attainment. And what is this attainment? It is realizing that our ultimate nature is nothing other than the three kayas or bodies of the Buddha nature – Nirmanakaya, Sambhogakaya and Dharmakaya of the Buddha. This is a realization in which we see that there is not, nor ever was, any ground for ego at all.

What is Kundalini (Shakti) Awakening?

"We do not meditate to attain God, because we have already attained Him. We meditate so that we can become aware of God manifest within us." – Swami Muktananda Paramahamsa

"To be Awakened means to see Reality as it is, not as we think it is. To see Reality is to gain true wisdom and this wisdom will free us. We are not trapped by external conditions, but by our misperceptions and prejudices. Whatever we do, our actions create reactions that come back to affect us. Because of this, we are responsible for our own actions. Also because of this, we are responsible for our own salvation. And exactly because of this, each one of us is capable of achieving Perfection. We just need to know how. The Dharma teaches us how. There are many ways of practice, many "Dharma gates" to achieve Enlightenment, and they all fall into these general categories: performing good deeds, meditation, and studying the Dharma." – Ven. Jian Hu, Introduction to Buddhism

Forms of Qi created in the body

Therefore, the high quality Zong Qi from the food (Gu Qi) we eat and from the air (Kong Qi) we breathe from nature supplement the Yuan Qi, balance, unblock and cleanse the Ying Qi in the meridians, and develop the energy bubble or Wei Qi field of Qigong practitioners which is necessary for healing and returning to oneness with the Higher Self.

Ocean waves release negative ions by breaking the surface tension of the water. Negative ions of hydrogen have more concentrated fresh air with abundant Kong Qi.

Today we have more positive ions, creating an imbalance. Positive in this instance being negative. Free radicals (positive ions) can be produced by: heating and cooling systems, TVs, radios, computers, exhaust, smoke, smog, radiation, and harmful chemicals. They damage cells and may affect the chances of cancer and increase aging. Plants (trees, green grass, gardens), mountains (forests), oceans, waterfalls, beaches and lakes all contain good, negative ions.

Sunshine, negative ions increase endorphins, the hormone that can help you feel better. Why do we feel so good walking or practicing Qigong in the woods, on a beach or near a river, breathing fresh air in the mountains, or just breathing fresh air after rain or storm? Simple … We feel like that due to benign properties of negative ions that are so abundant in these environments. Nature generates negative ions.

May the following excerpts from the book "Kundalini: the Secret of Life" by Swami Muktananda Paramahamsa enlighten those people seeking answers to a very important question: What is Kundalini (Shakti) awakening? I have included excerpts from the book "Kundalini: the Secret of Life" to describe a perspective from Kashmir Shaivism on the nature of Kundalini (Shakti) or Qi and its vital importance in spiritual awakening – a pathway to one's Self – as the Siddha way to return to oneness through the practice of meditation and Qigong.

Excerpts from Kundalini: the Secret of Life by Swami Muktananda Paramahamsa:

Almost every tradition speaks of Kundalini in one form or another and describes Kundalini in its own way. In Japanese it is called ki; in Chinese, chi (Qi); the scriptures of Christianity call it the Holy Spirit. What is Kundalini? It is the power of the Self, the power of Consciousness.

Kundalini is Shakti, supreme energy, whom the sages of India worship as the mother of the universe. Shakti is the consort of Shiva. She is the active aspect of the formless, attributeless Absolute. People who follow the tradition of bliss call her Ananda. Yogis make her the goal of their yoga. Devotees sing her name with love, and She becomes the object of their love. Enlightened men of knowledge perceive Her in all the forms and objects in the universe, and seeing everything as one in That, they merge in That. There is nothing higher, nothing greater, nothing more sublime and beautiful than Shakti. Dwelling within the center of the heart, She shines with all the colors of the morning sun, and when She is awakened within us, we can see Her there, blazing in all Her effulgence.

What is the nature of this Shakti? She is the supreme creative power of the Absolute Being. Just as heat, which has the power to burn, is not different from fire, Shakti, which has the power to create this universe, is identical with Parabrahman, the supreme Absolute. She is Brahman in the form of sound, the sound vibration of the Absolute, which manifested the universe…

The Shiva Sutras, the principal scripture of Kashmir Shaivism, state: "She is the willpower of God, the ever-young maiden called Uma." She is called ever-young because She is always playing; Her play is the creation, sustenance and dissolution of this world.

Another name for Kundalini is Chiti, universal Consciousness. The first aphorism of the Pratyabhijnahridayam, another of the principal scriptures of Shaivism, describes Her, saying, "Universal Consciousness creates this universe by Her own free will." Chiti is supremely independent. No one compels her to create this universe; She does it on Her own, in supreme freedom, without depending on anything outside. Moreover, as the second aphorism states: "She unfolds this universe upon Her own screen."

She creates this universe out of Her own being, and it is She Herself who becomes the universe. She becomes all the elements of the universe and enters into all the different forms that we see around us. She becomes the sun, the moon, the stars and fire to illuminate the cosmos which She creates. She becomes prana, the vital force, to keep all creatures, including humans and birds, alive; it is She who, to quench our thirst, becomes water. To satisfy our hunger, She becomes food. Whatever we see or don't see, whatever exists, right from the earth to the sky, is nothing but Chiti, nothing but Kundalini. It is that supreme energy which moves and animates all creatures, from the elephant to the tiniest ant. She enters each and every creature and thing that She creates, yet never loses Her identity or Her immaculate purity.

This divine power is the power of our own Self…

Kundalini is the support of our lives; it is She who makes everything work in our bodies…

A verse in the Shiva Mahimna Stotram says, "How can I describe You when You are beyond the mind, body and senses?" When the Self is limitless, unborn and eternal, how can It be known? Only through the medium of Shakti can we gain entry to the Self. Shakti is the pathway to God. Shakti is the face of Shiva. When we look at someone's face we know who he is; in the same way, when we perceive the Shakti working within, we come to know God.

That is why it is essential to awaken the inner Kundalini Shakti. According to Shaivism, when one acquires the strength of Kundalini, one expands infinitely, and one assimilates this whole universe; one is able to see the whole universe within one's Self. One no longer remains a limited, bound creature; one achieves total union with God. One merges with Shiva and becomes Shiva.

Although Kundalini pervades the human body, She has a special abode at the center of the body, in the muladhara chakra at the base of the spine...

Different modes of awakening the Kundalini have been described in the scriptures. However, the easiest and best method is through Shaktipat from the Guru, when the Guru directly transmits his own divine Shakti into the disciple. It is the divine function of the Guru to awaken the dormant Shakti; when the Guru transmits his power into a disciple, the inner aspect of Kundalini is automatically activated and set into operation.

Shaktipat is a great and divine science. It is the secret initiation of the greatest sages and has been passed on from Guru to disciple from the beginning of time...

If you want the Shakti to work with its full power, you have to take care of it. This Shakti creates a new life in man. After receiving it, you should be able to digest it. You should not lose it or throw it away by undisciplined living or by neglecting your sadhana (spiritual practice). Instead, you should try to understand it and enhance it. Meditation, chanting, the repetition of the mantra, faith and love for the Guru, a pure and regular life, all make the Shakti increase. Generally speaking, once you have received the Shakti, love for God and the desire for sadhana begin to arise in you on their own. The Shakti itself leads you on the proper path.

The samadhi that follows Kundalini awakening is not the kind of samadhi which makes you inert. It is a conscious samadhi; it makes you more alert, more aware. This state has been called in the Shiva Sutras: "The bliss of the world is the ecstasy of samadhi." In this state, one recognizes the presence of God in everything. The whole purpose of Kundalini awakening is to attain the natural samadhi while continuing to function in the world...

The awakened Kundalini transforms us on every level of our being, and this means that She will take care care of our worldly life as well. When Kundalini is awakened, She transforms our outlook and makes us see the world around us in a new way. What has seemed difficult and frustrating begins to seem enjoyable and full of flavor, and one has new enthusiasm for one's activities and pursuits.

Kundalini generates supreme friendliness among people. She makes us able to see each other as divine, to see our husband and wife, our friends and neighbors, our children and parents, as filled with God. She improves our daily life and makes perfect whatever is not perfect in our lives. Where you have deficiencies, She strengthens and fills you. She will make you able to look after your family in a better way and take care of your business or profession more skillfully and intelligently. She improves a student's memory and concentration. She makes an artist a better artist, a doctor a better doctor. Kundalini is the source of poetry, of music, of the power of intuitive reasoning, of the scientist's capacity of invention, of the statesman's ability to administrate. All talents, all inspiration, all creativity, lie in the womb of Kundalini, and when She is awakened, She releases great creative powers. There are people who after this awakening become great poets or compose significant philosophical works. For some, Kundalini takes the form of Lakshmi, the goddess of wealth, and they come into a lot of money. In others it takes the form of authority, and they become great leaders...

The truth is, this very body is the temple of God. There is no greater temple than this human body. Everyone should contemplate this and understand that God lies within him. Just as one says, "This is my property," or "This is my house," one should earn the right to say, "God is within me." Tukaram Maharaj said, "I went to look for God, but didn't find God. I myself became God. In this very body, God revealed Himself to me." And this is absolutely true.

This is the knowledge that arises as Kundalini merges in the sahasrara. This is the state of Parabhakti, supreme devotion, in which there is no devotee, no God, and no world, but only oneness. Just as a river, after flowing for a long time, merges in the ocean and becomes the ocean, when Kundalini has finished Her work and stabilized in the sahasrara, you become completely immersed in God. All your impurities and coverings are destroyed, and you take complete rest in the Self. The veil which made you see duality drops away, and you experience the world as a blissful play of Kundalini, a sport of God's energy. You see the universe as supremely blissful light, undifferentiated from yourself, and you remain unshakeable in this awareness. This is the state of liberation.

A being who has attained this state does not have to close his eyes and retire to a solitary place to get into samadhi. Whether he is meditating, eating, bathing, sleeping, whether he is alone or with others, he experiences the peace and joy of the Self. Whatever he sees is God, whatever he hears is God, whatever he tastes is God, whatever words he speaks are God's. In the midst of the world, he experiences the solitude of a cave, and in the midst of people, he experiences the bliss of samadhi. This the state which the Shiva Sutras describe as lokanandah samadhi sukham – "The bliss of the world is the ecstasy of samadhi."

It is to attain this that we should meditate, that we should have our Kundalini awakened. We do not meditate to attain God, because we have already attained Him. We meditate so that we can become aware of God manifest within us...

And this is why I always tell everyone, "Meditate on your Self, honor your Self, worship your Self for God dwells within you as you."

NOTE by Acharya Ricardo B Serrano: As an initiated Siddha yogi in the Nityananda lineage, I have included excerpts by my beloved Baba Muktananda's books because they are originally instrumental in my spiritual transformation 23 years ago (June 1989). I would recommend the practice of Enlightenment Qigong forms, as my contribution, to further build or enhance the foundational Shakti or Yuan Qi for healing and enlightenment. As you keep repeating the mantra *Hamsa*, as through the Guru's grace you become aware that it is going on within, the inner Kundalini energy, which has been dormant, awakens automatically.

The Upanishads say: "The Kundalini Shakti operates through the power of *Hamsa*, which is not different from the Self. *Hamsa* flows with the prana, and the prana flows through the nadis...

Divine Mother Lalitha Tripura Sundari

(See Sri Devi Khadgamala Stotram, page 92)

Guruji Amritananda Natha Saraswati

Raja Choudhury, Ricardo's kundalini teacher

After experiencing the bliss of samadhi through successfully awakening my kundalini and seven chakras returning to oneness with Divine Mother's grace under the guidance by my kundalini teacher **Raja Choudhury**, Gopi Krishna's theory that yoga and kundalini are interchangeable terms, that there is no yoga or union of individual consciousness with cosmic consciousness unless kundalini is activated, is experientially true.

As a Qigong teacher, I have integrated Qigong with kundalini meditation because Qigong builds the Yuan Qi and Wei Qi field, and grounds the practitioner to mother earth that are necessary for expansion of consciousness and avoidance of kundalini syndromes. Sri Vidya kundalini meditation powerfully boosts Qi-healing and Qigong practices when integrated together. **Read Awakening your Kundalini, p. 138 and my book "Return to Oneness with Shiva."**

"If the mind is not filled with divine light, bliss, and peace, then all the efforts of yoga are useless." – Aphorism No. 53, Fire without Fuel

The word Yoga is synonymous with Truth, One-ness, Samadhi, Nirvana, or Moksha.

"Moksa or liberation is nothing else but the awareness of one's true nature." - Abhinavagupta, Tantra I, p. 192

Forms of Qi created in the body

Qi is life-force that animates the forms of the world. It is the vibratory nature of life phenomena – the flow that is happening continuously at molecular, atomic and sub-atomic levels. In Japan it is called "ki," and in India, "prana" or "shakti." The ancient Egyptians referred to it as "ka," and the ancient Greeks as "pneuma." For Native Americans it is the "Great Spirit" and for Christians, the "Holy Spirit." In Africa it's known as "ashe" and in Hawaii as "ha" or "mana." Wilhelm Reich also called it as orgone, negative ions or negative entropy. The fundamental insight of Qigong and Chinese Medicine (acupuncture and herbal medicine) is that balanced and free-flowing Qi results in health; while stagnant or imbalanced Qi leads to disease.

Qigong and Inner Alchemy practitioners understand their bodies to be the meeting-place of Heaven and Earth, and actualize this by working with Heaven Qi and Earth Qi – drawing Heaven Qi down from above, and Earth Qi up from below through the five energy gateways – the entry points of Qi through the palms of the hands, soles of the feet and the crown. Also commonly used in Qigong practice is the Qi of mountains, lakes, rivers and trees. Even when we're not consciously doing Qigong practices, with every breath we take, we absorb Heaven Qi, and through the food we eat, we absorb Earth Qi.

> Qigong is the interchange of Qi between man and the universe.

How Are The Major Forms Of Qi Created Within The Body?

According to Chinese Medicine, the energy used to sustain our bodies is of two major types: (1) Congenital (or Prenatal) Qi, and (2) Acquired (or Postnatal) Qi. Congenital Qi is the Qi we were born with – the energy/intelligence that we inherited from our parents, and that is associated with DNA and RNA codes (our "karma" from previous lives). Congenital Qi includes both Jing/Essence and Yuan Qi (Original Qi), and is stored in the Kidneys. Acquired Qi, on the other hand, is the Qi that we generate within our lifetime from the air that we breathe, the food that we eat, and Qigong practice, and is associated primarily with the Lung and Spleen Organ-Systems. If our eating and breathing patterns are intelligent, and our Qigong practice strong, we can generate a surplus of Acquired Qi, which can then be used to supplement our Congenital Qi.

Included within the category of Acquired (Postnatal) Qi are: (1) Gu Qi – the essence of the food we eat; (2) Kong Qi – the energy of the air that we breathe; (3) Zong Qi (also called Pectoral Qi or Gathering Qi) – which is the combination of Gu Qi and Kong Qi; and (4) Zheng Qi (also called True Qi) – which includes both Ying Qi (also called Nutritive Qi), which is the Qi that flows through the meridians, and Wei Qi (also called Defensive Qi). The terminology is complex, but basically what is being described is the process by which the food that we eat and the air that we breathe are metabolized internally, to produce the Qi that flows through the meridians, and the Qi that flows outside of the meridians as protection.

It works something like this: The food that we eat is processed by the Spleen/Stomach Organ-System to produce Gu Qi. The air that we breathe is processed by the Lung Organ-System to produce Kong Qi. The essence of the food (Gu Qi) is sent up to the chest where it mixes with the essence of the air (Kong Qi) to produce Zong Qi. In terms of western physiology, this is the rough equivalent to the oxygenation of the blood that happens in the lungs. Supported by Yuan Qi (Congenital Qi, stored in the Kidneys), Zong Qi is then transformed into Zheng Qi (True Qi), which in its yin aspect becomes Ying Qi (what flows through the meridians) and in its yang aspect becomes Wei Qi (which protects us from external pathogens).

What is the Self?

"I am not this body; I am that same divine light of which the whole cosmos is an extension." – Mansur Mastana

The seven books of author Ricardo B Serrano cover the basics of advanced combination of meditation and enlightenment Qigong forms for attaining oneness with higher Self or Self-realization – to become a self-realized being (Zhenren) or Srivatsa symbolized by Swastika.

Swastika: Swa means higher self, asti means being, and ka is a suffix. The word maybe understood as "being with higher self." It symbolizes *Shakti*. It has an especially strong connection to Buddhism in India, which was then transmitted to China. The srivatsa is often found on Buddha sculptures, and it is believed to be a sign displayed by Buddhas to the people who first depicted it – a symbol with profound and heavenly meanings. It has been understood over the ages as a symbol of good luck, a symbol of purity, and other positive attributes.

Swastika represents the turning of the "Dharma Wheel," and thereby promotes goodwill, compassion, and generosity to all sentient beings.

"True compassion is letting go of the self and putting others first." – Buddha

"Take refuge in me (our inner consciousness) alone." – Lord Krishna

May the readers gain an understanding of a very important fact about the inner Self according to Kashmir Shaivism based from excerpts from "Getting Rid of What You Haven't Got" by Swami Muktananda Paramahamsa which describe that God is not outside of you but within you – when you are aware of the Self – by returning to oneness through meditation and Qigong.

Excerpts from Getting Rid of What You Haven't Got by Swami Muktananda Paramahamsa:

The truth is that we get what we have already got, not what we haven't got. We get rid of what is not – what we don't have – not what we have. This is Vedantic philosophy in its subtle and highest form. In Vedantic philosophy there is nothing to be done; the only important thing is understanding. Through understanding comes liberation.

A great philosopher-sage of our country, Shankaracharya, says in a Sanskrit verse: "The Self or soul is always present, it has always been there and will always be there; it is wrong to think that you got it just a while ago or will get it after you have done some spiritual practices." But, though the Self is eternally present within us, it appears as though it were not present, because we do not understand it and are not aware of it.

First we have to overcome our wrong idea. I say that we are not aware. We have made a mistake, as a result of which we don't achieve awareness of what is already there. Once we rectify our mistake, we will experience what we already have.

We look all over the place for the Self which is always present within. We look here and there, and there, and there. We look for inner consciousness, or we look for inner spaces in things which are outside us, and when we don't find them where they are not, we feel disappointed. The Self has always been there. No matter where you are, you can experience the Self as it has always been, right here and now. This is the awareness of subtle philosophical truths.

Another poet-saint says: "O man, look within, go into your own inner spaces, and you will see that the Self, the light of the Self, is reflected through the intellect." You will also realize that you are not the body, that you are not a separate entity, that you are something else. We should try to find out who is the seer, the observer, the knower of the waking state and the dream state; who remains separate from them while watching them; and who exists within. That is the highest truth. Anyone who experiences that truth, that truth as "I," as "I am That," becomes that very truth. Compared to this understanding, all spiritual practices are futile. Practices have a secondary place. The first place is occupied by knowledge, by this understanding, and it's enough just to hear it.

The fact is that the truth always exists, and we always have, already have, the Self within us. If it did not exist within us now, it would not be real, because something is real only if it exists all the time. This is something which one should try to grasp through refined intelligence. Anyone whose intellect has been refined can know the truth directly within himself. There is another poet-saint who sings, "Why are you looking for Him by wandering from forest to forest and mountain to mountain and temple to temple and place to place? Because He is right within you." Alakh is a word which means the invisible or impalpable, that which cannot be perceived by the mind or the intellect or the ego or the imagination. It is present in your heart; you have only to look there and you will see it, as you see your reflection in a mirror, as clearly as that.

One looks for it in the East, another in the West, but none is able to find it, because to find it you need a Guru who can show it to you and explain it to you. Without a Guru you can't perceive it. Manpuri says that the Lord is within – why do you wander from place to place in search of Him? This is Vedanta. It is Vedanta in its purest form, the philosophy called ajatavada. Another poet-saint says, "There is a great mystery which I cannot figure out: though the Lord is within everyone, yet we do not experience Him." God's light can actually be seen. Whether you are confronted with unity or diversity, you must remain aware that the same one being has become diverse, and you will be able to realize this truth if you can see within. Know that to be the supreme deity. He dwells right within your body, just as bubbles dwell in water.

Manpuri says that the Lord is within your body and yet you wander from place to place in search of Him. (It is just like somebody holding a child in his lap, who sends a town crier around to announce that the child has been lost.) So Manpuri says that God dwells right within your body, and yet you are seeking Him from place to place.

There was another ecstatic saint called Mansur Mastana. He used to soar in the inner spaces, and he saw the highest truth right there. He began to say, "Analhaq, analhaq, I am God, I am God, the truth is within me, the truth is within me, I am in the midst of truth, and the truth is in my midst!" He began to dance. "I have found it, I have found it, I have got it, I have got it!" The orthodox clerics, who never understand a thing, got after him accusing him of uttering blasphemous heresy, and Mansur said, "I do not mean to utter heresy. I am only speaking the truth which I have experienced directly. From that, an understanding has spontaneously arisen within: I am not this body; I am that same divine light of which the whole cosmos is an extension." He continued, "You may break a mosque, you may break a temple, you may break any other holy place, but you must not break the human heart, because there the Lord Himself dwells. Inside a temple you worship an idol, inside a mosque you worship the void, but in the temple of the heart the divine light is scintillating, sparkling all the time, and that is the true house of the Lord."

Because he said this, he was hanged, and he proclaimed the same truth even from the hanging noose. From there he began to shout: "Down with all priests, down with all scriptures. Fling them into water. Go around proclaiming fearlessly, 'I am God, I am God, I am God!' Mansur Mastana says, 'I have recognized my true Master in my own heart.'"

To many it is not given to hear of the Self.

Many, though they hear of it, do not understand it.

Wonderful is he who speaks of it.

Intelligent is he who learns of it.

Blessed is he who, taught by a great Guru,

is able to understand it.

- Katha Upanishad

What is it that keeps us from experiencing our Self all the time? It is our mind that is totally out of control which needs to quiet down through chanting, meditation and Qigong. The poet-saint Bhartrihari writes:

O my mind, my friend,

Because of your fickleness,

I descend into hell.

Because of your unsteadiness,

I ascend into heaven.

The ten directions cannot contain you.

And yet, never once, even by mistake,

Do you think of the Self within.

- Vairagya-Satakam, verses 70-71

* Self: the source of joy, being and Consciousness, the Witness of the other three states, the inner Knower, the One who illuminates our mind and understanding, the One who watches all our thoughts and deeds. Satchitananda. We are the Self.

* Grounding and rooting to mother earth through the practice of Enlightenment Qigong forms especially Hanuman Qigong, Meditation on Three Hearts and Eight Extraordinary Meridians Qigong are added to Siddha spiritual practices to balance the Shakti Qi flow in the body, avoid post-kundalini syndromes often seen in yoga practitioners and Self-realization.

Swastika, seal of Buddha's Heart

Swastika was a symbol of the revolving sun, infinity or continuing creation. Western cultures call it the wheel of light, in Mandarin Chinese it is called the WAN symbol. WAN is a homophone for ten thousand in Chinese and Japanese, a number often used to encompass all of the universe's creations. One of the oldest known Swastikas was painted on a Paleolithic cave at least 10,000 years ago. It was widely utilized in China, about 2000 years ago, when Buddhism was brought to China from India. During the Chinese Tang Dynasty, Empress Wu Zetian (684-704) decreed that the swastika would also be used as an alternative symbol of the Sun. In India, the swastika is an auspicious mark – worn as jewelry or marked on objects.

Swastiska, a symbol of Shiva Shakti. The vertical line in swastika indicates Swayambhu Jyotirlinga. This Shiva-linga is the main source of the origin of the world. The horizontal line indicates the extension of the world. The world has grown with the union of Shiva and Shakti.

For Western cultures the swastika was also a very important symbol. It is used mostly in the area of art in clothing, architecture, pottery, and sculpture. In ancient Greece we found it in many ancient pottery. In Eastern cultures, the swastika is a symbol of Buddha. In Buddhism, swastika is usually found in the images of Buddha on his chest (seal of the Buddha's heart – Shen, true Spirit, within the heart that manifests as loving-kindness), and the palms, or soles of feet and crown – five energy gateways where Qi or Shakti enters during meditation and Qigong.

Swastika represents the continuous movement – a movement like the movement of a windmill or a water mill, and a chakra. It continuously spins clockwise (energizing) and counter clockwise (sedating). When it turns clockwise it represents universe's energy, strength, and intelligence; when it turns counter clockwise it represents mercy. It also represents universal harmony and the balance of the opposites (yin – yang). Yuan Qi (Original Qi) is represented in the center of Swastika which indicates that opening the heart to the love or Qi of the universe aligned with the navel chakra connected to the center of earth, and the crown chakra connected to Yuan Shen or Original Spirit is the key to enlightenment or returning to oneness with higher Self. See *Atma Yoga*, p. 103; *Da Bei Zhou*, p. 109

The four arms of the swastika remind us that during the cycles of birth and death we may be born into any one of the four destinies: heavenly beings, human beings, animal beings, (including birds, bugs, and plants) and hellish beings and represents a higher inner meaning that our aim should be liberation (Self-realization or Soul-realization) and not rebirth.

The word Swastika is Sanskrit: swa means "higher self," asti means "being," and ka is a suffix. The word may be understood as "being with higher self." The seven books of author Ricardo B Serrano cover the basics of advanced combination of meditation and enlightenment Qigong forms for attaining oneness with higher Self or Self-realization – to become a numinous self-realized being (Zhenren) or Srivatsa symbolized by Swastika. See Atma (Soul) Yoga, p. 103 "Heal the soul first; then healing of the mind and body will follow." - Dr. Master Sha

When our practice harmonizes breath, postures or movements and hara (lower dantian) *kundalini shakti meditation* we become numinous Self-realized beings at one with the Dao. To become NUMINOUS is to seek everything in life that arouses the magical, spiritual or mystical in me and everyone I share it with.

How to Quiet the Mind

"One's own thought is one's world. What a person thinks is what he becomes – That is the eternal mystery. If the mind dwells within the supreme Self, One enjoys undying happiness." – Maitri Upanishad

Five Agreements (Toltec Wisdom) taught by Don Miguel Ruiz and Jose Ruiz:

1. Be impeccable with your word.
2. Don't take anything personally.
3. Don't make assumptions.
4. Always do your best.
5. Be skeptical but learn to listen.

The Five Levels of Attachment by Don Miguel Ruiz, Jr: Authentic Self, Preference, Identity, Internalization and Fanaticism, an expansion of the Five Agreements, are simply a framework to help us become aware of where we are at this moment in relation to the various things in our life. We can look at any situation and determine what is driving our thoughts and behavior as far as a particular attachment is concerned.

With awareness of how attached we are to a particular belief or idea, we regain something very important: our ability to make a choice, to say yes or no all over again. The true freedom we have as individuals is to be able to choose with full awareness of what we want and don't want, instead of allowing our knowledge to dictate what we are supposed to be or choose. Our freedom to choose is true freedom; it is free will. "Is knowledge controlling you, or are you controlling knowledge?" The answer is the truth of where I am at this moment, and the truth will set me free.

The key to all forms of transformation is awareness (the Authentic Self) with love and respect for self and others. To get a fuller understanding, please read "Fanatical Attachment", page 110

Our lives are filled with stress reflected by our mental attitude and emotional experience. Because of our own ignorance, instead of turning within to experience the love of Self we look for love, happiness, peace, joy and contentment outside where they are not.

May the following excerpts from "Mystery of the Mind" by Swami Muktananda Paramahamsa according to Kashmir Shaivism show that the one great obstacle in experiencing the joy and inner love of the Self within is the constant chatter of the ego-mind which quiets down by returning to oneness through the practice of chanting, meditation and Qigong with the help of the Shakti of the Guru.

Excerpts from Mystery of the Mind by Swami Muktananda Paramahamsa:

There is one great obstacle that keeps us from knowing the Self, and that is the mind. The mind veils the inner Self and hides it from us. It makes us feel that God is far away and that happiness must be found outside. Yet the same mind that separates us from the Self also helps us to reunite with it. That is why the ancient sages, who were true psychologists, concluded that the mind is the source of both bondage and liberation, the source of both sorrow and joy, our worst enemy as well as our greatest friend. That is why, if there is anything worth knowing in this world, it is the mind.

The sages of the Upanishads said that the mind is the body of the Self (Consciousness). The Self shines through the mind and makes it function. But although the Self is so close to the mind, the mind does not know it. The mind is always moving outside, focusing on external objects, and as a result it has become very dull. It has lost the capacity to reflect the radiance of the Self, just as a lake whose waters are filled with silt loses its capacity to reflect the sun. However, when we practice meditation, the mind goes deeper and deeper within, and becomes more and more quiet. When it is truly still, we begin to drink the nectar of the Self. That is why yoga and meditation came into existence: to quiet the mind, to make it free of thoughts, and to enable it to touch its own source...

True psychology is born of meditation. The scriptures of meditation are the greatest works of psychology. Psychology is not just talking, talking, talking. Real psychology is yoga. There was a great sage called Maharshi Patanjali whose Yoga Sutras are the authoritative text on yoga. Patanjali said that through yoga one can still the movements of the mind. That is true psychology. One cannot cure the troubles of the mind by talking, nor can one steady the mind by using herbs or drugs. Drugs may calm the mind for a while, but once the effect of the drugs fade away, the mind will return to its former state. One can straighten out the mind only by making it still, by calming the thoughts and feelings that cause it to become agitated. If psychotherapists truly understood what the mind is and improved their own minds with meditation, they would be be able to practice great therapy...

In our yoga scriptures, the mind is represented as the horse that pulls a chariot. The reins are In your hands. If you let the horse go where it wishes, it will take you into a pit. You should not be defeated by your own mind. You should still the mind, purify the mind, discipline the mind. You should bring it under control with your intellect..."

* Grounding and rooting to mother earth through the practice of Enlightenment Qigong forms especially Hanuman Qigong, Meditation on Three Hearts and Eight Extraordinary Meridians Qigong are added to Siddha spiritual practices to balance the Shakti Qi flow in the body, avoid post-kundalini syndromes often seen in yoga practitioners and Self-realization.

Hamsa-So'ham, Hamsa-So'ham – it goes on and on.

The Sadguru unravels its secret and makes your mind still.

Brahmananda says: "Yogis who sit and meditate on this every morning attain the state of liberation. They are not born again."

Affirmation of the Soul

I am the Soul.

I am Divine.

I am a Child of God.

I am a vessel of Divine Light, Divine Love, Divine Power.

I am a vessel of abundance; material & spiritual.

I attract and radiate health, wealth & success.

I am the epitome of health: physical, mental, emotional & spiritual.

I am the Soul. I AM THAT I AM. (3 X)

KODOISH, KODOISH, KODOISH, ADONAI, TSEBAYOTH. (3 X)

HOLY, HOLY, HOLY IS THE LORD, GOD OF HOSTS.

The affirmation above is based on one taught by Grand Master of Pranic Healing and Arhatic Yoga, Master Choa Kok Sui. This has proven a most useful and worthwhile affirmation for building up of the self – physical, emotional, mental and spiritual. Those experiencing crises such as depression, anxiety, or financial difficulty are encouraged to recite this affirmation three times a day for as long as necessary. Thereafter, once a day may be enough.

Sri Maha Varahi Mantra

Aeem gloum Aeem - namo bhagavati -vartaali vartaali - varahi varahi

varaha mukhi varaha mukhi - andhe andhini namaha

rundhe rundhini namaha - jambhe jambhini namaha

mohe mohini namaha - stambhe stamhini namaha

sarva dushta pradushtanam - sarvesam sarva vakcitta

caksar mukha gatijihva - stambhanamm kuru kuru

seeghram vashyam - aim gloum

thah thah thah thah - hum astraya phat

Ganapathi mantra: Om Shreem Hreem Kleem - Gloum Gam - Ganapataye Vara varada

Sarva Jnanam Me Vasham aanaya Svaha

See Virgin and the Unicorn, p. 82

The Guru is the Means

"The Guru is the Grace-bestowing power of God." – Shiva Sutra 2.6

Invocation for Divine Blessings

To the Universal Supreme Being,

To Amitabha Buddha,

To Buddha Sakyamuni,

To Buddha Kuan Yin (Buddha Avalokiteshvara),

To Boddhisattva Mei Ling (Boddhisattva Padmasambhava),

To all the Great Buddhas and Boddhisattvas,

To all the Spiritual Teachers and Spiritual Helpers,

Thank you for the blessings of compassionate, purifying light and soothing

healing energy.

Thank you for the divine guidance, help and protection.

Invocation to Ganesh

Om Gannaanaam Tvaa - Ganna Patim Hava Amahe -

Kavim Kaviinaam - Upama Shravas Tamam -

Jyessttha Raajam Brahmannaam - Brahmannas Pata Aa Nah Shrunnvan

Nuutibhih Siida Saadanam - Sri Maha Gannadhipataye Namaha

Hari Om - Sri Guru Bhyo Namaha - Hari Om (Sri Vidya Mantras, p. 27)

May the following excerpts from chapter The Guru from the book "I Have Become Alive" by Swami Muktananda Paramahamsa enlighten the readers on the vital importance of a true Guru to enable the seeker to return to oneness because – The Guru is the Means – to know one's Self according to the Siddha Guru's path of Kashmir Shaivism.

Excerpts from the book I Have Become Alive by Swami Muktananda Paramahamsa:

Life is great only for a person who is truly alive. What does it mean to be truly alive? To be truly alive means to know your own Self, to know the Consciousness that pervades everywhere in the universe and lives within the human heart. A person who does not recognize his own Self, a person who identifies with his body, a person who thinks that only worldly life is real and that God does not exist – such a person is not really living.

Anyone can repeat mantras, anyone can meditate, anyone can practice different kinds of sadhana. But the saints tell us that without the grace of the Guru none of this will bear fruit. It is only the Guru who can erase your false ego and make you realize the Self.

According to Kashmir Shaivism, gururupayaha – "The Guru is the means." Through the Guru, one attains the power of the Self. The word "Guru" has two syllables: gu and ru. "Gu means darkness and ru means light." Gu represents the darkness which envelops the Self, and ru represents that principle which destroys the darkness of ignorance and reveals the light of wisdom. It is the Guru who gives knowledge of the Supreme Principle, the Self, and absolute bliss.

The Shiva Sutra Vimarshini says, "The Guru is the grace-bestowing power of God." The Guru is not a body made of flesh and blood. The Guru is not a man or a woman. The Guru is not an individual being. He is the embodiment of God's power, the power of the Self. It is not a particular individual who is the Guru, but the power, the Shakti, that flows through that individual. Such a Guru has the ability to transmit God's energy into others, to awaken their own divine inner power. When this power awakens and unfolds in someone, yoga takes place on its own. Spiritual attainment happens on its own. By awakening this inner power, the Guru removes the cataracts of ignorance and ego that cover our eyes and prevent us from seeing God. Then individuality is changed into Godhood...

Discipleship is a great and mysterious yoga. Jnaneshwar said, "All scriptures arise from one who serves the Guru's feet." The path of discipleship is the surest and easiest path to the Truth. Just by serving the Guru, just by worshipping the Guru, just by loving the Guru, a disciple attains all the Guru's knowledge. There are countless types of sadhana that rely on effort alone, countless paths that require a person to practice mantras and meditation techniques. But in none of these paths is it guaranteed that the goal will be reached. However, the path of the Guru is a direct path, because when a disciple surrenders himself to the Guru, the Guru takes full responsibility for his progress. The Guru guarantees that he will lead the disciple to the goal...

I used to visit Nityananda Baba everyday. At his place there were piles of food; so much that it would just sit there and rot. But I never asked for anything. I just obeyed his command. The result is that I received the most divine shaktipat. And now, even though I don't know English, I have been able to do a lot of work all over the world. Ordinarily a saint can give shaktipat to only two people in a week. If he transmits his energy to more than two people, he will become very weak. Not only that, a saint ordinarily can give shaktipat only after purifying the seeker for at least one year. He has to make the seeker do many different kinds of practices. But I have not had to follow all these rules. I have been able to give shaktipat to anyone who has come to me, knowing that whatever my Guru wants to make happen will happen. It is because I have surrendered completely to my Guru that I have been able to transmit Shakti to so many people all over the world. This is the power of Guru's grace; this is what you attain by following the Guru's path.

There is something that you should remember: A person who becomes aware of his own ignorance is drawn to the Guru's feet, but the pride of knowledge gleaned from dry books leads one to look for scriptures rather than for a Guru. Although the scriptures emphasize surrender, vows, and discipline, they are lifeless, so one does not really have to surrender to them; one can interpret them in any way one likes. But one cannot interpret the Guru. You may change the scriptures, but the Guru will certainly change you. He will begin by awakening you, by telling you that you have forgotten your own Self. Lacking knowledge of your Self, you are deep in the sleep of ignorance. The Guru will open your eyes to your darkness, ignorance, and forgetfulness. Only after knowing darkness is it possible to find light. Only one who falls can get up. Unless a seeker knows what it is to fall down, it is difficult for him to rise. After the Guru has made you aware of your condition, he will give you the vision of your own Self.

A great saint describes in one his poems the state the Guru gives us:

When I met that pure one I also became pure.

From him I received grace, and after that I begin to meditate. As I meditated, my individuality vanished,

And I myself became Consciousness. I myself became the Guru ...

When my inner ego was struck by the sword of my Guru's love, That love began to kill my ego,

So that even though I was alive, I experienced death. My death died, and I became immortal.

When I received the Guru's touch, he took away my sleep of delusion.

The fire of knowledge was kindled in me, And it burned up all my involvements.

It burned away my bondage and I became completely free.

When I met the Pure, when I merged into the Pure, I also became pure.

When I met that ecstatic being, my individuality vanished. And I became God.

Another verse in the Guru Gita further explains the significance of the Guru:

- dhyanamulam guror murthihi,
- pujamulam guroho padam;
- mantramulam guror vakyam,
- mokshamulam guroho krupa.

- The first line of this verse is "The root of meditation is the Guru's form." Meditation on a tangible object is superior to meditation on something intangible and imagined, because a person can easily picture in his mind an object that he has already seen. As Patanjali says in one of the aphorisms of the Yoga Sutras – "Focus the mind on one who has risen above passion and attachment." By meditating on a being whose mind is free of attachment and hatred and who has become one with Parabrahman, a person becomes identical with that being.
- The second line of the verse is "The root of worship is the Guru's feet." Because the Kundalini Shakti flows continuously from the Guru's feet, it is beneficial to worship and touch them.
- The third line is "The root of the mantra is the Guru's word." Because the Guru has the power to infuse a mantra with Consciousness, he is the root of the mantra, His word is a mighty mantra.
- Finally, "The root of liberation is the Guru's grace." The Guru's compassionate glance is the means to liberation and supreme peace – but the Guru must be a Siddha who has a lineage and who has completely conquered his senses. Without the grace of such a Guru, there is no knowledge and no state of meditation. Without the Guru's company, it is difficult to contemplate the Self. Without the Guru's teaching, there is no discipline in one's life. Without the Guru's blessing, there is no love. Without the Guru's knowledge, there is no end to desire, the intellect does not receive the light of wisdom, the delusion and pain created by duality are not eradicated, nor are doubts dispelled. Happiness and virtue arise from the Guru. When iron comes in contact with the philosopher's stone, it is transmuted into gold. Sandalwood infuse their fragrance into the trees around them. In the same way, Shri Gurudev makes a true disciple like himself.

NOTE from Acharya Ricardo B Serrano: May these short essays on my spiritual practices assist those on the path to Self-realization. Thank you for taking the time to read this short essay which is dedicated to my beloved Sadguru Bhagawan

Nityananda who through his Gurukripa, his Grace, was instrumental in my enlightenment and liberation or Self-realization, and also in the bliss of liberation of others through my transmission of Shakti by Shaktipat to my meditation and Qigong students, as my guruseva, as well. As a final note, I leave you with a quote from my beloved Siddha Guru Baba Muktananda:

"After Shaktipat, when the disciple becomes fully aware of the nature and importance of the Shakti, total devotion to the Guru springs up in his heart naturally. If the disciple were to become aware of the fact that the Kundalini Shakti which pervades the universe, which has limitless power, which creates the universe, is now running through every cell and fiber of his being since the Guru has awakened it in him – in fact, it is the Guru himself who entered him in the form of Shakti – devotion would arise in him spontaneously." – Baba Muktananda

May all who read these words be uplifted and filled with God's Grace and the All-Pervasive Love of the Endless One, Bhagawan Nityananda (everlasting bliss) of Ganeshpuri. You are all, and all are you. Om guru, jaya guru. O Shri Guru, I hail you. Sadgurunath maharaj ki jay.

* Grounding and rooting to mother earth through the practice of Enlightenment Qigong forms especially Hanuman Qigong, Meditation on Three Hearts and Eight Extraordinary Meridians Qigong are added to Siddha spiritual practices to balance the Shakti Qi flow in the body, avoid post-kundalini syndromes often seen in yoga practitioners and Self-realization.

Way of Qi by Ricardo B Serrano, R.Ac. (Why Jedi's Force is same as Qi)

"If a so called Jedi Master is not a Qigong master, he is not a true Jedi Master." – Jedi Master Ricardo

NOTE by Ricardo B Serrano, R.Ac.: Unbelievable as it may sound, I believe that Jedi Master fictional characters such as Jedi Masters Qui-Gon Jinn, Obi-Wan Kenobi and Grand Jedi Master Yoda appear to be highly advanced Qigong masters because I have personally experienced and witnessed the empty force (Jing Qi) being used by real Qigong masters to heal and move or knock down people without touching.

According to Empty Force Qigong master Paul Dong, "Ling Kong Jing, the "Empty Force," is the highest martial arts skill in China. This extraordinary technique harnesses the power of Qi, the body's vital energy, enabling masters of the art to defend themselves against opponents without making physical contact."

In Star Wars, the Jedi Masters owe their powers to the Force that they acquire through years of training. In the universe of Star Wars, this Force is all-pervasive, yet elusive, and the Jedi Masters hold the secret to harnessing and utilizing the Force for good.

In Chinese Medicine philosophy, the whole Universe and its contents are interconnected by Qi (chi, ki, prana, life force, tenaga hayat). It sustains every creature and every plant in the web of life, and is responsible for our every action. The more Qi we have flowing uninterrupted in us, the healthier we are. It gives us life and vitality.

In practicing Qigong and similar exercises, you will build up your Qi level and ensure its efficient flow. This will charge-up your cells to perform all their functions efficiently.

Qigong (Chi Kung) means cultivating energy, it is a system practiced for health maintenance, healing and increasing vitality. A Qigong master is someone who can pull in (and emit) a lot of energy, which the Chinese call Qi, for healing and self-defense.

The parallel between Qi and the Jedi's Force is so obvious. No wonder Obiwan Kenobi's master was called Qui-gon Jinn (Spirit of the Living Force). They were all actually Qigong masters!

The following facts are reasons for calling a Jedi master a Qigong master also:

- A Qigong master relies in the empty Force (Jing Qi) which is all around us in nature for a sense of peace, and for healing and self-defense like Wing Chun Kung Fu.
- To become a Qigong master, you start training as a student of a real Qigong master to learn how to experience returning to oneness by being in the flow of Qi.

- A Qigong master has to feel his Qi flow around the eight psychic channels and energy body to become proficient in the use of the empty force (Qi) for healing and self-defense like Wing Chun Kung Fu.
- A Qigong master has to go with the flow of benevolent Qi rather than oppose it with the dark side of the force such as attachments and negative emotions such as fear, anger, aggression and hate which lead to suffering.
- A Qigong master has to know and realize that he is not the body, mind and emotions but rather a luminous spiritual being having human experiences.

Qi is not only energy, but a lot more. Just like the saying about Tao: if you know it, it is not Tao. So it is at the moment with Qi. If you can fully describe it, it is not Qi!

And just as physicists discovered that the energy/particle nature of the smallest units of matter is determined by the observer, the nature of Qi is also determined by the master. The Qigong master who understands most the variabilities and capabilities of Qi will most likely be able to utilize more of the potential of Qi in healing, and in many other areas.

Qigong (personal energy cultivation) is the missing half of the problem in healing and global climate change protocols. Everyone is dealing with half of the issue - external energy. They are missing the other half - internal energy, without which it can't work. That would be like pouring the highest quality fuel into a bucket with a hole in the bottom. Qigong is the missing half.

To the uninitiated, it could easily seem so, for when Qi is summoned, it becomes a force of power, bravery, fearlessness and determination. When Qi is summoned for healing, it becomes a force of compassion, empathy, gentleness and softness.

Qi can also be harnessed as a force of peace and wisdom. The Jedi Masters of the Star Wars are the best examples of masters who use the Force for self-defense, peace and wisdom. May God's Force, Peace and Wisdom be with you, too. God is a creative principle and energy, not a personality.

"There are many paths to take, Obi-Wan. Not all of us are fortunate enough to find the one with heart, the path the Force has set before us." - Qui-Gon Jinn, to Obi-Wan Kenobi

As a Qigong teacher/practitioner, I have experienced returning to oneness by being in the flow of Qi – feeling the Qi flow from natural energy sources such as trees, earth, sun, moon, planets, stars and ocean through Qigong for healing, self-defense and spiritual awakening.

This oneness phenomenon as being in the flow of Qi is based from the Taoist Chinese medicine philosophy of Qi cultivated by Qigong via body meridians and dynamic flow process of Wei Qi field (torus, lightbody, electromagnetic field, energy bubble, merkaba or aura).

When nature's divine energy is felt as a divine presence, he feels himself at one with the Universe through this felt presence of divinity. This feeling of oneness is explained by the western God concept of Pantheism - All is God. When Force (Qi) awakens, it is seen in the eyes.

Sri Vidya Guru Mantra (Read Sri Vidya Mantras, Return to Oneness with Shiva)

Guru: Imagine Guru's feet on top of your head, washing them and bathing in the waters. That purifies you and invokes grace. Best done as soon as you get up before getting up from bed.

Aeem Hreem Shreem – Aeem Kleem Souh – Hamsah Shivah Soham- Hasakhaphrem- Hasakshamalavarayum Hasoum – Sahakshamalavarayim Sahouh – Svaroopa Niroopana Hetave Sva Gurave – Sri Anna Poornamba Sahita Sri Amritananda Natha

Sri Guru Sri Padukam Poojayami Tarpayami Namah

The Sri Vidya bija mantras Hreem and Shreem affect the ida and pingala nadis in the body balancing and reuniting them both, while Aeem affects the sushumna to facilitate healing and kundalini awakening. The mantras Aeem Kleem Souh balance and reunite the three suns or dantiens. Ham is the sound of Prana moving upwards in pingala and is Shiva embodied, and Sah is Shakti moving in the ida to both reunite in the bindu via ajna chakra.

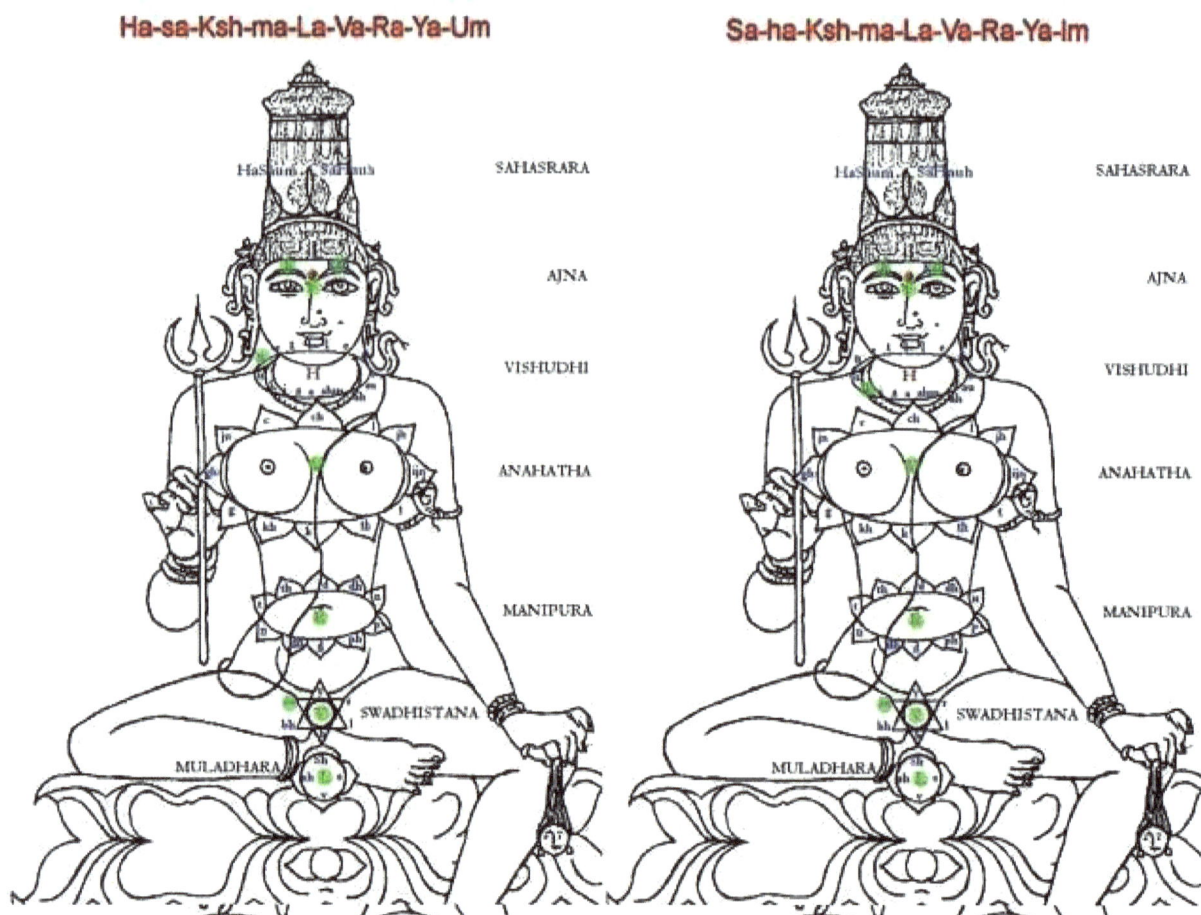

Oh Devi, You are existing in each and every form, in each and every step, in each and every movement of this world. - Abhinavagupta

Lalitha Tripura Sundari Devi is a Goddess who is representative of three Goddesses on form, Kali, Lakshmi and Saraswathi. Om Aeem Saraswatyai Namaha. Saraswati Mantra attracts this sacred power of the goddess, giving worship to her wisdom, health, creative energy, bliss and quieting thought. Saraswati mantra: Aeem Vada Vada Vac Vadini Swaha (27x) along the 9 chakras (3x in each chakra). Top to bottom. Saraswati (essence of Self) represents the free flow of wisdom and consciousness that are essential to achieve liberation. See Sri Devi, page 32; Atma (Soul) Yoga of Immortality, page 103; Sri Vidya Upasana, page 140

The key to growth is the introduction of higher dimensions of consciousness into our awareness. - Lao Tzu

So once you have chosen your Devatas, create a space for them, learn or develop rituals around them, practice their Mantras with devotion and surrender completely to them and ask them to guide you to the other side. This is the Yoga of Ishta Devata. When we tune in to them through *numinous* sound, concentration and devotion, they make themselves visible to us in a way we can understand - as deity or beings, as light, as angelic beings, as a Guru in dreams, as sacred geometries etc.

Drama is like a dream, it is not real, but it is really felt! - Abhinavagupta

Garland of Letters

Source:The Goddess and the Guru by Michael Bowden, 2017

See Chakras with Petal Letters and Bija Letters, page 126

The Nectar of the Inner Self

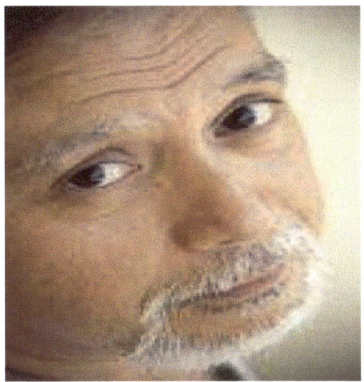

"When Force (Qi) awakens, it is seen in the eyes."- Acharya Ricardo

"The love of the inner Self is nectarian by nature." – Narada

"The really blissful life - not wonderful food and beautiful women, but unlimited love for Primordial Nature."

"Feel yourself as rich as a king. On the way everyone can be happy even if he is a beggar."

"Every man has *reichi* – divine wisdom, and *reinoh* – divine power – within himself." – Okada Torajiro, Words of the Master

Om Gate gate paragate parasamgate Bodhi svaha

"Form is emptiness, emptiness is form." – Heart Sutra

Where there is no breath there is no thought, and where there is no thought there is no mind; where there is no mind, the Self stands revealed. This space between the breaths is like a door in the mind, a secret panel that allows us to escape the room of our finite consciousness. Meditate on the space between breaths. The essence of all things is emptiness.

According to Hanuman Qigong, "In that space of Nothingness all that is left is love – nothing but Love. In an ultimate act of giving, the final movement seeks to root out whatever is left of one's individuality to offer oneself in service to the highest truth. That pure love melts into the Oneness – the truth of the universe. The merging is complete."

"It is empowering to learn that we can be architects of our own happiness and health - or our misery. It is tremendously important to nurture ourselves, foster meaningful relationships, seek the good in others and in situations, live lives of purpose and meaning, share our blessings, and remain hopeful and optimistic. This positive attitude will not only improve our own lives, but that of people around us. Happiness is socially contagious! A smile begets a smile, a kind deed is paid forward - and slowly, the world becomes a better place for all of us." – Dr. Werner Spangehl, MD, author of One Minute Medicine

May the following excerpts from the book "The Perfect Relationship" by Swami Muktananda Paramahamsa describe for you from the perspective of Kashmir Shaivism, the nectar or elixir of the inner Self, which is supreme love, that lies within everyone of us, and can be attained through the knowledge of the Self with Guru's help by returning to oneness with Shiva.

Excerpts from The Perfect Relationship by Swami Muktananda Paramahamsa

There is a mantra that describes a being who is established in the Self: "[one] whose eyes are unblinking and whose gaze, though appearing to look outside, is fixed within." In this way, although our eyes may appear to look outward, our gaze should be directed within. We should also turn our hearing inward. Meditating yogis slowly direct their outer hearing toward the divine inner music and listen for a long time to the divine inner sounds, or nada. The Upanishads refer to this nada as om. Om is not merely a mantra to be repeated; it is the sublime and indestructible sound of the Self which continuously reverberates within us. It is the divine music of our true inner existence arising spontaneously without two objects being struck together. It has been resounding since the beginning of time and is the eternal Truth. The entire universe exists within this sound. Because it exists, all the activities of the world takes place. It makes the sun rise and set and the wind blow. The creation, maintenance, and dissolution of the universe occur within this vibration, which in Kashmir Shaivism is called spanda, the original throb. One who wishes to know it must hide his eyes from outer forms and colors. He must shield his tongue from outer tastes, and his nose from outer fragrances. He must free his hands from outer contacts. Only then will he experience that divine vibration.

Jnaneshwar Maharaj wrote, "One tastes and attains this elixir by stealing it from the senses." When the senses become free from all outer contacts, for the first time in one's life one experiences the inner sensation of joy that lies at the core of one's being. When one sees and hears the Self, one touches that inner love. When one tastes one's own Self, one experiences satchidananda. Whoever has tasted this sublime elixir has tasted the mystery of life and essence of the entire world.

The divine sage Narada said, "Knowing this, the devotee becomes intoxicated and still, reveling in the Self." By attaining and experiencing the nectar of the Self, which is supreme love, one becomes ecstatic. One who is completely established in Self becomes utterly quiet and serene; he becomes the Self. When the love of God, the ambrosia of the Self, is revealed, one finally attains the Truth and begins to dance like a madman. The intoxication that arises from the love of the divine Self is overwhelming. I often say, "Why do you use marijuana, opium, and cocaine? If you want real intoxication, drink the elixir of the Self. That will take you higher and higher; you will never come down from it."

When a flowing river merges into the ocean, it becomes the ocean and so takes on the ocean's delight. The ocean of Self is complete in itself. Intoxicated with love, it billows ceaselessly with its own joy. A person who is immersed in the Self becomes drunk with love. Sometimes he dances out of sheer joy. Sometimes he is lost in a state of overwhelming bliss. At other times, he is engrossed in discussing the Self. Narada said, "The love of the inner Self is nectarian by nature." That inner love is not far from us; since its source lies within us it is not, and cannot be concealed. We ourselves have obscured it. Our blindness makes us think that it is hidden, but it is manifest within us.

The Guru's help is essential to one who wants knowledge of the Self. Without the wisdom of the Guru, the notion of one's individuality will never be rooted out. Without the Guru's grace, one cannot be uplifted, and without the Guru's knowledge, the darkness of one's ignorance can never be destroyed. All individuals are bound by the noose of time, but one who keeps Guru's company will not feel the blows of death. Kabir Sahib said that without the Guru, birth and death will never be annihilated. Without the Guru, life is full of darkness. For many lifetimes we have been trapped in worldliness; only the Guru can release us. We should contemplate this and understand it. The subtle path to the Self is most easily attained through the Guru. Kabir said that the Guru makes one perfect; he unites the individual soul with Shiva. Therefore, one should keep the company of the Guru and remain respectfully at his feet. When one has his darshan and listen to his words, delusion flees and cheerfulness, joy, and compassion arise. Gurudev is like the philosophers' stone; he makes his disciples just like himself. This is the true Guru-disciple relationship.

"Chanting the divine name is the most sublime way to develop inner love. The divine lover pursues God through his divine name." See Hare Krishna Mantra, page 123

"Chant the mantra with great feeling. Chant with all your heart and the bliss will come. No negativities can withstand the bliss of the Lord's name." OM NAMAH SHIVAYA

By constant meditation on *So'ham*, the ego and the awareness caused by the three gunas vanish.

The Blue Pearl

Svarupananda says: "Then all that remains is the effortless enjoyment of your own inner bliss."

Baba Muktananda said, "The fourth body is the Blue Pearl, the subtlest covering of the individual soul, and when we see this tiny blue light in meditation, we should understand that we are seeing the form of the inner Self. To experience this is the goal of human life."

"Meditation on the Soul is very powerful. The essence of this spiritual practice is to concentrate and be aware of the "seed of consciousness" or the "blue pearl" at the center of the head, and eventually become one with the higher soul.

What exactly is the blue pearl? The blue pearl is the "seed of consciousness" or the mental permanent seed, found in the crown chakra, and located in the pineal gland. Through regular and prolonged meditation on the blue pearl or the seed of consciousness, one gradually experiences one's true nature, which is called the "Buddha Nature" in Buddhism or "Shiva" in Hinduism."

Master Choa Kok Sui, Om Mani Padme Hum: The Blue Pearl in the Golden Lotus, p. 55

THE HEART OF PRAJNA PARAMITA SUTRA (Heart sutra)

When Avalokiteshvara Bodhisattva was practicing the profound prajna paramita, he illuminated the five skandhas and saw that they are all empty, and he crossed beyond all suffering and difficulty. Shariputra, form does not differ from emptiness; emptiness does not differ from form. Form itself is emptiness; emptiness itself is form. So, too, are feeling, cognition, formation, and consciousness.

Shariputra, all dharmas are empty of characteristics. They are not produced. Not destroyed, not defiled, not pure, and they neither increase nor diminish. Therefore, in emptiness there is no form, feeling, cognition, formation, or consciousness; no eyes, ears, nose, tongue, body, or mind; no sights, sounds, smells, tastes, objects of touch, or dharmas; no field of the eyes, up to and including no field of mind-consciousness; and no ignorance or ending of ignorance, up to and including no old age and death or ending of old age and death. There is no suffering, no accumulating, no extinction, no way, and no understanding and no attaining.

Because nothing is attained, the Bodhisattva, through reliance on prajna paramita, is unimpeded in his mind. Because there is no impediment, he is not afraid, and he leaves distorted dream-thinking far behind. Ultimately Nirvana!

All Buddhas of the three periods of time attain Anuttarasamyaksambodhi through reliance on prajna paramita. Therefore, know that prajna paramita is a great spiritual mantra, a great bright mantra, a supreme mantra, an unequalled mantra. It can remove all suffering; it is genuine and not false. That is why the mantra of prajna paramita was spoken. Recite it like: Om, Gate gate paragate parasamgate bodhi svaha! Om, Gone, gone, gone over, gone fully over, Awakened!

Sri Devi

Sri is all aspects of the awakening of Kundalini Shakti that leads to living a completely fulfilled, abundant, healthy, compassionate, kind, beauty-filled, and gracious life. Understanding Sri behind Sri Vidya is understanding how to live fully and become a full Shakti. Sri fills our hearts with divine bliss. Sri ensures we are completely looked after while we gaze at the awesome beauty of Adi Shakti. Sri prepares us for union with Shiva. But most importantly Sri makes this life beautiful. Sri is the golden energy of the Sukshma. Sri is the white lotus in our hearts. Sri is Maha Lakshmi. Sri is Tara, Durga, Kali, Saraswati, Guanyin, Kamla. And to them all we chant Shreem.

The Maha Lakshmi Beej Sound **SHREEM**

- SH Auspicious, Grace, Beauty, Abundance – Maha Lakshmi
- RA The Fire to activate - Durga/Kali
- EEM The river of consciousness from Shiva Shakti to the body and up again – Maha Saraswati

SHREEM the condensation of the universal energy into one point at the bindu. **See Sri Devi, pages 112, 119, 120, 122, 138, 140**

Ishta Devata Yoga (chosen deity meditation): One of the critical aspects of Tantra and advanced mental Yoga is the selection of an Ishta Devata or a spirit companion for the inbetween space between you and the bliss of Source and the Void. In the vibratory universe between absolute source (Para - Brahman, Mahadev, Aditi) and your body (Sthulla) is the realm of vibratory intelligence in Sukshma - the spiritual plain - which is filled with wonderful levels of intelligence that can influence and affect our lives. Once you have chosen your deities to focus on (and yes you can have more than one) - my primary Devatas or windows into the Void or spirit guides and companions are first and foremost Maha Lakshmi and then Maha Kali, Tripura Sundari, Bhairav, Saraswati, Guruji Amritananda and the Sri Chakra Meru.

Om Aeem Hreem Shreem Kleem Mahalakshmayi Namaha
AEEM HREEM SHREEM AEEM KLEEM SAUH

Om Shreem Hreem Shreem Kamle Kamlalaye Praseeda Praseeda Shreem Hreem Shreem Om Maha Lakshmiye Namah

See Kundalini Awakening, p. 12; Garland of Letters, p. 28 and 126; Sri Yantra, pages 40, 44, 47, 52, 92, 125, 128

Drugs and Self-Awareness

"Don't seek the aid of drugs; they will dull the refined sensory nerves in your brain. Those who meditate with the aid of drugs always remain insecure and dissatisfied."

"Peace comes from within. Do not seek it without." – Buddha

Chapter 11

Can you fix your concentration at the Soul Center (Tsu Chiao) and never stray? Can you clear the eight psychic channels until your body is totally purified? Can you control your prenatal breath until your body becomes soft and supple like a child?

Can you become enlightened and penetrate every realm of existence? Can you empty the mind and still the breath until you have finally gained Tao? Mysterious virtue always resides in Tao, Therefore, seek Tao and everything shall be added unto you.

Chapter 52

Therefore, train yourself to circulate your Inner Light Along the Microcosmic Orbit, Ren Mai and Du Mai. Only when the Microcosmic channels are cleared, Can a man truly finds Salvation in life. All else and all claims are only empty talks.

Sages and immortals have realized this final truth. The clever, worldly people are still sleeping in the dark dungeon of their own ignorance. Clever people are getting so used to the darkness of their own faith or beliefs.

Quotations from The Secrets of Eternal Life: Tao Teh Chieng by Victor Shim, 1985.

Most people resort to legal and illegal drugs and alcohol to deal with their physical, mental and emotional traumatic pain. There are natural alternative therapies that can assist people to deal with their pain such as acupuncture, herbs, meditation and Qigong. As a registered acupuncturist, and Qigong teacher, I can vouch for their effectiveness in dealing with their physical, emotional pain. However, a more effective way to deal with their addiction is to love oneself identifying with their soul instead of their body by realizing the compassionate Higher Self (Soul) within themselves through the practices of Atma (Soul) Yoga, see 103.

May the readers benefit from the excerpts on drugs and Self-awareness from "I Have Become Alive" by Swami Muktananda Paramahamsa which talk about attaining the nectar of the Self through knowledge of the Self as a better natural alternative than drug dependency. I love these excerpts because I clinically use meditation and Qigong to rehabilitate my drug dependent clients together with acupuncture and natural detoxification strategies.

Excerpts from I Have Become Alive by Swami Muktananda Paramahamsa

What do you feel about the use of drugs for attaining Self-awareness?

Self-awareness does not depend on anything. But if you take drugs in the name of attaining Self-awareness, you will become dependent on the drugs. Kabir Sahib said, "Never have the hope that you will attain the Self while taking intoxicants." The Self has its own effulgence. The intoxication of drugs is derived from the light of the Self. When this is the case, how can drugs make the light of the Self reveal itself?

A person becomes addicted to drugs, and then to keep himself from admitting this mistake, he says they give him Self-awareness. When your mind turns within, when you become very, very pure and subtle, the Self reveals itself to you. Every day we chant and meditate and observe good conduct. We do not do these practices to attain the Self, because we have already attained the Self. We do them to make our mind purer and subtler, so that we can perceive the light of the Self. The Self is very subtle, and our mind and intellect must become extremely refined in order to experience it.

If the mind becomes intoxicated and too excited, it becomes rajastic and impure. That is why a person who is addicted to outer intoxicants will find it very difficult to experience the intoxication of the inner Self. Meditation affects extremely refined sensory nerves for which drugs are much too strong. These nerves cannot even bear strong coffee. That's why drugs are forbidden by the scriptures.

You should become intoxicated only on God's love. A saint said that a person whose mind has been completely cleansed and whose heart has become pure becomes intoxicated on God's love. And it is the best intoxication. When you get drunk on the intoxication of love for God, all outer drugs will seem insipid by comparison.

Even if you get high on marijuana, you don't get very high, and when the effect wears off, you come down, perhaps even lower than before. To get high again you have to use more marijuana; otherwise, you might not be able to bear your own company. But as you get higher and higher on the intoxicants of the Self, you will reach a state from which you will never come down. So if you want to get high, get high on God's love. You cannot experience this intoxication through drugs.

Meditation is far more potent than marijuana, but before you can get meditation you first have to give up drugs completely. There are no "downs" in meditation; there are only "ups," because the high of meditation will never desert you. It keeps getting stronger and stronger, so powerful is the inner intoxication. No drug, however potent, can influence a real meditator. It is said that Mira was given poison to drink, yet it caused her no harm for she was under the influence of a far mightier "poison" – the ecstasy and nectar of her love for Krishna. I am not speaking of any miracle or siddhi; this happens naturally to one who is divinely intoxicated.

Therefore, meditate with love and interest. Don't seek the aid of drugs; they will dull the refined sensory nerves in your brain. Those who meditate with the aid of drugs always remain insecure and dissatisfied.

The Guru's help is essential to one who wants knowledge of the Self. Without the wisdom of the Guru, the notion of one's individuality will never be rooted out. Without the Guru's grace, one cannot be uplifted, and without the Guru's knowledge, the darkness of one's ignorance can never be destroyed. All individuals are bound by the noose of time, but one who keeps Guru's company will not feel the blows of death. Kabir Sahib said that without the Guru, birth and death will never be annihilated. Without the Guru, life is full of darkness. For many lifetimes we have been trapped in worldliness; only the Guru can release us. We should contemplate this and understand it. The subtle path to the Self is most easily attained through the Guru. Kabir said that the Guru makes one perfect; he unites the individual soul with Shiva. Therefore, one should keep the company of the Guru and remain respectfully at his feet. When one has his darshan and listen to his words, delusion flees and cheerfulness, joy, and compassion arise. Gurudev is like the philosophers' stone; he makes his disciples just like himself. This is the true Guru-disciple relationship.

"Chanting the divine name is the most sublime way to develop inner love. The divine lover pursues God through his divine name." See Hare Krishna Mantra, page 123

"Chant the mantra with great feeling. Chant with all your heart and the bliss will come. No negativities can withstand the bliss of the Lord's name." OM NAMAH SHIVAYA

Brahmananda said, "As you contemplate this mantra So'ham, you attain the supreme state."

Namdev, another great saint, said, "Just keep repeating So'ham, So'ham all the time, and you yourself will become God."

Quotations from Tai Chi Grand Master Victor Shim

You can feel the chi running within the the energy lines{meridians}. When they are not open you only feel a bit of tingling sensations instead of a line like electric current.

Transferring chi to a student can help to speed up opening the students' chi channels in a shorter time frame and also boost up a weak student's chi. A true master has all the chi channels opened. He can at will intake through Bai hui, yongchuan, laogong and even all the fingers or toes instantly. I've used the chi projection techniques to heal many people with fatigue syndrome or extreme tiredness due to aura leaks. Aura leaks are caused by impact injuries. I help thousands to eradicate pain ..

CHI projection can help to heal others suffering especially from arthritis, rheumatism or poor circulation problems. An advanced tai chi master can instantly cure a person suffering migraines, back pain or minor health problems by a mere wave of his hand PROVIDED THE RECIPIENT IS SPIRITUALLY OPENED. A SKEPTIC HAS ITS DOORS CLOSED thus the chi cannot enter to effect a miraculous cure. What we term as miracles is an exact science to an enlightened mind, cause he is in UNION WITH THE CREATIVE FORCE.

* Grounding and rooting to mother earth through the practice of Enlightenment Qigong forms especially Hanuman Qigong, Meditation on Three Hearts and Eight Extraordinary Meridians Qigong are added to Siddha spiritual practices to balance the Shakti Qi flow in the body, psychic self-defense, avoid post-kundalini syndromes often seen in yoga practitioners.

There are many names for the invisible auric field that surrounds the physical body in various traditions such as torus, Lightbody, Electromagnetic Field (EMF), energy bubble, Merkaba or aura. The auric field is also called Wei Qi Field in Medical Qigong.

"A torus consists of a central axis with a vortex at both ends and a surrounding coherent field. Energy flows in one vortex, through the central axis, out the other vortex, and then wraps around itself to return to the first incoming vortex. The simplest description of its overall form is that of a donut, though it takes many different shapes, depending upon the medium in which it exists. For example, a smoke ring in air or a bubble ring in water are both very donut shaped. And yet an apple or an orange, which are both torus forms, are more overtly spherical. Plants and trees all display the same energy flow process, yet exhibit a wide variety of shapes and sizes. Hurricanes, tornadoes, magnetic fields around planets and stars, and whole galaxies themselves are all toroidal energy systems. Extending this observation of the consistent presence of this flow form into the quantum realm, we can postulate that atomic structures and systems are also made of the same dynamic form." - Cosmometry.net

Torus is synonymous with Wei Qi Field in enlightenment Qigong forms where the lower dantien is the sea of Qi. It is the dynamic flow process of Wei Qi field (torus) that explains that all is interconnected – All is God (pantheism) – and makes healing, self-defense and oneness with God possible.

See Way of Qi, pages 27-28 and Wei Qi Field in Medical Qigong, page 62

Shakti-Yoga Philosophy by Swami Shivananda of Saraswati, Rishikesh, India

Mother worship is the worship of God as the Divine Mother, as the power of the Lord or the cosmic energy. Shakti, then, is energy. Just as one cannot separate heat from fire, so also one cannot separate Shakti from Shakta. Shakti and Shakta are one. They are inseparable.

She lies dormant in the Muladhara Chakra in the form of a serpentine power coiled up energy known as Kundalini Shakti. She is at the center of the life of universe. She is the primal force of life that underlies all existence. She vitalises the body through Her energy. She is the energy in the sun, the fragrance in the flowers, the beauty in the landscape, the Gayatri or the Blessed Mother in the Vedas, She is the colour in the rainbow, intelligence in the mind, devotion in worship.

Kundalini is Shakti power symbolized by Divine Mother. She is pure blissful consciousness. She is the Mother of nature. It behooves, therefore, that the aspirant should approach the Mother first, so that She may introduce Her spiritual child to the Father for its illumination or Self-realization.

Divine Mother is everywhere triple. She is endowed with the three gunas, Sattva, Rajas, Tamas. She manifests as will (Icha-shakti), action (Kriya-shakti) and knowledge (Jnana-shakti). She is Brahma-shakti (Sarasvati) in conjunction with Brahma; Visnu-shakti (Lakshmi) in conjunction with Lord Vishnu; Shiva-Shakti (Gauri) in conjunction with Lord Shiva. Hence She is called The Tripurasundari.

The abode of Tripurasundari, the Divine Mother, is called Sri Nagara. This magnificent abode is surrounded by twenty-five ramparts which represent the twenty-five tattvas (principles or qualities). The resplendent Cintamani palace is in the middle. The Divine Mother sits in the Bindu Pitha in Sri Chakra in that wonderful palace. There is a similar abode for Her in the body of man also. The whole world is Her body. Mountains are Her bones. Rivers are Her veins. Ocean is Her bladder. Sun and moon are Her eyes. Wind is Her breath. Agni is Her mouth.

The Sakta enjoys Bhukti (enjoyment of the world) and Mukti (liberation from all worlds). Shiva is an embodiment of Bliss and Knowledge. Shiva Himself appears in the form of man with a life of a mixture of pleasure and pain. If you remember this point always, all dualism, all hatred, jealousy, and pride will vanish. You must consider every human function as worship or a religious act. Answering calls of nature, micturition, talking, eating, walking, seeing, hearing become worship of the Lord if you develop the right attitude. It is Shiva who works in and through man. Where then is egoism or individuality? All human actions are divine actions. One universal life throbs in the hearts of all, sees in the eyes of all, hears in the ears of all. What a magnanimous experience it is, if one can feel this by crushing this little 'I'! The old samskaras, the old Vasanas, the old habits of thinking, stand in the way of your realizing this experience - whole.

The aspirant thinks that the world is identical with the Divine Mother. He moves about thinking his own form to be the form of the Divine Mother and thus beholds oneness everywhere. He also feels that the Divine Mother is identical with Parabrahman.

The advanced Sadhaka feels "I am the Devi and the Devi is in me." He worships himself as Devi instead of adoring any external object. He says "Saham", "I am She" (Devi, Divine Mother). Shaktism is not mere theory or philosophy. It prescribes systematic sadhana of yoga, regular discipline according to the temperament, capacity and degree of evolution of the sadhaka. It helps the aspirant to arouse the Kundalini and unite Her with Lord Shiva and to enjoy the Supreme Bliss of Nirvikalpa Samadhi. When Kundalini sleeps man is awake to the world. He has objective consciousness. When She awakes, he sleeps. He loses all consciousness of the world and becomes one with the Lord. In Samadhi the body is maintained by the nectar which flows from the union of Shiva and Shakti with Sahasrara.

Guru is indispensable for the practice of Shakti Yoga sadhana. He initiates the aspirant and transmits the divine Shakti.

Worship of the Divine Mother with intense faith and perfect devotion and self-surrender will help you to attain Her grace. Through Her grace alone you can attain knowledge of the Imperishable.

Glory to Sri Tripurasundari, the World-Mother, who is also Rajarajesvari and Lalitha Devi. May her blessings be upon you All!!!
See Kundalini Awakening, p. 12; Garland of Letters, p. 28 and 126; Sri Yantra, pages 44, 47, 52, 92, 125, 128; Sri Devi, pages, 32, 112, 119, 122

How to Experience Love Now

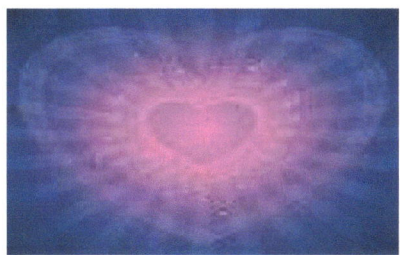

"If you want to experience love, you have to start by loving yourself. First you have to love your body, then those who are related to your body, and then the master of the body, the inner Self." – Baba Muktananda

"Personal and spiritual transformation are dependent upon the opening of the heart chakra. As our heart centers open wider and we begin to feel greater compassion and empathy for all living things, we move closer to expressing the divine unconditional love of the Christ Consciousness, which is the supreme facet of spiritual awakening towards which we are all gradually evolving.

The expression of love is perhaps one of the most important lessons that humans have incarnated upon the physical plane to learn. Without love, existence can be dry and meaningless. It is necessary that we learn to love not only those around us but also ourselves.

What I have discovered is that the most powerful healing force in the universe is love, unconditional love. When you work from that level you begin to open up whole vistas of discovery in self-exploration and spiritual transformation. You begin a new level of healing, not just fixing the body, but helping the individual to grow to a whole new understanding of their life and their awareness as an evolving spiritual being." – Richard Gerber, Vibrational Medicine: New Choices for Healing Ourselves, 1988

Jesus says in John 14:6, "I AM the way and the truth and the life. No one comes to the Father except through me." Does Jesus literally mean that he is the way, the truth and the life, or does he mean that the I AM or higher soul within you is the way, the truth and the life? The higher soul is the source of life. It is called the I AM. This is the meaning of "I AM the life." The voice of conscience is actually from the higher soul. It is from the higher soul that one knows right from wrong. It is from the I AM that a person receives inner guidance or intuition. The higher soul is the source of truth. This is the meaning of "I AM the truth."

Happiness is your nature. It is not wrong to desire it. What is wrong is seeking it outside when it is inside. – Ramana Maharshi

The truth that happiness or bliss is your nature is experienced through Sri Vidya kundalini awakening with Qigong, chanting and Sri Chakra Yantra meditation.

By devotion and surrender to the Goddess Shakti within me through Sri Vidya upasana, I manifest healing and desires through my heart that is connected to the Source (Adi Shakti). I am Shakti! - Acharya Ricardo B Serrano

Bahá'u'lláh Shen Gong is a Torus Qigong practice that is dedicated to oneness with God and awakening of Yuan Shen (Original Spirit) by connecting to God through the Holy Spirit (I AM) and Manifestation of God, Bahá'u'lláh. It generates a tremendous downpouring of spiritual Light, Love and Power for healing oneself and others by blessing humanity with loving-kindness.

May the readers of these excerpts "How to experience love" from I Have Become Alive by Swami Muktananda Paramahamsa based from Kashmir Shaivism experience the bliss of the inner love from within the inner Self – the true source of love – by returning to oneness through meditation and Qigong.

Excerpts from I Have Become Alive by Swami Muktananda Paramahamsa:

If you want to experience love, you have to start by loving yourself. First you have to love your body, then those who are related to your body, and then the master of the body, the inner Self.

You must understand the value of this body and then make it strong through hatha yoga, meditation and chanting God's name. This body is your greatest friend, and treachery against a friend is not good. Feed your body regularly and with self-control. Take good care of it; make it an abode fit for God to live in. Then love all those who are related to your body: your mother, father, brothers, sisters, friends, relatives, husband or wife, and children. That is how love expands.

The truth is that God has no physical body; the only body he has is the body of love. If the love you experience in your daily life – the little love you feel for your friends, your relatives, your pets and even your possessions – could be turned toward the inner Self that would be enough to bring you liberation.

You once told me to teach my mind to love myself. What is the best way to do this?

Question your mind. Ask your mind whether it finds happiness in fickleness or stillness. Tell your mind that it has been wandering here and there according to its own whim without finding anything or attaining anything. Tell it that for this reason it should try to enter the Self. Teach the mind good things about your Self. Talk to the mind about the love of your own Self. Then you will experience that love.

To follow the path of love you do not need any outer qualifications. You do not need to be beautiful or come from an important family. You do not have to be well educated. You do not need degrees or money. Even the simplest person can experience the sweetness of love.

Love of the Inner Self

Love is our only reason for living and the only purpose of life. We live for the sake of love, and we live seeking love... Love is essential for all of us...

It is not surprising that we keep looking for love, because we are all born of love. We come out of love. All of us are nothing but vibrations of love. We are sustained by love, and in the end we merge into love... According to the great scriptural authors, when the ocean of love of Shiva and Shakti, the supreme Reality and His creative power, overflowed, it took birth as this world and all the creatures in it. So the world is an expansion of God's love and, like Him, it is full of love...

Yet the love we experience through other people is just a shadow of the love of the inner Self. There is a sublime place inside us where love dwells. Just as electric bulbs derive their power from a power plant, all the love we experience comes from the inner source. Only because that love exists within us are we able to love our friends, our families, our parents, and our children. Even our everyday experience shows that the real abode of love is within us... That is why, if we want to experience complete love, we must plunge within to the place that is its source. That is why we meditate. Through meditation the inner love is unfolded. As we constantly meditate, we get drunk on this inner love, and that is when we begin to realize what love really is...

To find the love of the Self you have to leave everything behind. If you carry any burden on your heart, you cannot attain the inner love. You have to rid yourself of ego. Only then can you experience that love. When you become immersed in love, you become one with love. You merge in the ocean of love. In the Shrimad Bhagavatam there is a story about Radha. Radha was so devoted to Krishna that she thought of nothing else. Finally, she became so
immersed in Krishna that she became Krishna and began to ask her friends, "Where is Radha? She had lost herself completely with love. In the same way, you must lose yourself in the Self. When you become one with the inner love, that love will saturate your entire being and you yourself will become the embodiment of love. See Hare Krishna Mantra, page 123

Who Am I?

"We are all children of God. In each person, there is a divine essence or a divine spark. In Buddhism, there is a Buddha in each person. In Christian religion, there is a Christ in each person. In Hinduism, there is a Shiva or a Krishna in each person.

What is the name of this divine essence? When Moses saw the burning bush, he asked, "If the people ask me what is your name, what shall I tell them?" From within the burning bush God answered, "I AM THAT I AM." (Exodus 3:13-14) In Hebrew, this is called Eieh. In Sanskrit, this is known as So Ham or Tatwamasi. There is a universal or planetary I AM. There is a micro I AM in every person.

Jesus says in John 14:6, "I AM the way and the truth and the life. No one comes to the Father except through me." Does Jesus literally mean that he is the way, the truth and the life, or does he mean that the I AM or higher soul within you is the way, the truth and the life? Does Jesus mean himself as the way to the Father or is this a reference to the I AM or higher soul within every person? "The Divine Father" here refers to the divine spark in every person.

The divine spark in every person is a part of God. It is made in the essence of God. The divine spark is one with God and one with all. The divine spark extends a portion of itself "downward", manifesting as the higher soul. The
higher soul extends a portion of itself "downward", manifesting as the incarnated soul. In Hindu teachings, the incarnated soul is called Jivatma. It literally means "embodied soul." The higher soul is called Atma. The divine spark is called Paramatma. This is why St. Paul said that you have a body, soul, and spirit (1 Thessalonians 5:23).
Here, "spirit" refers to the divine spark in each person. To achieve union with the divine spark or the Divine Father within you, you must first pass through the I AM or the higher soul."

The correspondence of the Divine Spark, Higher Soul and Incarnated Soul in different traditions:

- Nothingness – Ain | Sunya or Paramatma (Divine Spark) | Father | Kung
- Infinite Source – Ain Soph | Atma (Higher Soul) | Son | Higher Buddha Nature
- Infinite Light – Ain Soph Aur | Jivatma (Incarnated Soul) | Holy Spirit | Buddha Nature

Affirmation on I AM (similar to Meditation on the Soul) by Master Choa Kok Sui

I AM THAT I AM. I Am not the body. I Am not the emotion. I Am not the thought. I Am not the mind. I Am the soul. I Am a spiritual being of Divine Intelligence, Divine Love, Divine Power.

I Am one with my higher soul. I AM THAT I AM. I Am one with the Divine Spark within me. I Am a child of God. I Am connected with God. I Am one with God. I Am one with all.

I am Spirit Soul. Aham Brahmasmi.

YOUR OWN SOUL IS YOUR GURU. QUIET THE MIND AND LISTEN TO YOUR HIGHER SELF.

Atma (Soul) Yoga, page 103

"The key to Mahatma Gandhi's greatness comes from his Samadhi (unity consciousness) by soul-force cultivation shown in his quotations." – Acharya Ricardo B Serrano

"In the attitude of silence, the soul finds the path in a clearer light."

"There is force in the universe, which, if we permit it, will flow through us and produce miraculous results."

"Soul-force comes only through God's grace and never descends upon a man who is a slave of lust."

"The mantra becomes one's staff of life, and carries one through every ordeal. It is no empty repetition. For each repetition has a new meaning, carrying you nearer and nearer to God."

Inside of me there's a mantra going on that reminds me of who I am. It's that place inside – that niche in the wall where the candle flame never flickers. Always bringing me right to my heart where we dwell eternally. Mantra is the repetition of the names of God. Mantra is usually recited silently in the mind. When practiced daily, it has the ability to steady the mind and transform consciousness. To be most effective, mantra should be repeated frequently; any time, any place – walking, taking a shower, washing the dishes. I used to do mantra while waiting in line, so as not be bored. Now I practice being here now in line... See Hare Krishna Mantra, page 123

Ka-e-i-la-hreem Ha-sa-ka-ha-la-hreem Sa-ka-la-hreem

For many millennia the **Sri Yantra** has been used to bring good fortune, wealth, health, protection and as an energetic aid to meditation and healing for Sri Vidya practitioners.

Focus your eyes in bindu point of Sri Yantra while chanting the panchadasi mantra 15x and SHREEM 9x.

I experience the bliss of samadhi while doing the mudras with the bija mantras of each 9 avaranas in the Sri Chakra Yantra. – Acharya Ricardo B Serrano

See Kundalini Awakening, p. 12; Garland of Letters, p. 28 and 126; Sri Yantra, pages 44, 47, 52, 92, 125, 128

How to Experience Heaven Now

"Heaven is real and you can experience heaven now." – Ricardo B Serrano

"When you do meditations, you have to practice character building. Without it, there is a tendency to become worse…

During prayer or meditation, the spiritual cord becomes big. Every time a person breaks the virtues, the connection becomes thinner. When you do what you are supposed to do, the spiritual cord becomes bigger. Every time you refrain from unwholesome action, the connection with your higher Buddha nature increases." – Master Choa Kok Sui

Buddha was asked, "What have you gained from meditation?"

He replied, "Nothing! However, let me tell you what I have lost: anger, anxiety, depression, insecurity, fear of old age and death."

"If you truly loved yourself, you could never hurt another."

"Those who experiences the unity of life sees their own Self in all beings, and all beings in their own Self, and looks on everything with an impartial eye."

"Those who knows life flows, feels no wear or tear, needs no mending or repair."

"In the end these things matter most: How well did you love? How fully did you live? How deeply did you let go?" – Buddha

Chant Shyama Mula Mantra

Aeem Hreem Shreem Aeem Kleem Souh- Om Namo Bhagavathi Sri Matangiswari

Sarva Jana Manohaari- Sarva Mukhranjini- Kleem Hreem Shreem

Sarva Raja Vasankari- Sarva Sthri Pursha Vasamkari - Sarva Dustha Murgavasankari- Sarva Sapta Vasamkari

Sarva Loka Vasankari- Sarvamme Vashamanaya Swaha - Souh Kleem Aeem Shreem Hreem Aeem

We are only fascinated by the light, we miss the whole point of our source. The Void. It is time to embrace the Void. The destroyer of ego and time. The vast black soup that is our real mother, Maha Kali. All balance with Kali from the heart center. Kali is Tara. So Kali is Lalitha at the top as she is Bhairavi at the bottom. So just chant KREEM and know your true mother who bestows moksha (liberation). **Om Kreem Kreem Kreem Hum Hum Hreem Hreem Dakshine Kalike Kreem Kreem Kreem Hum Hum Hreem Hreem Svaha**. See Sri Devi, pages 32, 44, 112, 119, 122, 140; Maha Vidyas, p. 120

There are good books you can read on author's experiences on heaven after near death who have written their heavenly experiences after being revived. However, you don't need to believe these authors and wait for near death to experience heaven while still breathing, aware and living fully your day to day joys and stresses.

Heaven is real and you can experience heaven now. The most important question is how to unite individual consciousness with Universal God consciousness to experience heaven, our true spiritual home, regularly and continuously while still alive and consciously aware.

Notes from one of my personal heavenly merkabah meditation experience during my October 25-26, 2003 meditation with Alton Kamadon in Alberta, Canada:

"Lots and lots of love and light pouring in my heart opening it to a greater degree which brought tears to my eyes... There is no other reason for your existence – to ascend while you are still living ... It is time to Self-Realize I AM THAT I AM ... Align with I AM Presence (your God-Self, Angelic Self)... which in turn releases the perfect solution or advice in any given situation."

The reality of this whole universe is God consciousness. It is filled with God consciousness. This world is nothing but the blissful energy (shakti) of the all-pervading consciousness of God. God and the individual are one, to realize this is the essence and goal of meditation and Qigong.

My seven books covered thoroughly in You Hold the Keys to Healing together with Workshops will show you how to experience heaven now by returning to oneness.

Excerpts from Sheng Zhen Wuji Yuan Gong: A Return to Oneness

"All journeys end where they begin. From Love you came to manifest love in the world. Then you return to the heart of Love. In that truth is found the essence of life."

"Understand that the purpose of life is to reach for and attain the highest experience of love."

"One cannot hold happiness because it is in constant motion. One has to ride it."

"The gateway to Heaven is the gateway into your heart."

"The natural state is the highest level in the world. It is the state of a loving heart. After you have acquired that state, whatever you do is always in the flow."

"As long as you have love and the willingness to help others, people can receive love from you."

"In truth, when you help others, you are also helping yourself. Gratitude from others together with your own virtue further uplifts you. Through helping others, you continuously awaken and elevate your soul."

"Where does one's true home lie? The saying "Home is where the heart is," does not mean only that one's affections lie where one's home is. Its deeper meaning is that the Heart is where the true home is.

Home is not just a place, or structure, or people. It is a state of consciousness where one experiences a sense of oneness. To return to one's true home is to return to one's original nature – to rediscover one's real Self – to regain the awareness of the wholeness which was never lost but only forgotten.

The journey back to one's true home is a journey into one's own Heart – a journey into the heart of existence – back to that "nothingness" from which everything arises. To attain this state is to know one's place in the scheme of things – to always be at home no matter where one is – to always experience wholeness no matter what the circumstances of one's life may be. To attain this state is to merge with all and to know that there is only One."

Dr. Eben Alexander MD, author of Proof of Heaven: A Neurosurgeon's Journey into the Afterlife, is a doctor who believes that true health can be achieved only when we realize that God and the soul are real and that death is not the end of personal existence but only a transition.

He is adamant that "the theory that the brain, and in particular the cortex, generates consciousness and that we live in a universe devoid of any kind of emotion, much less the unconditional love that I now know God and the universe have toward us," is drastically incorrect.

"What happened to me destroyed it, and I intend to spend the rest of my life investigating the true nature of consciousness and making the fact that we are more, much more, than our physical brains as clear as I can, both to my fellow scientists and to people at large."

Rather than dismissing all his scientific training, he is combining his spiritual and scientific views. "I'm still a doctor, and still a man of science every bit as much as I was before I had my experience. But on a deep level I'm very different from the person I was before, because I've caught a glimpse of this emerging picture of reality," said Dr. Alexander.

So-ham Quotations

In the still space where the breath merges, the feeling of duality disappears, and you become conscious of equality of all things. Jnaneshwar Maharaj said: "As you become aware of *So'ham*, the body-consciousness dissolves, and the senses, which have been wandering among outer objects, automatically turn within." Then you experience the union of Shiva and Shakti within yourself. Outside and inside become one.

The mantra of the pure "I"-consciousness destroys the duality of this world and reveals that God who is one. Jnaneshwar Maharaj said: "Just as light pervades everywhere, the *So'ham* consciousness extends from the embodied Self to the supreme Self. When men becomes fully immersed in the *So'ham* vision, he spontaneously merges in the supreme being."

Quotations from Tai Chi Grand Master Victor Shim

"The ego represents human nature. As long as we cling onto our human nature, we cannot unite with the divine self, that is your true self or true spirit. Only the true self can go beyond the mind of reasoning and techniques. Therefore one enters the mysterious gate when he is in union with his Buddha nature or Christ image or you can call the creator's image whatever.

In all my demos I've used the chi with restrain and gentleness. If I were to use my master's explosive outburst of chi, I could easily injured my beloved students. When you are good with chi, you eliminate the pride and boastfulness or to impress someone. Anyway, everyone can attain a high level as long as you peel off your ego!

Chi has no secrets. When your 8 psychic channels are opened, you will be able to extend the chi outside your physical body. Starts with REN mai and DU mai.

To build up the Chi, you must be in harmony with breath, mind and synchronized with your movements with the tip of tongue touching the upper palate."

Quotes on Lord Krishna's intimate and infinite divinity from the Bhagavad Gita:

Behold my forms, O Partha, by the hundreds, or by the thousands - Divine, of various types, and of various colors and appearances. - BG 11.5

But you are unable to see me with only this, your own eyes. I [therefore] give divine eyes to you - behold my supremely powerful yoga! - BG 11.8

Having seen what never has been seen before, I am exceedingly pleased, yet my my mind is distressed and filled with fear. O divinity, allow me to see that very [intimate] form. Bestow upon me your grace, O Lord of Divinities, dwelling place of the universe. - BG 11.45

Only by the offering of one's love to none other, O Arjuna, am I able, in such a form, to be known and to be truly seen, and to be attained, O Fighter of the Enemy. - BG 11.54

Acting for me in one's actions, being devoted to me, having no attachments, Free from enmity toward all beings - this is the one who comes to me, O Son of Pandu. - BG 11.55

And remembering - remembering over and over that most wondrous beautiful form of Hari, My amazement is great, O King, and I feel rapturous bliss again and again! - BG 18.77

Sri Devi is Durga, Kali, Lakshmi, and Saraswati.

Durga is Kali. Ma Durga is the benevolent face of Maha Kali. See Sri Devi, pages 32, 112, 119, 120, 122, 140

Sri Yantra Sarvayoni Mudra

See Kundalini Awakening, p. 12; Garland of Letters, p. 28 and 126; Sri Yantra, pages 40, 47, 52, 92, 125, 128

Theme of the Song Imagine

"And you will know the truth, and the truth will set you free." – John 8:32

"Character-building is very important because it is a means to purify the incarnated soul. As you purify yourself thoroughly, your incarnated soul will be able to function on a higher level of consciousness until it can unite with your higher soul."

"By meditating on the Higher Soul, we become One with the "I AM" or "God Nature" within all of us."

"The Higher Soul is a seed of God's Divinity within all of us. Through the Higher Soul we are made in the image of God! Being One with our Higher Soul, we become One with the "I AM", the Christ, the Buddha Nature or the Shiva within us." – Master Choa Kok Sui

Quotes from Bhagavad Gita about God-realization through Lord Krishna's Bhakti Yoga:

Even among all yogis, one whose inner self has come to me, Who is full of faith, who offers love to me - that one is considered by me to be the most deeply absorbed in yoga. - BG 6.47

I am the taste in water, O Kaunteya; I am the radiance of the moon and the sun, the sacred utterance in all the Vedas, the sound in space, the prowess in men. - BG 7.8

You are the supreme Brahman, the supreme dwelling place, the supreme means of purification; The eternal divine Person, the original Divinity, the unborn, all pervading one. - BG 10.12

Whatever form of existence possesses abounding power, contains the beautiful, or is well-endowed with excellence - Understand that every such form has become fully manifest from but a part of my splendor. - BG 10.41

"All you need is love (Krishna)." – Bhakti Yogi George Harrison (Beatles) 31/3/70 see Everybody is looking for Krishna, page 48

The following teachings from Kashmir Shaivism, embodied in the song Imagine, will shed light on the necessity of the practice of Qigong meditation to help people find peace, love, happiness from within themselves rather than focus their dependency from outside.

The sages and saints have said that to end suffering and attain happiness, one must have knowledge of the Self, which is the true source of joy. "Knowledge is the supreme state." The bliss of the Self is attained only through knowledge. In the Bhagavad Gita the Lord says, "In the world, there is nothing as pure as knowledge."

That is why it does not matter where you are or where you live, but rather who you are and what your inner state happens to be. The problem lies in your ignorance of your own essential nature. You will gain nothing by changing your country, town, or home; since you take your own destiny with you, you will only be welcoming pain again. It is very good to want freedom, but instead of looking for it in the wrong place, you must discover where it really dwells. The difference between a spiritual being and a politician is this: The politician says, "Bondage is external – break it and then you will obtain the joy of freedom." But the knower of the Truth says, "O my friend, bondage is not outside, but within you." No matter how much you try to break your outer fetters, your bondage will only increase. Therefore, you must go where there is supreme freedom – to the inner Self in the heart.

You are entirely responsible for your own state of dependency; in fact, you have become addicted to it. Because you think that the elixir of love is found in dependency, you have made it the abode of your love, and if you were ever to tear down the wall of dependency, you would only build another one somewhere else. However, you must free yourself in every way. Lord Buddha said again and again, "You can certainly come to me, but do not become bound by me." In the same way, when people ask me, "Is it alright to meditate on you?" I tell them, "Meditate on your own Self." Although it is difficult, you must escape from the prison of the non-Self. Who is a Hindu? Who is a Jain, a Buddhist, a Sufi, or a Christian? If you are imprisoned in one of these false identities, how can you find freedom of the self? That is why Lord Krishna said, "Give up all religions and take refuge in me (our inner consciousness) alone." Discard all false identification with religion. Go to the inner Self for shelter and revel there.

Ascended Master Thoth said, "As we change our personal energy field to the Hologram of Unconditional Love Merkaba we break down linear time and disintegrate the veil. If we understand the concept of this pattern it will take us into the time continuum of the eternal life form of Adam Kadman in the higher dimensions.

As the universe is sustained by unconditional love, true divine manifestation can only occur within love. It is natural to conceive that the Hologram of Love is the pattern of unconditional love. The Universe was born from it and the finest particle of our atomic cell structure is that pattern. This means we have always had the seed of unconditional love within us and and all we need to do is recognize it and activate this wonderful original essence. This would seem to mean that if you activate a Light field of this hologram pattern around your physical body, that also extends through your body cells and anchors in your heart, you are indeed activating your true being of unconditional love."

A great master said, "And you will know the truth, and the truth will set you free." When you know that the truth is what you are, the next step is to see the truth, to see what you are. Only then are you free. Free of what? Free of the emotional drama that is the consequence of believing in lies. When the truth sets you free, the symbols and agreements you learned and believed are true are no longer ruling your world.

IMAGINE (by John Lennon)

Imagine there's no heaven

It's easy if you try

No hell below us

Above us only sky

Living for today ...

Imagine there's no countries

It isn't hard to do

Nothing to kill or die for And no religion too

Imagine all the people Living life in peace ...

You may say I'm a dreamer But I'm not the only one

I hope someday you'll join us And the world will be as one

Imagine no possessions I wonder if you can

No need for greed or hunger A brotherhood of man

Imagine all the people Sharing all the world ...

You may say I'm a dreamer But I'm not the only one

I hope someday you'll join us And the world will live as one

Prana Pratishtha

Our Sri Chakra Yantras and Merus are brought to life using the Prana we have developed in ourselves. This infusing of sacred breath is called Prana Prathishta and by doing this ritual, your Sri Chakra becomes a living portal and vehicle for your communication with Lalitha Tripura Sundari (The Adi Shakti) and your highest self. It also attracts only good and grace-filled energies into your life as you move towards the middle Bindu. The Sri Chakra is a map of Kundalini's journey and the Chakras with bija mantras relate to the 9 levels. The Sri Chakra Yantra and the Kundalini Chakra System are related to the body of the Goddess being equivalent to your body. Meditating on her, on the Sri Yantra, and on your body become the same thing.

Prana Pratishtha and Sri Chakra Yantra

By infusing the Sri Chakra Yantra with prana by Prana Pratishtha ritual, it becomes a living portal and vehicle for your communication with Adi Shakti and your highest Self. – Acharya Ricardo B Serrano

See Kundalini Awakening, p. 12; Garland of Letters, p. 28 and 126; Sri Yantra, pages 40, 44, 52, 92, 125, 128

By infusing the Sri Chakra Yantra with prana by Prana Pratishtha ritual, it becomes a living portal and vehicle for your communication with Adi Shakti and your highest Self.
— Acharya Ricardo B Serrano

Everybody is looking for KRISHNA. Some don't realize that they are, but they are.

KRISHNA is GOD, the Source of all that exists, the Cause of all that is, was, or ever will be. As GOD is unlimited HE has many Names. Allah-Buddha-Jehova-Rama: All are KRISHNA, all are ONE.

God is not abstract; He has both the impersonal and the personal aspects to His personality which is SUPREME, ETERNAL, BLISSFUL, and full of KNOWLEDGE. As a single drop of water has the same qualities as an ocean of water, so has our consciousness the qualities of GOD'S consciousness... but through our identification and attachment with material energy (physical body, sense pleasures, material possessions, ego, etc.) our true TRANSCENDENTAL CONSCIOUSNESS has been polluted, and like a dirty mirror it is unable to reflect a pure image. With many lives our association with the TEMPORARY has grown. This impermanent body, a bag of bones and flesh, is mistaken for our true self, and we have accepted this temporary condition to be final.

Through all ages, great SAINTS have remained as living proof that this non-temporary, permanent state of GOD CONSCIOUSNESS can be revived in all living Souls. Each soul is potentially divine. Krishna says in Bhagavad Gita: "Steady in the Self, being freed from all material contamination, the yogi achieves the highest perfectional stage of happiness in touch with the Supreme Consciousness." (VI,28)

YOGA (a scientific method for GOD (SELF) realization) is the process by which we purify our consciousness, stop further pollution, and arrive at the state of Perfection, full KNOWLEDGE, full BLISS.

If there's a God, I want to see Him. It's pointless to believe in something without proof, and Krishna Consciousness and meditation are methods where you can actually obtain GOD perception. You can actually see God, and Hear Him, play with Him. It might sound crazy, but He is actually there, actually with you.

There are many yogic Paths--Raja, Jnana, Hatha, Kriya, Karma, Bhakti--which are all acclaimed by the MASTERS of each method. SWAMI BHAKTIVEDANTA is as his title says, a BHAKTI Yogi following the path of DEVOTION. By serving GOD through each thought, word, and DEED, and by chanting HIS Holy Names, the devotee quickly develops God-consciousness. By chanting:

Hare Krishna, Hare Krishna - Krishna Krishna, Hare Hare, Hare Rama, Hare Rama - Rama Rama, Hare Hare

one inevitably arrives at KRISHNA Consciousness. (The proof of the pudding is in the eating!)

I request that you take advantage of this book KRISHNA, and enter into its understanding. I also request that you make an appointment to meet your God now, through the self liberating process of YOGA (UNION) and GIVE PEACE A CHANCE. – by George Harrison (Beatles) 31/3/70 See To Feel the Love of one's Soul, page 100 and Hare Krishna Mantra, page 123

How to Conquer Death Now

"We have to realize our identity with the Universal Consciousness. We have to merge with that Consciousness, just as a river merges with the ocean. When a being has attained this state of oneness, he has gone beyond death." - Swami Muktananda Paramahamsa

Another term for Universal consciousness is Buddhic consciousness, Christ consciousness or Krishna consciousness. This state of being manifests as a person feels oneness with all, oneness with the Creator. This is the state of feeling Loving-Kindness for all.

When Shiva and Shakti reunite, you become one with everything. – Acharya Ricardo B Serrano

According to the excellent article "*Death and Dying in the Tibetan Buddhist* Tradition" by Ven. Pende Hawter, "Contemplation and meditation on death and impermanence are regarded as very important in Buddhism for two reasons : (1) it is only by recognising how precious and how short life is that we are most likely to make it meaningful and to live it fully and (2) by understanding the death process and familiarizing yourself with it, we can remove fear at the time of death and ensure a good rebirth. The three roots are described below:

A. DEATH IS CERTAIN
B. THE TIME OF DEATH IS UNCERTAIN
C. THE ONLY THING THAT CAN HELP US AT THE TIME OF DEATH IS OUR MENTAL/SPIRITUAL DEVELOPMENT

To ripen our inner potential now, without delay is the inner conviction.

"Goodbyes are only for those who love with their eyes, because those who love with heart and soul there is no such thing as separation."
"My soul is from elsewhere, I am sure of that, and I intend to end up there."
"This place is a dream. Only a sleeper considers it real. Then death comes like dawn, and you wake up laughing at what you thought was your grief." - Rumi

May the following Kashmir Shaivism based excerpts from the book "Does Death Really Exist?" by Swami Muktananda Paramahamsa enlighten those people seeking answers to the ever most important question: how to conquer death – end the cycle of death and rebirth – in this lifetime. I believe that we can conquer death now by returning to oneness – uniting our individual consciousness with the universal consciousness through the practice of meditation and Qigong. See Atma (Soul) Yoga of Immortality, page 103

Excerpts from Does Death Really Exist? by Swami Muktananda Paramahamsa:

How can a person free himself from this wheel of death and rebirth? He can do so only by going within and through meditation discovering his own inner Self. As we meditate, we become established in the seat of the inner Self, and then we are liberated from death. In meditation, we discard our individual ego and merge with the Self. The ego is a veil which hides the Self and keep us bound to the body. The ego is nothing but our sense of limited individuality, an identification with the body and the mind, with our sex, our family, our country, our position. Although the Self is completely stainless, when it is enveloped in the three impurities (malas) the ego is born, and we become bound.

The purpose of spiritual life is to become free of these impurities, and to do that we must perform only good actions. If we perform bad actions – if we hurt ourselves or other people – then over and over again we are enveloped by these malas. As long as we are covered by them, we are mere human beings. But once we become free of them, we are nothing but Supreme Consciousness.

Within every human being is a great and divine energy called Kundalini (Shakti)… When it is awakened through the grace of the Guru, a spontaneous process begins within. Then the awakened energy moves through our system, burning all the impurities in the body. Through the meditation which takes place after Kundalini awakening, one easily comes to see the Self within the heart. The fire of that knowledge of the Self destroys the three malas, and one expands more and more. Once one has completely evolved, one knows, "I am God." Instead of having the awareness that one is the body, one very naturally becomes aware, "I am the Self." When one realizes that God dwells within as one's own inner Self, the fire of that knowledge burns all one's accumulated karma…

"Because of the three malas – anavamala (awareness of imperfection), mayiyamala (awareness of duality), and karmamala (awareness of doership) – an individual soul is born again and again. When the malas are removed through spiritual practices and the grace of a pure being, the individual soul goes beyond birth and death and is never born again.

"The truth is that it is our own ego which is death for us. When we have gone beyond the ego, death no longer exists.

"In the same way, our ego brings us again and again to our death. In order to conquer death, we have to transcend the ego, to overcome our limited individuality. We have to realize our identity with the Universal Consciousness. We have to merge with that Consciousness, just as a river merges with the ocean. When a being has attained this state of oneness, he has gone beyond death. The Gita says: "The embodied one, having gone beyond the three gunas – sattva (purity), rajas (activity), and tamas (inertia) – out of which the body is evolved, is freed from birth, death, decay, and pain and attains immortality."

"Whatever being a person thinks of at the last moment when he leaves his body, that alone does he attain." Therefore, whatever is in one's mind at the moment of death is extremely significant. For this reason we hold regular recitation of sacred texts at our Ashrams. If one memorizes good words, they keep reverberating inside. If one studies the Bhagavad Gita, the Bible, and the Upanishads, they keep coming to one's mind. One who remembers God constantly in this way will attain the state of God at the time of death. One who meditates and prays every day has no fear of death.

We forget to contemplate, "Who am I? Why was I born? What is the goal of my life? What am I supposed to accomplish here?" We forget the reason we are here, and we eat and drink and make merry. We indulge in sense pleasures, and one day we leave this body. Kabir wrote: "O friend, listen to me: through chanting God's name, great beings go across in this way. One day the body will drop away. In this world, everything that comes also goes. But the Self does not die. The inner Self is ageless and unchanging. Death cannot reach it. Therefore, live with the awareness: "The Supreme Truth lies within me; the flame of Supreme Truth is shimmering and shining inside me." That light is the Self.

May your awareness turn inward. May you live with the knowledge, "I am the Supreme Truth; pure Consciousness lies within me." Through the fire of knowledge, may death die for you. I wish this for you all.

Within this body the taintless string of beads goes round and round day and night.

It goes up and down with each breath.

Not understanding this, worldly people let their breath go to waste and walk into the jaws of death.

Without the aid of tongue or teeth every living being repeats the *So'ham* mantra.

Day and night, awake or sleep, it doesn't stop even for a moment.

Hamsa-So'ham, Hamsa-So'ham – it goes on and on.

The Sadguru unravels its secret and makes your mind still.

Brahmananda says: "Yogis who sit and meditate on this every morning attain the state of liberation. They are not born again."

"Finally, as you pursue this self-born yoga, as the inner Shakti unfolds, you reach the sahasrara, the topmost spiritual center in the crown of the head. This is the culmination of the spiritual journey, and here the light of the Self reveals itself. In the sahasrara there is a divine effulgence. That light has the radiance of a thousand suns. In that center, there is no pain and no pleasure. Only the bliss of consciousness exists there. In the center of that divine effulgence in the sahasrara, there is a tiny subtle blue light, which yogis call the *nila bindu*, the blue pearl. Watching this tender, infinitely fascinating light, you become aware of your true glory. Though smaller than a sesame seed, the blue pearl contains the entire universe. It is the light of God, the form of God within you. This is the divinity, this is the greatness that lies within a human being...Therefore, perceive that light. Only if you discover that light will you recognize who you truly are." – Muktananda

Negative Ion Therapy

If your are desperately ill or hopelessly sick and modern medicine including surgery gives you little or no help, you may think you need a miracle to get back your health. This "miracle" may be provided by Qigong and a new electromagnetic healing technology that promises to correct what is wrong with your body.

Most ailments are the result of an imbalance in the body's electrical Wei Qi field, usually due to a drop in supply of anions or negatively charged ions.

Qigong aims to correct this imbalance by bombarding the body with anions or negative ions from nature until the right yin-yang balance is achieved.

When this is accomplished, the human body will go back to its normal functioning self, free of any disease. See Nature generates negative ions, page 56

Another way to correct the ionic imbalance is by an electrotherapy device which is described as a multi-functional machine invented in the Philippines that can stimulate and rebuild the body's natural electric field. Safety precautions and expert guidance for its use are recommended.

The negative ions are provided by electricity from an electromagnetic healing machine that is strapped for a number of hours each day through the feet in the Yong Quan point (Kidney 1) of the patient supplying the healing Qi into the kidneys' adrenals building the Yuan Qi. This is similar to the effect of internal and external Qigong in the body's storage of Source Qi in the lower dantian to cultivate the Three Treasures Jing, Qi and Shen for healing and enlightenment.

The **Sri Chakra Yantra** is a map of your consciousness and cosmology that goes from the center of your highest being to living in the world of elements and planets. It is a map to navigate through consciousness and to take you from earth consciousness to the heavenly realms of your divine nature. Become one with your Sri Yantra or Meru and allow it to guide your life and attract power and the blessings of the Devis (Shaktis) into your life; the Meru is a communication and transmission portal between dimensions and between you and your highest self.

The Universal Mother (Source) is attained via a journey through the 9 (Nava) levels (Avaranas) of Sri Yantra: Three tantric bodies (shariras) and 5 Koshas - (1) Universal Mother (Source) Anandamaya Kosha (2) Sukshma (the Spirit Astral Realm) - Vigyanamaya, Manamaya & Pranamaya Kosha, and (3) Sthula (the Body) - Annamaya Kosha.

"You become a living Sri Yantra Meru by reuniting Shiva and Shakti within you through the Sri Yantra and Mantra meditation." – Acharya Ricardo B Serrano

See Kundalini Awakening, p. 12; Garland of Letters, p. 28 and 126; Sri Yantra, pages 40, 44, 47, 92, 125, 128

Origin of the Heart (Hanuman Qigong)

The basic idea for this qigong is to integrate qi with Heaven, to integrate the heart with the spirit in dance-like movements. The spirit we refer to here means both the human being's soul and also the soul of the Universe. This qigong is beneficial to health when the practitioner reaches a state of integrating himself and heaven. In comparison with other Sheng Zhen Wuji Yuan Gong, this qigong practice may not be as effective in treating disease because the health benefits will only occur when the practitioner has reached a very high level of practice. So this form is recommended for those who have practiced Sheng Zhen Wuji Yuan Gong for more than three years. Beginners are not encouraged to study.

The true meaning of Nothingness lies in the dropping away of all resistance. Nothingness means the end of separation. At this point, attachment and selfish desire dissipate, leaving at once both Nothingness and complete union into Oneness. It is here that the practitioner has become truly empty. There is no more individuality. Nothingness frees the person. All that is left is the One. In essence, Nothingness and Oneness are the same.

"Oneness or Qigong state (Samadhi) is experienced by cultivating the Three Treasures Jing, Qi and Shen in the Three Dantians through the practice of Qigong." – Master Ricardo B Serrano

"The teaching focuses essentially on the purification of Jing-Chi-Shen into its final product: the elixir of pure-person." – Door to All Wonders, Tao Te Ching

"Health is the greatest possession. Contentment is the greatest treasure. Confidence is the greatest friend. Non-being (samadhi) is the greatest joy." – Lao Tzu

In this Qigong practice when the qi is integrated, dancing is the state of gong. When the practice integrates Heaven's qi, dancing becomes expressed in a state of wholeness. The whole body dances as it joins in the movements. This helps qi and blood to move, too. With these dancing movements, one's thoughts gradually melt from the mind, merging with the purest qi and the most sincere love in the universe. At this moment, the practitioner becomes integrated with nature, his heart is integrated with spirit, Heaven is integrated with Earth, and everything in this world returns to its most original state. This is the state we are trying to reach in this qigong practice.

Unconditional love is the fulcrum of this universe, the original point of the universe. In the practice of Meditation on Three Hearts and Hanuman Qigong, efforts must be made to integrate the mind and heart, to feel the interaction between Love and Qi, restoring the experience of harmony in the world, in nature, and the Universe. In starting the day with the practice of Hanuman Qigong, one holds within, the desire to integrate heart and spirit, to arrive at the experience of Oneness. The rest of the day unfolds naturally from this sublime intention. At this moment, this is the highest service a human being can perform to humanity, to the universe, to Heaven.

When one finds true Oneness, there will be no words. Nothing can explain what Oneness truly is. One will only have the experience of Love and a smiling heart. No words can express that happiness and peace. It is beyond words. Oneness is everything. Oneness is the only truth worth seeking. Oneness is a gift from Heaven.

- Hanuman Qigong, Origin of the Heart, a form of Sheng Zhen Gong

*Prerequisite: To take this course, you must know, and practice well, at least one Sheng Zhen standing form.

NOTE by Acharya Ricardo B Serrano during the July 20-29, 2012 Sheng Zhen Teacher Training in Rosemary Heights Retreat Center, Surrey, B.C. with teacher Li Junfeng and his daughter Li Jing where we practiced Hanuman Qigong, origin of the heart: The practice of Hanuman Qigong was an unforgettable heart opening experience where my heart integrated with spirit and heaven integrated with earth. I strongly felt my mind quieting down merging with the most purest Qi and love in the universe. The practice of Hanuman Qigong, origin of the heart, expresses these truths.

> When I think of myself as a body, I am your servant;
>
> when I think of myself as an individual soul, I am part of you;
>
> but when I realize I am atman, you and I become one. — Valmiki Ramayana

Hanuman qigong practice includes 24 movements with every three movements considered a session, making eight sessions in all.

The First Session

(1) Wind, (2) Rain, (3) Sign (Climate) of the times

The Second Session

(4) Sun, (5) Moon, (6) Star

The Third Session

(7) Consciousness (Yi), (8) Thought (Nian), (9) Awakening (Xing)

The Fourth Session

(10) Heaven (Tian), (11) Earth (Di), (12) Humanity (Ren)

The Fifth Session

(13) Fullness (Bao), (14) Emptiness (Xu), (15) Roundness (Yuan)

The Sixth Session

(16) Light (Guang), (17) Qi, (18) Essence (Jing)

The Seventh Session

(19) Tao, (20) Dharma (Fa), (21) Love (Ai)

The Eighth Session

(22) Origin, (23) Nothingness, (24) Oneness

Glossary of Sheng Zhen Wuji Yuan Gong Terms:

Qigong is the interexchange of Qi between people and the universe. When the exchange of Qi takes place, the Qi works. It is this exchange of Qi that creates an energy that brings about health in living beings and in the natural environment. When there is Qi, there is life. When there is no Qi, there is no life.

Qigong is a science. But it transcends modern science. Qigong as a science should be used to improve people's lives – to teach them to be more natural and to attain a sense of total well-being. True Qigong must be something that is not just an intellectual pursuit or something to study but should be applied to life.

The three functions of Qigong:

1. Qigong is good for health. Through the exchange of Qi, diseased Qi is removed and fresh Qi is gathered.
2. Qigong brings about the removal of negativities that lead to worry, sadness, anger, nervousness, fear, and a stressful life. As a result, one is free to lead a happy and carefree life. Modern medicine is good but only provides a temporary solution. If people want to maintain their health, the energy level in the body must be in balance; the emotions must become balanced and even. Since emotions can affect the physical body, the emotions and the physical body must be in harmony.
3. Qigong opens the heart. As one experiences the opening of the heart, this allows the Qi from the universe to go to the entire body, removing the negativities that rob one of a life of perfect well-being. When the heart is open, immersed in the experience of love, the interflow of Qi can naturally take place making the Qi work. Unconditional love is the root, is the key. It is this purpose that Sheng Zhen Wuji Yuan Gong serves.

Nature generates negative ions

Why do we feel so good walking or practicing Qigong in the woods, on a beach or near a river, breathing fresh air in the mountains, or just breathing fresh air after rain or storm? Simple ... We feel like that due to benign properties of negative ions abundant in these environments:

- Increase the flow of oxygen to the brain resulting in higher alertness, decreased drowsiness, and more mental energy.
- Help recovery from physical exhaustion and fatigue – achieved by increasing oxygen levels in the blood and stabilize brain function – effect – relaxation and calmness.
- Aid in blood purification by increasing the levels of calcium and sodium (healthy salt intake) in the blood stream, negative ions help restore a healthy (slightly alkaline) pH balance to the blood.
- Increase metabolism by stimulating exchange of electronic substances in cells.
- Strengthen immune system – high levels of negative ions promote production of globulin (proteins that are found extensively in blood plasma) in the blood, resulting in stronger resistance to illness.

Negative ions balance autonomic nervous system by balancing the opposing sympathetic and parasympathetic branches of the autonomic nervous system. Promote better digestion – by counteracting over-arousal of the sympathetic nervous system, negative ions help ease tension in the stomach and intestines, promoting the production of digestive enzymes and enhancing digestion. Promote cell rejuvenation by revitalizing cell metabolism, negative ions enhance vitality of muscle tissue and strengthening internal organs.

Conclusion

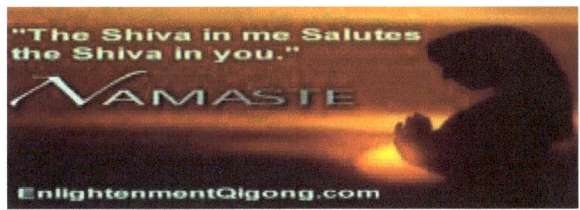

"Let Love light your path, Truth guide your way, and Joy sing from your soul."
– Sananda

When you meditate on the Self as the Self, you become one with Shiva, the Self of all.

YOUR OWN SOUL IS YOUR GURU, QUIET THE MIND AND LISTEN TO YOUR HIGHER SELF.
Atma (Soul) Yoga, page 103

Buddha Palm

"Qi is real, but takes time to cultivate. No ego should be expressed. One should be in harmony with Heaven, Earth and one's true self. When one becomes a vessel that can accumulate the Qi, permanent Qi will be harnessed in the 'Dan Tien' (the field of elixir." – Tai Chi Grand Master Victor Shim

"As a BC registered acupuncturist, Qi-healer and Qigong master for 30 years, I absolutely agree with GM Victor Shim's Qi demonstrations on empty force or ling kong jing. Only experience with Qi projection for healing and self-defense with a master will dispel most people's doubt about the reality of Qi. Qi is real and it takes time to cultivate it via regular tai chi or Qigong practice. Ego has to be defeated to experience Qi flow from emptiness (void). Thanks, GM Victor Shim."

"By focusing on breathing and movement exercises that emanate from our power center, the lower dantien – the physical center of gravity of our body located an inch or two below our navel and an inch or two inside our bellies – we can become more attuned to the Torus Wei Qi fields of energy, particularly human energy, that surround us so we can become healthier, perform better, be happier, and connect with ourselves, others and nature at a higher level of existence." – Ricardo B Serrano

I am grateful and fortunate to have studied within the span of 30 years with my pranic healing, meditation and Qigong teachers that made me realize my long-time dream of mastering energy healing, and eventually returning to oneness in the process.

How is it done? What are the necessary keys to healing stress-related diseases, and self-mastery, Self-realization or Soul-realization? These inquiries assisted me to search for the answers to these questions from the ancient eastern yoga, pranic healing and Qigong perspective.

How do I know that I am on the right path? I know I am on the right path because of the blissful and heart opening gift of oneness I am continuously experiencing when I practice the spiritually empowering Qi-healing (Buddha Palm), Eight Extraordinary Meridians Qigong, Hanuman Qigong, Meditation on Three Hearts, and Merkaba meditation regularly integrating heaven and earth, and integrating my heart with spirit – my soul and the soul of the universe.

"Let Love light your path, Truth guide your way, and Joy sing from your soul." – Sananda

I have lovingly recorded and written these ancient eastern yoga of Kashmir Shaivism teachings, meditation and Qigong techniques – Techniques of a Master – integrated path on how to become a divine medium through this book with Return to Oneness with Shiva and the other four books of the You Hold the Keys to Healing to benefit those serious seekers seeking a real ancient, time-proven, safe, grounded and balanced approach to energy healing and soul-realization.

"The most beautiful thing we can experience is the Mysterious. It is the source of all true science." – Albert Einstein

"As long as one is substantially connected to the higher soul, one remains whole and healthy." – Pranic Healing Grand Master Choa Kok Sui

"To better the quality of qi, to improve the circulation, human hearts must open. Unconditional love is the key that unleases the power of Qi. When the heart is open, immersed in the experience of love, the interflow of qi can take place making the qi work." – Sheng Zhen Gong Master Li Jun Feng

Love is. Love will always be. Love is eternity.

"Pranic Healing is a bridge to spirituality."

"Healing is Active Meditation. Healing is Meditation in Motion."

"A Healer's attitude is very important. It is only when you are humble that you become a Powerful Healer."

"You are a Soul with a body, not a body with a Soul."

"Inner forgiveness is therapeutic. If you do not forgive, you cannot be internally healed. Forgiving heals the soul. Make a list of all your enemies and those who have hurt you. Mentally visualize forgiving each one of them."

"The Soul is the Gateway to Heaven within you."

"When you are filled with soul energy you become magnetic."

"Soul-realization is nothing more than the incarnated soul realizing that it is not the body and it is one with the I AM or the higher soul."

"Character building is very important because it is a way to purify the incarnated soul. As you purify yourself thoroughly, your incarnated soul will be able to function on a higher level of consciousness until it can unite with your higher soul." – Grand Master Choa Kok Sui

The Goal: To discover the Truth within our Heart via Maha Kali, Maha Lakshmi and Tripura Sundari mantras

Om Kreem Kreem Kreem Hum Hum Hreem Hreem Dakshine Kalike Kreem Kreem Kreem Hum Hum Hreem Hreem Svaha.

Om Shreem Hreem Shreem Kamle Kamlalaye Praseeda Praseeda Shreem Hreem Shreem Om Maha Lakshmiye Namah

Tripura Sundari mantra, p. 40 See Sri Devi, pages 32, 41, 44, 112, 119, 122, 140; Maha Vidyas, p. 120

To discover the Truth within our own heart is the goal – and for this we need to perform spiritual practices.

The Siddha practices are not aimed at attaining God. God, according to the Siddhas, is already attained. The purpose of the practices is to purify the mind and break the chain of inner words, for when the mind is quiet and clear, the awareness of Self naturally reveals itself from within.

This is the goal of all spiritual practices – whether they be Qigong, meditation, chanting, mantra repetition, discipline, selfless service (guruseva), study, or satsang, spending time in the company of saints. These practices purify the atmosphere within and without. God is revealed by his own light, however, in the end.

The difference between Siddha meditation and other meditation techniques of other traditions is that instead of stilling the mind through our human efforts alone, we take the aid of a greater power, the Siddha Guru and the awakened Kundalini.

The result of the integration of the Siddha Guru and awakened Kundalini is a meditation that is very powerful. For very little self-effort, we get extraordinary and immediate results.

Turn Attention Within

Turn your attention deep within. Where Attention goes, energy flows. Where energy flows, awareness follows. Great power is created by focusing within. Focus on the soul above your head and the sphere of light which envelopes the body.

Meditate on the Self

Meditate on the Self, not on the thoughts of your mind. The Self is the one who watches your thoughts, the witness of your mind. Watch the watcher.

Meditate on the Self as the Self

Meditate on the Self as the Self. You are the Self. Become the Self. Stop identifying with your physical body, your mind, or your emotions. Become one with Shiva, the Self of all.

Meditate on a great being

Patanjali recommends that we meditate on a being who is "beyond attachment and aversion." Choose whatever form of God you love, or meditate on the form of the Guru, or on a saint. As you do, you will absorb that being's state and qualities. Sadguru Nityananda is the saint or the Guru we meditate on in our Siddha lineage.

Meditate on the space between the breaths

Where there is no breath there is no thought, and where there is no thought there is no mind; where there is no mind, the Self stands revealed. This space between the breaths is like a door in the mind, a secret panel that allows us to escape the room of our finite consciousness. Touch the tip of your tongue to upper palate while meditating on the space between the breaths (So'ham).

See the thoughts that arise as a play of consciousness

Even if thoughts continue to arise in your mind, detach from them. See them all as Consciousness. Look at the material of your thoughts, rather than at their "meaning." Every thought, no matter how interesting or how unappealing is only Consciousness in a different form, just as every wave is a part of the sea. Watch the waves of your thoughts arise and subside. From where do they arise? And what do they dissolve back into?

Chant the Adi Shakti, the Beej and the Om Nama Shivaya Mantras and listen deeply to your body trying to reconnect your Muladhara to your Ajna. Shiva and Shakti will reunite again one day in you.

Adi Shakti Mantra: **Adi Shakti Namo Namaha - Sarva Shakti Namo Namaha - Prathama Bhagavati Namo Namaha - Kundalini Mata Shakti - Mata Shakti Namo Namaha**

Kundalini Beej Mantra: **Lam Vam Ram Yam Ham Om**

Shiva Mantra: **Om Na Ma Shi Va Ya**

After Meditation

The Yoga Vashistha says, "The world is as you see it." When you see the world as Consciousness, it becomes Consciousness. When you regard yourself as Shiva, you yourself become the Lord. It's not only our thoughts and emotions that are made of Consciousness. This whole world, the Siddhas tell us, is made of Consciousness as well. Even after you come out of meditation, hold the awareness that the world is God's manifestation; see mother earth, sun, moon as the body of the divine Shakti. See everything that happens to you, good or bad, as God's play of consciousness. Regard everyone you meet as the light of God.

"God consciousness is the reality of everything." – Shiva Sutra 1.1

- Siddha: a perfected yogi; one who has attained the highest state and become one with the Absolute.
- Grounding and rooting to mother earth through the practice of Enlightenment Qigong forms especially Hanuman Qigong, Eight Extraordinary Meridians Qigong, and Drawing in Heaven and Earth via Wei Qi field activation are added to Siddha spiritual practices to balance the Shakti Qi flow in the body, build the Lightbody, psychic self-defense, avoid post-kundalini syndromes often seen in yoga practitioners and Self-realization.

Ling Kong Jing, or Powerful Empty Force: A standing meditation Buddhist method of the Hsing-I school of internal martial arts made famous by Wang Xiang Zhai.

The style of Qigong called Ling Kong Jing, or "empty force," has several applications. Among these are health promotion, fitness, increased longevity, and emission of Qi for healing or for martial arts purposes.

Standing Like a Tree is based on fundamental principles of Chinese medicine – the oldest continuous medical tradition in the world. The aim is to regulate the flow of vital energy by helping your whole system to relax while, at the same time, strengthening the ability of your body and mind to withstand stress. Research in China into its effects has shown increased blood circulation, greater breath capacity, enhanced muscle tone and strengthened immunity.

Summing up this rare system of energy cultivation, the US quarterly "Internal Arts Journal" told its readers: "These deeply spiritual and mysterious exercises contain the seeds of real internal power. In Zhan Zhuang Chi Kung one learns to return to the source of all power, to enter back into the very womb of universal energy and to experience the truth of the power of the void, the still point, the wuji".

Sifu R. Mooney said, "I respect each person's opinion, for that is how he or she is; but to those who discount this ability, I have a challenge: if you would dismiss it as fraud or magic, train in it yourself to get to the truth of the matter." Ling Kong Jing, the "Empty Force," is the highest martial arts skill in China. This extraordinary technique harnesses the power of chi, the body's vital energy, enabling masters of the art to defend themselves against opponents without making physical contact. It is based on the principle of directability and interconnectedness.

To cultivate the "Empty Force" or *Lin Kong Jing*, I practice regularly Tai Chi, Maitreya Shiva Shen Gong, Omkabah Lightbody Activation, Hanuman Qigong and the Eight Extraordinary Meridians Qigong with Meditation on Three Hearts to develop the Wei Qi Field, *Zhan Zhuang Qigong* with *Wing Chun Kung Fu* forms, Merkaba or Lightbody for healing and self-defense purposes. This advanced form of Qigong is best learned from an expert rather than learning on your own. For more information, see Psychic Self-Defense on page 132

External Qi-healing (Wai Qi Liao Fa)

The basis of Chinese medicine exists due to the belief that all living things have Qi. Without Qi there is no life. The theory of External Qi Healing (projection) follows the same theory of acupuncture: Reduce what is excessive, and stimulate what is deficient.

In doing External Qi Healing (Wai Qi Liao fa), the practitioner gains the benefit of doing Qigong, and after a healing session, the practitioner and recipient should feel the same as if they had just done a set of standing meditation (zhan zhuang) exercises; a sense of calm alertness, euphoria, and all-around good feelings that can last for quite a few hours after the session is done.

The ancient healing practice where cannabis oil is integrated with external Qi-healing as done 2000 years ago by Jesus Christ and the Classical Chinese Medicine practitioners has been rediscovered by Qigong master Ricardo B Serrano, R.Ac. See Jesus and Cannabis, page 136

Wei Qi Field in Medical Qigong

"This field of Qi protects the body from the invasion of external pathogens and communicates with, as well as interacts with, the surrounding universal and environmental energy fields."

– Chinese Medical Qigong Therapy

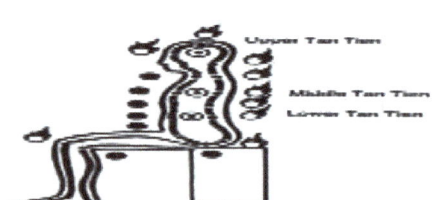

The Microcosmic Orbit is the key to balancing energies in the body to prevent kundalini syndromes, and the basic foundation for other advanced meditation practices.

There are many names for the invisible auric field that surrounds the physical body in various mystical traditions such as torus, Lightbody, Electromagnetic Field (EMF), energy bubble, Merkaba or aura. The auric field is called Wei Qi Field in Medical Qigong which will be under discussion.

Torus is synonymous with Wei Qi Field in enlightenment Qigong forms where the lower dantien is the sea of Qi. It is the dynamic flow process of Wei Qi field (torus) that explains that all is interconnected – All is God (pantheism) – and makes healing, self-defense and oneness with God possible.

Torus Qigong is synonymous with Baha'u'llah Shen Gong founded by Master Ricardo B Serrano. Baha'u'llah Shen Gong uses the Greatest Name chant instead of the Kototama chant. Baha'i prayers, songs, and meditations are used as contemplations. See Greatest Name in Dedication, page 3

Kototama (sacred Sound of Spirit) Chanting (Su Wa wo uuuu yeee iii) in resonance with this Wei Qi field (Torus) Qigong is taught as an aide to expanding one's consciousness to the Qi energy of the universe beyond the body. Kototama chant creates a resonant torus around the body. Could it be mere coincidence that the sequence of vowels is identical to the Hebrew name of God – "Yahweh" – that people were told not to speak aloud? Could this be the final ascension key to attain the Elixir of Immortality - the eternal Sahhu (Golden raiment) in Egyptian alchemy, or the rainbow lightbody in Tibetan Buddhism, which is not subject to dissolution of death or the after-death states of consciousness? See Way of Qi, page 27, Atma (Soul) Yoga of Immortality, page 103, Yuan Shen, page 130 and Torus Qigong with Kototama Chant, https://vimeo.com/628965833

According to Chinese Medical Qigong Therapy, "Qigong is a powerful system of healing and energy medicine from China. Qi means "Life-force energy" and gong means "skill," so Qigong (pronounced Chigong) is the skillful practice of gathering, circulating, and applying life-force energy. It uses breathing techniques, gentle movement, and meditation to cleanse, strengthen, and circulate the life energy or Qi and leads to better health and vitality and a tranquil state of mind. The primary goal is to purge toxic emotions from within the body's tissues, eliminate energetic stagnations, as well as strengthen and balance the internal organs and energetic fields.

All living bodies generate an external field of energy called Wei Qi (pronounced "whey chee"), which translates as "protective energy." The definition of Wei Qi in Medical Qigong is slightly different than that of Traditional Chinese Medicine (TCM). In classical TCM texts, the Wei Qi field is seen to be limited to the surface of the body, circulating within the tendon and muscle tissues. In Medical Qigong, however, the Wei Qi field also includes the three external layers of the body's auric and subtle energy fields. This energy originates from each of the internal organs and radiates through the external tissues. There the Wei Qi forms an energy field that radiates from the entire physical body. This field of Qi protects the body from the invasion of external pathogens and communicates with, as well as interacts with, the surrounding universal and environmental energy fields.

Both internal and external pathogenic factors affect the structural formation of the Wei Qi. The internal factors include suppressed emotional influences (such as anger and grief from emotional traumas). The external factors include environmental influences when they are too severe or chronic, such as Cold, Damp, Heat or Wind, etc. Physical traumas also affect the Wei Qi field.

Any negative interchange affects the Wei Qi by literally creating holes within the matrix of the individual's external energetic fields. When left unattended, these holes leave the body vulnerable to penetration, and disease begins to take root in the body. Strong emotions, in the form of toxic energy, become trapped within the body's tissues when we hold back or do not integrate our feelings. These unprocessed emotions block the natural flow of Qi, thus creating stagnant pools of toxic energy within the body.

The body has an energy field that is composed of energetic lines called meridians and channels. Energetic blockages in these channels cause imbalances in the energy field, which can lead to dis-ease. A free flow of energy is needed in the body and energy system for good health and well-being.

Medical Qigong consists of specific techniques that uses the knowledge of the body's internal and external energy fields to purge, tonify, and balance these energies. Medical Qigong therapy offers patients a safe and effective way to rid themselves of toxic pathogens and years of painful emotions that otherwise, can cause mental and physical illness. This therapy combines breathing techniques with movement, creative visualization, and spiritual intent to improve health, personal power, and control over one's own life."

The Schumann resonances are electromagnetic waves that exist in the space between the surface of the earth and the ionosphere. The frequencies include 7.83 Hz and is said to be the heartbeat of mother earth. When a person's brain waves resonate with 7.83 Hz, it has been shown in scientific studies to be an essential requirement for physical and psychological health. This demonstrated a direct link between humans and their connection with the pulse of the earth.

Many experts believe that wireless electromagnetic frequencies we are surrounded by everyday can cause us to feel more stressed, fatigued and out of balance. Therefore, by tuning into 7.83 Hz "alpha state" frequency, the Schumann resonance, we get back to a state of resonance or attunement with the planet's own magnetic frequency via the use of cannabis, acupuncture, meditation and Qigong that are necessary for spiritual awakening and healing chronic diseases. **OM SO-HAM**, see page 118

See Hanuman Qigong, page 53; Siddha meditation, page 59; Eight Extraordinary Meridians Qigong, page 65; Sheng Zhen Qigong, page 79; Mahashivaratri and Cannabis, page 96; Hare Krishna mantra, page 123; Meditation on Three Hearts, page 139

Glossary of Sheng Zhen Wuji Yuan Gong Terms:

Baihui – the acupuncture point located at the top of the head, the center of the crown.

Dantian – the storage place of Qi in the body, about two inches below the navel.

Five gateways – the entry points of Qi through the palms of the hands (laogong), the soles of the feet (yongquan), and the crown of the head (baihui).

Niwuan – the point located in the center of the head at the intersection between the center of the eyebrows (yintang) and the top of the head (baihui). Yintang – acupoint located at the center of the eyebrows.

Zhongmai – the primordial channel in the center of the body which connects the dantian to the niwuan – the dantian being earth and the niwuan being heaven.

The following principles are based on the principles of pranic healing and Ling Kong Jing:

Principle of Transmittability. Life force or vital energy can be transmitted from one person to another person.

Principle of Receptivity. A patient has to be receptive or at least neutral to receive the projected pranic energy. Being relaxed also helps increase the degree of receptivity. Without receptivity, the projected pranic energy will not be absorbed, or only a minimal amount of it will be absorbed. Patients may not be receptive because: they are biased towards this type of healing, they do not like the healer personally, they do not want to get well, or they are in general not receptive about anything.

Principle of Interconnectedness. The body of the patient and the body of the healer are interconnected with each other since they are part of the earth's energy body. On a more subtle level, it means that we are part of the solar system. We are interconnected with the whole cosmos. The principle of interconnectedness is also called the Principle of Oneness.

Principle of Directability. Life force can be directed. It follows where attention is focused; it follows thought. Distant pranic healing and Ling Kong Jing are based on the principle of directability and the principle of interconnectedness.

Sifu Rich Mooney explained his idea on Lin Kong Jing as to what was going on when used for healing and self-defense:

The Earth is the energy source (via laogong points of each hand), I am the conductor of the energy and the person I am projecting at is the ground. We all know that when you rub your feet on a carpet, and touch a person, or a pet, that a shock is felt. This is a discharge of static electricity. This also shows that we can induct, or take in energy. It is evident that we can store this energy, because it takes time for us to walk over and touch the friend or pet. We can emit, or discharge this energy upon touching the grounded target. The practice of Lin Kong Jing allows the practitioner to pull in (and emit) a lot of energy, which the Chinese call Qi. In all probability this is a type of electromagnetic bioenergetics force.

Eight Extraordinary Meridians Qigong

According to David Twicken, OMD, author of The Eight Extraordinary Channels – Qi Jing Ba Mai: A Handbook for Clinical Practice and Nei Dan Inner Meditation, "The eight extraordinary channels are one of the most fascinating aspects of the acupuncture channel system. These channels are the bridge between prenatal and postnatal influences in our life. The eight extraordinary channel's terrain is Jing, essence, and source Qi. These channels influence the yuan, or deep layers of our body, mind and spirit.

The jewel or pinnacle of Chinese medicine is that it enables us to work on the whole being, that includes body, mind and, spirit. One of the principal ways of achieving this is through the eight extraordinary channels, which are also called, the eight Psychic channels. These multi-dimensional channels can treat deep, chronic and old patterns that influences the three treasures of our life: the physical, emotional, and spiritual. These channels comprise the three dantiens and are the inner circuit system of communication between Jing and Shen (Zhi and Shen). The eight Psychic channels can release one from emotional and spiritual imbalances and realign one to their yuan shen – their original spirit. This experience can inspire and motivate a person to exert their will to live the type of life they desire, and they can apply their Zhi and passion to live from their spirit."

> *"To really understand the Eight Extraordinary Channels, one needs to cultivate them with Nei Dan (inner meditation/inner cultivation)."* – Master Li Shi-Zhen

The Eight Extraordinary meridians aka *Macrocosmic Orbit* is the basic anatomy and physiology of the human energy system, its structure and function, which is the control system and blueprint for everything else:

The four primary ones operate within the torso, and are known as:

1. Governor (Du Mo)
2. Conception (Ren Mo)
3. Belt (Dai Mo)
4. Thrusting (Chong Mo)

The four secondary ones, which support the primary set and run into the arms and legs, are:

1. Bridge (Yang Qiao Mo)
2. Bridge (Yin Qiao Mo)
3. Linking (Yang Wei Mo)
4. Linking (Yin Wei Mo)

These eight extraordinary meridians may be accessed and controlled by a special group of points called the Master and Coupled points: SI 3, Lu 7, GB 41, Sp 4; Bl 62, Ki 6, TH 5, PC 6

Together with some sub-branches and connecting channels, these 20 meridians / channels/ pathways constitute the full number of channels in the body familiar in Acupuncture.

However, there is another set of important centers used particularly in Qigong. These are called the *Three Dantiens*, which can be translated as the *Three Elixir Fields* or the Three Energy Centers. These are located in the core of the body along the *Chong Mo*. They are located in the lower abdomen, the center of the chest and the middle of the head.

The *Three Dantiens* contain the *Three Treasures*, which are known as *Jing, Qi,* and *Shen*, which can be translated as *Essence, Energy,* and *Spirit*. The Three Treasures are considered to be the most important possession a person has, and are nurtured, cultivated and protected.

Qigong works by operating these channels and centers – right balance and flow, increase the volume and heighten the frequency of your energy, and put it under your conscious control.

The applications of Qigong are: for Fitness, Sports, Martial Arts, Health and Healing, Sex, Longevity, Extraordinary human abilities, Spiritual development and Immortality.

If people learn how to effectively and use their own energy they will not be driven to use vast quantities of external energy to satisfy some internal need that could be equally satisfied by doing a simple internal practice. They will not be compelled and addicted to find external answers for internal imbalances – they will take care of themselves sitting quietly in a chair, and practicing. The more people that practice Qigong, the better for the planet, and everybody else.

Practicing Qigong is a process of personal evolution, and an act of social responsibility. Qigong holds the potential to make us healthy, sane and happy – and truly alive with Energy.

The Wei Qi Field

The human body is like a simple bar magnet, with a positive pole at one end and a negative pole at the other. Outside and around the body is a bio-electromagnetic field referred by the Chinese as Wei Qi, but is commonly known in the West as the Aura. This extends roughly as wide as your arms can reach.

The Wei Qi field/ Aura is an extension and reflection of your energy system. It is said to have seven distinct layers of increasing refinement and subtlety as it extends outward, each one corresponding to one of the seven energy centers along the central Thrusting Channel/ Chong Mo. This Wei Qi field is like an antennae and connects you with the external energy outside you – for instance, it resonates with Earth's magnetic field. It is also affected by such natural events as the weather, the seasons, and the moon cycles, as well as the location you are in.

It is important for your health and well-being to keep your Wei Qi field clear, clean and strong, because it reflects and affects your meridian energy and can be beneficial or detrimental to your organs, functions, and overall health.

The purpose of Drawing in Heaven and Earth:

- to activate your Wei Qi field around your body through the Belt Channel (Dai Mo) so that you can draw external energy in to you.
- to recharge yourself.
- to borrow the energy of heaven and earth when you need to.
- to plug yourself into the universe.

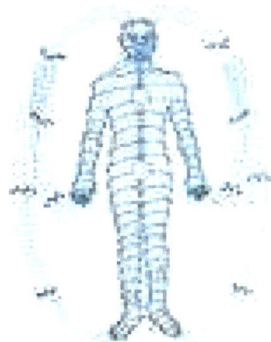

The Belt channel (Dai Mo) is the meridian that circulates horizontally around the body. It is the only meridian that moves on a horizontal level, and it wraps around all of the other channels, holding them together like a belt.

It activates and strengthens the Wei Qi field around your body to smooth, repair, balance and equalize your protective personal energy envelope, and access the only horizontal channels circling and spiraling around your body.

It acts as a protective field, an envelope, and can function as an energy overcoat to keep out undesirable energetic, psychic and emotional influences.

The pathways of the eight extraordinary meridians are **rooted** in the *Lower Dantian / Mingmen*.

Pan Gu Shen Gong, Primordial Wuji Qigong, Sheng Zhen Gong, Guo Lin Gong, Maitreya Shen Gong with *8 Extraordinary Vessels Qigong* complement Drawing in Heaven and Earth practice.

For more information on how to use the Wei Qi field for drawing in heaven and earth energy & 8 extraordinary vessels Qigong, please visit keystohealing.ca or contact Ricardo for instructions.

Source: globalqiproject.com/the-eight-extraordinary-meridians.html and healingtaousa.com

With thanks/acknowledgement to M.Winn and James MacRitchie, originator of this Qi project.

This practice involves extending the Belt Channel / Dai Mo up into heaven and down into Earth, and then reversing it to draw the essence and energy of Heaven and Earth into you.

Ascend Up Into Heaven

First open your whole personal Wei Qi field. Put your mind into your navel, open it. Then, draw your Qi up the Dai Mo, to crown point / Bai Hui. At this stage it is condensed to a 3 inch diameter circle.

Using your mind to control your energy, extend it 3-12 inches above your head. Rotate to left 3-9 times. This point is where the external Qi/energy aligns with your own unique personal energy frequency.

Then extend it above your head to the very edge of your personal field. Rotate to the left 3-6 times. This point is the 'transformer' that adjusts your own unique personal energy frequency to the universal field outside of yourself. It extends outside of your own personal energy field, to join with the external energy of the universe.

Directing your energy with your mind, spiral out 9 times, in ever increasing diameter, from the edge of your own personal field into the further reaches of the heavens above you. For you this may be to the edge of the atmosphere around our planet, or it may be to the outer edge of the universe, which according to the most recent observations and theories of science of astrophysics is an opaque plasma-field bubble. Extend out to whatever feels comfortable for you.

Rest in this space and place. Hold your mind and attention there. Experience this expanded sense of your relationship to the universe, and place in it. Breathe deeply in and out.

Then, rotating the direction of the spirals to the right, reverse the same scale and proportion over 9 spirals, and as you breathe in return back to the point above the outer-most edge of your personal field.

At this point circle 3-9 times. This acts like a 'transformer' and adjusts the universal energy to your own personal Qi/energy frequency and vibration.

Then, continuing to the right, drop down to the point 3-12 inches above your head. This adjusts it to your personal energy even more.

Then, descend to down to your Crown/Bai Hui point.

From here continue down, spiraling to the right, through each level of the Microcosmic orbit – brow, throat, chest, solar plexus, navel, sexual point, perineum, knees, to the soles of your feet.

Descend down Into Earth

Focus your Qi at the Bubbling Spring/ Yong Quan point on the soles of your feet. At this stage it is condensed to a 3 inch diameter.

Then, using your mind to control your energy, extend it 3-12 inches below your feet. Rotate to the right 3-9 times. This point is where the external Qi/energy aligns with your own unique personal energy frequency.

Then extend it below your feet to the very edge of your personal field. Rotate to the right 3-9 times. This point is the 'transformer' that adjusts your own unique personal energy frequency to the Earth energy outside of yourself. It extends outside of your own personal energy field, to join with the external energy of the Earth.

Directing your energy with your mind, spiral out 9 times to the right, in ever increasing diameter, from the edge of your own personal field down to into the Earth. This may progress from the immaculate environment of the room or open space you are in, to the building, block, city, country, state, continent, hemisphere while at the same time descending directly down to the center of the planet. Geologists believe there is a molten iron core at this center.

Rest in this space place – the center of gravity. Hold your mind and attention there. Experience this expanded sense of your relationship to planet Earth, and your place on it.

Breathe deeply in and out. Rest.

Then, rotating the direction of the spirals to the left, reverse this same scale and proportion over 9 spirals, and as you breathe in, slowly return back to the point below you, at the outer-most of your personal field.

At this point circle 3-9 times. This acts like a 'transformer' and adjusts the Earth energy to your own personal Qi energy frequency and vibration.

Continuing to the left, draw up to the point 3-12 inches below you. This adjusts it even more.

Then, draw it up to the Bubbling Spring/ Yong Quan point on the soles of your feet.

From here continue upwards, spiraling to your left, through each level of the Microcosmic orbit – knees, perineum, sexual point – back to the navel.

Close and Seal at your Navel: To end at this stage, close and seal your energy at your navel by spiraling out 9 or 36 times, and back-in 6 or 24 times.

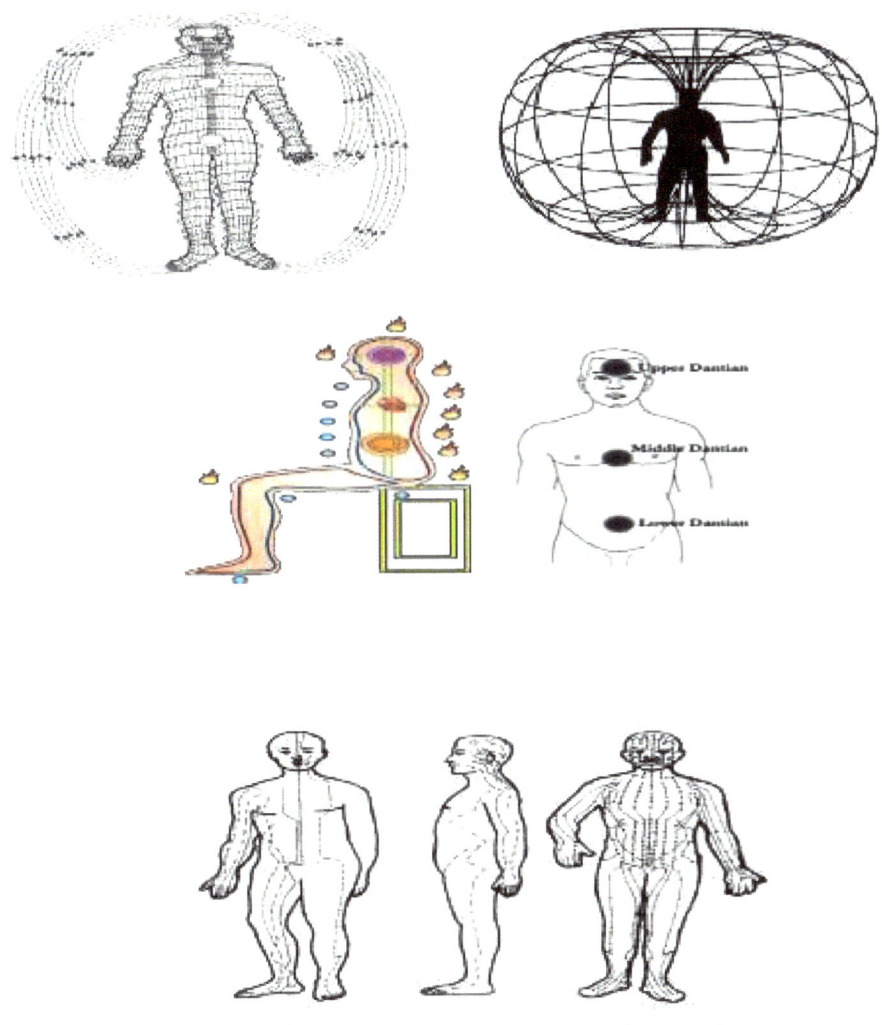

Shown are the body's complex network of yin and yang energy pathways, called Meridians, that flow along both sides of the body and connect to organs. Also shown are what are called extraordinary meridians, that balance and feed the others.

Kundalini syndrome and its treatment

Kundalini syndrome is just over active Prana in areas that need clearing and redistribution. Do the Prana work and all will balance...also mix up the practices so you don't get bored - most Kundalini syndrome is due to boredom. - Raja Choudhury

Theorists within the schools of Humanistic psychology, Transpersonal psychology and Near-Death Studies describe a complex pattern of motor functions, sensory, affective and cognitive-hermeneutic symptoms called the Kundalini Syndrome.

This psychosomatic arousal and excitation is believed to occur in connection with prolonged and intensive spiritual or contemplative practice (such as meditation or yoga) or as a result of intense life experience or a near encounter with death (such as a near-death experience).

According to these fields of study the Kundalini syndrome is of a different nature than a single Kundalini episode, such as a Kundalini arousal. The Kundalini syndrome is a process that might unfold over several months, or even years. If the accompanying symptoms unfold in an intense manner - that de-stabilizes the person - the process is usually interpreted as what Stanislav Grof has termed "spiritual emergency".

Interdisciplinary dialogues within the mentioned schools of psychology (see references below) have now established some common criteria in order to describe this condition, of which the most prominent feature is a feeling of energy travelling along the spine, or progressing upwards in the body.

Motor symptoms are said to include tremors, other spontaneous or involuntary body movements and changes in respiratory function.

Sensory symptoms are said to include subjective changes in body temperature - feelings of heat or cold - a feeling of electricity in the body, persistent sexual arousal syndrome, headache and pressure inside of the head, tingling, vibrations and gastro-intestinal problems.

Cognitive and affective symptoms are said to include psychological upheaval, stress, depression, depersonalization or derealization, intense mood-swings, but also moments of bliss, deep peace and other altered states of consciousness.

Within the mentioned academic traditions this symptomatology is often referred to as the Physio-Kundalini syndrome or Kundalini-experience Awakening.

Transpersonal literature emphasizes that this list of symptoms is not meant to be used as a tool for self-diagnosis.

Any unusual or marked physical or mental symptom needs to be investigated by a qualified Sri Vidya meditation and Qigong teacher who specializes in treating kundalini syndrome.

I practice Qigong to redistribute and balance my Qi after Sri Vidya meditation to prevent and treat kundalini syndrome. It works! - Acharya Ricardo B Serrano

Q and A on Kundalini awakening and Qigong:

Question: Hi Raja Choudhury, How can I explain to somebody that she needs kundalini awakening despite her insisting that she doesn't need it and Qigong is enough for spiritual enlightenment and awakening?

I know that Qigong only affects the energy body (Qi field) - prana kosha - and doesn't go further up the Anandaya Maya Kosha which kundalini awakening can affect. Would that be enough of an explanation? - Ricardo B Serrano

Answer: Don't call it Kundalini Awakening. Call it adding Shakti or any other language she likes to her QiGong practice. You can show her the beauty but you don't have to drag her there kicking and screaming. You can also say that the Chinese integrated many of the Tantric teachings from Buddhism and Hinduism into Taoism and QiGong is a synthesis of that. Every one hears truth and magic through their own lenses and filters. I can even teach Kundalini to a born-again Christian by showing them the power of the Holy Ghost. - Raja Choudhury

See Kundalini Awakening, pages 12, 138, 140; Garland of Letters, p. 28 and 126; Sri Yantra, pages 40, 47, 52, 92, 125, 128

Eight Extraordinary Meridians Qigong By Michael Winn

1. **Ocean Breathing**: open lower dantian, mother of 8 Extraordinary Vessels
2. **Thrusting Channels** (Chung Mo): (3x each, wt. on heels, body still, holds axis)
   a. Both hands scoop and down chest (L. & R. core channels) while standing.
   b. Core channel extends above head, both palms holding single ball of heaven Qi, divide into two channels at head as descend, bend waist to scoop Earth Qi.

3. **Belt Channel** (Dai Mo): hands circle waist to ming men (pull in belly & inhale to spine), exhale & bring palms to Navel (Sea of Qi). (Reverse breathing). Repeat 3X.
4. **Microcosmic Orbit** (Du Mo & Ren Mo): facing palms move in small circles at navel, solar plexus, heart, throat, third eye, crown; whole body & pelvis moves, bend knees.
5. **Leg Bridge Channels** (Yin & Yang Qiao Mo):
   a. Hands go down inside of leg to heel, up outside of feet/ankles/outside of legs (weight 100% on heels) as body straightens.
   b. Rise up Spine: Marriage of Heaven & Earth, first rising movement. As both palms raise (facing body), feel Qi move up bladder meridians on either side of spine. Hands behind head, elbows open wide behind head.

6. **Left & Right Arm Channels** (Yin & Yang Wei Mo):
   [Short version] **Embrace Heaven**: arms/fingertips extend up to sky.
   a. Shift wt. to rt. foot, left arm scoops down, shoulder spirals straight out to left.
   b. Right hand passes over top of left arm to fingertip (weight shifts left), then passes under arm back to armpit.
   c. Transition: Right hand passes over neck/back of head as weight shifts right.
   d. Repeat same movement, mirror on right side. Right hand scoops out horizontally.
   e. Balance left/right brain: gather Gall Bladder/Triple Heater Qi: Palms face ears, make 3 circles, each bigger, around each ear. Then palms/ elbows behind head.
7. Descend head/chest (Yin Qiao Mo) **Marriage Heaven & Earth** over head, down face.
   a. Focus internally on lao gong beaming into Bladder 1 point (inside of eyes), then center of two palms meet at chin and continue to well of throat, out to L & R side.
   b. As palms descend right and left sides of chest, bend over down inside of legs to feet.
8. Closing: **Fountain of Yin, Shower of Yang** combines all eight channels together.
   a. Palms scoop up core and expand out above head (Earth rising), with half squat.
   b. Reverse, scoop down core and out below waist (Heaven Descends).

Palms face dantian, feel them move, pulse out into Qi ball and back. Internally guide Leg & Arm Channels, then circulate Orbit. Practice Inner Smile to all 8 Forces.

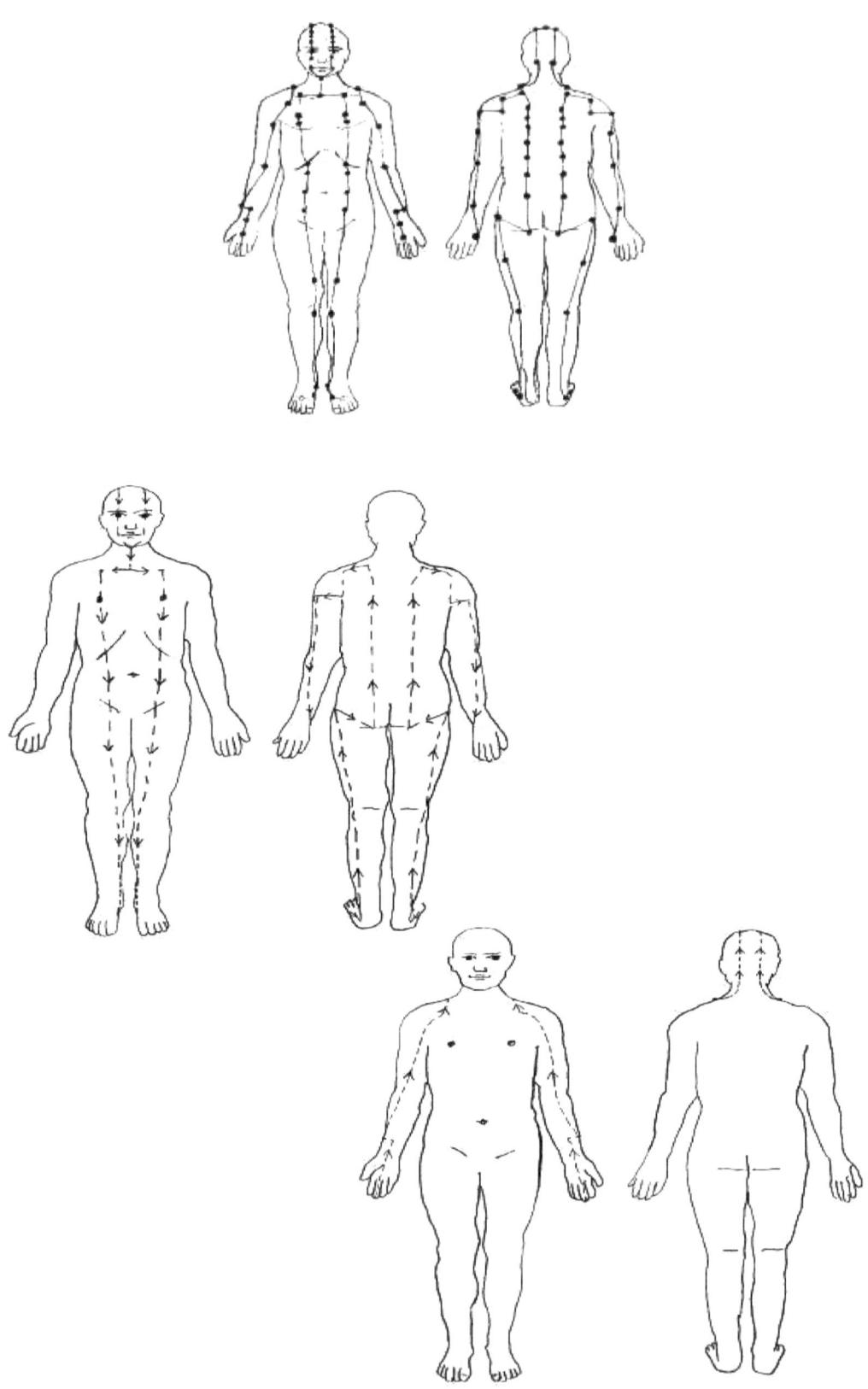

Extraordinary Meridians Master Points and Energy Flow

The Eight Extraordinary Meridians

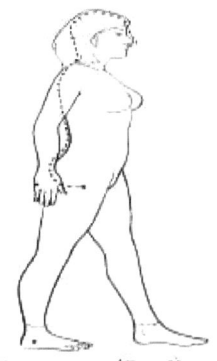
Governor/Du Mo

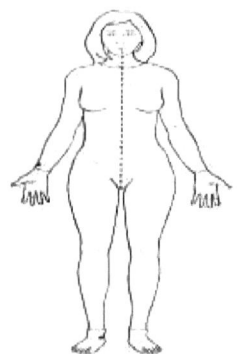
Conception/Ren Mo

Bridge/Yang Qiao Mo

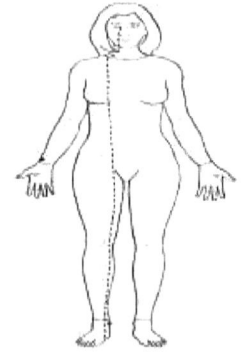
Bridge/Yin Qiao Mo

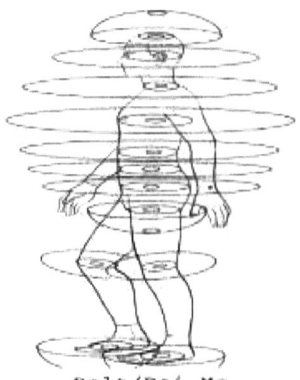
Belt/Dai Mo

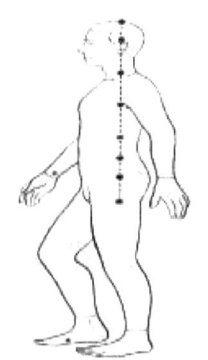
Thrusting/Chong Mo

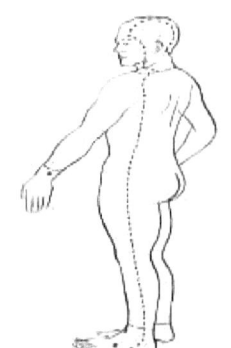
Linking/Yang Wei Mo

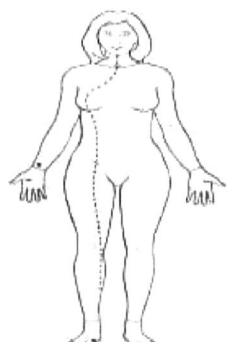
Linking/Yin Wei Mo

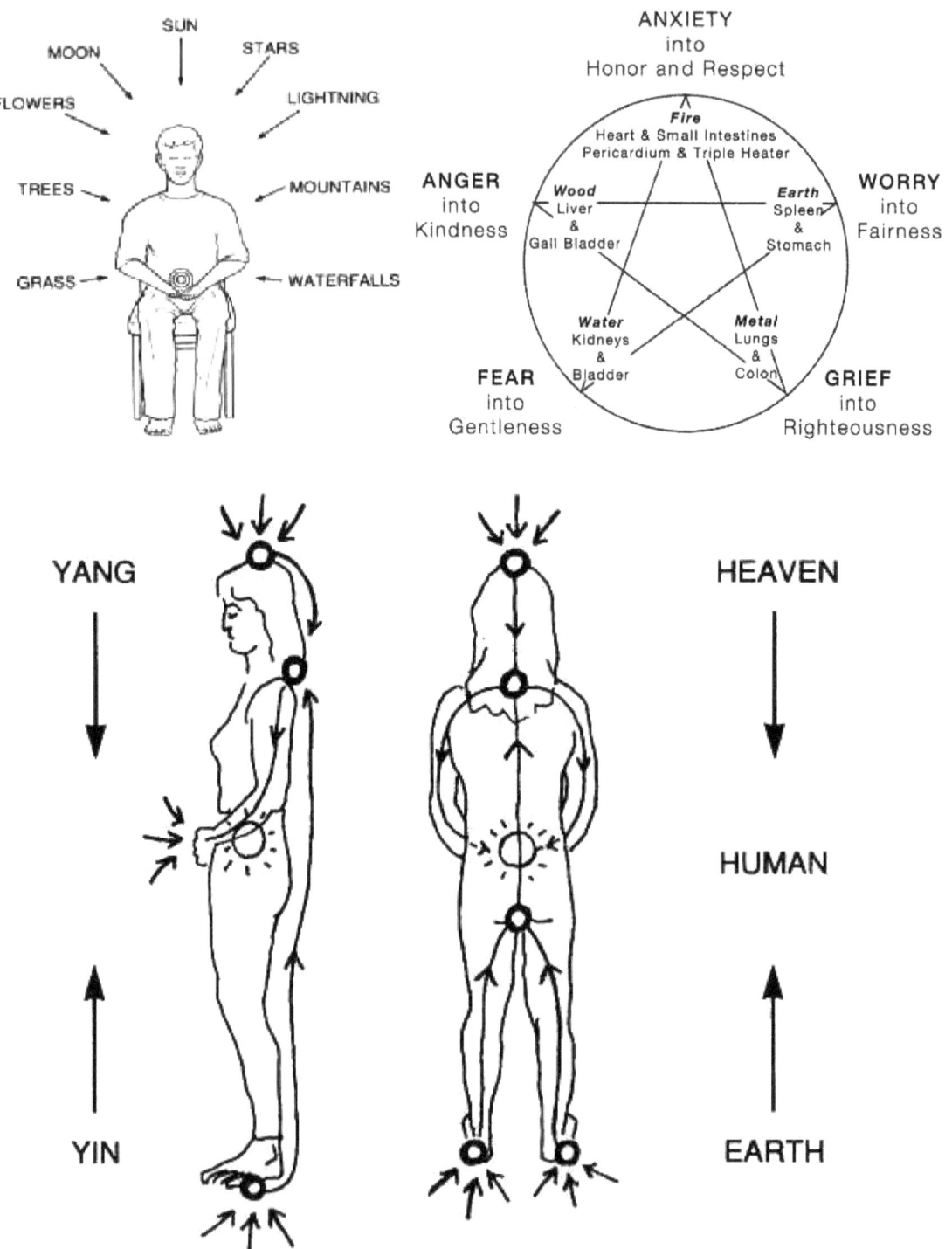

Drawing heaven and earth into you

Benefits of Eight Extraordinary Meridians Qigong Practice

1. Build a more powerful Energy Body by making conscious the deep energetic structure of your body-mind. You become far more powerful energetically in all spheres of your life. Everyone needs more energy; few understand where to find it and how to keep it balanced. It offers a template for a dynamic, flexible, grounded, and continuously flowing Energy Body.
2. These 8 channels are the deep pathways the 5 inner "body spirits" of our heart-mind ("xin") use to energetically manage our biology, our psychology, and our spirituality.
3. Open Qi flow internally in the Macrocosmic Orbit. It balances internal yin-yang Qi flow. The Macro orbit adds in the arm and leg channels, which balances the Qi flow between the environment and our body. It functionally integrates the Qi flow between our inner self and our outer self/world. The Macro orbit creates a wonderful feeling of deeper harmony with all that is around us.
4. Gain a powerful tool for self-healing especially chronic illness and "mystery illnesses" that don't respond to other treatments. Since the healing with the 8 extraordinary vessels occurs at a deeper level, it dissolves chronic diseases that are hard to cure, and stubborn mental-emotional patterns that do not respond to standard medical or psychological techniques.
5. Learn to tap into the most secrets of Classical Chinese Medicine (CCM). Traditional Chinese Medicine (TCM invented about 60 years ago) does not use the 8 extraordinary vessels. It is because the 8 extraordinary vessels are deep meridians, mostly below the skin level, thus not easily accessible to acupuncture. These 8 deep 'reservoirs and canals' feed the 12 superficial (vital organ) meridians. If the 8 deep channels are balanced, all 12 of the regular channels will automatically self-balance. Private studies show that 8 extraordinary vessel treatments work faster and have a higher success rate of healing than regular 12-meridian acupuncture.
6. When you activate 8 deep channels awareness in the body, you become a highly intuitive or psychic person. You begin to spontaneously receive more information from the larger Qi field of the environment.
7. Supercharge the spinal cord, its physical nerve plexus and its subtle energy wiring. This intense practice is like charging your body's internal communication system from slow dial up to high speed internet.
8. The two most important are using the belt channels for grounding and psychic protection, and activating the left, right and center thrusting channels to clear internal blockages and extend your awareness deep into earth or high into heaven. When core channels flow in continuous yin-yang circuits, they form an energetic torus (donut shape aura) that is self-charging. They open pathways of communication between your Original Spirit, prenatal self and your post-natal (physical) self.

To activate the Eight Extraordinary Meridians with or without the *Eight Extraordinary Meridians Qigong*, apply acupressure bilaterally to each of the following **Eight Master / Coupled points**:

Governor: Small Intestine 3 **Yang Qiao:** Bladder 62

Conception: Lung 7 **Yin Qiao**: Kidney 6

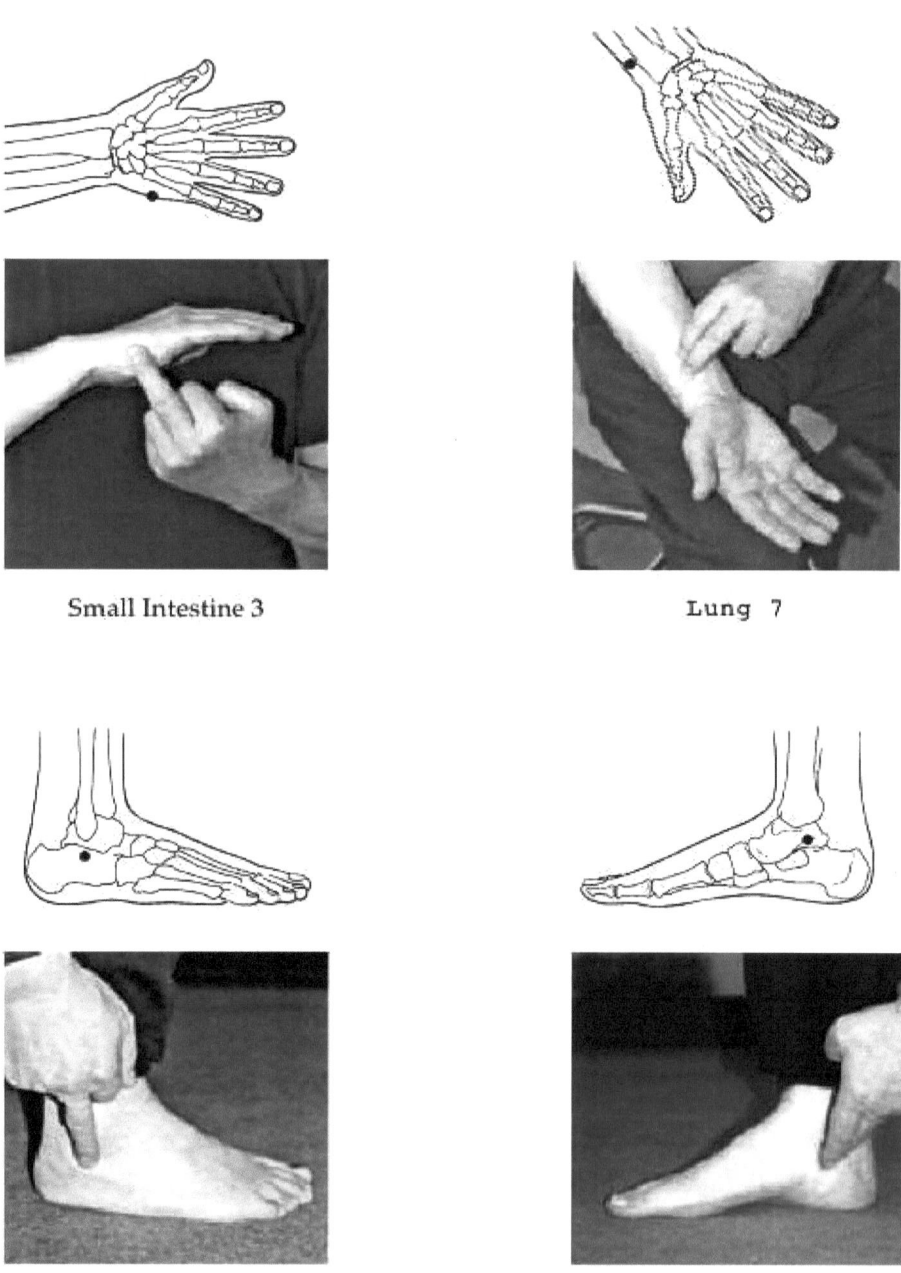

Belt: Gall Bladder 41 **Yang Wei:** Triple Heater 5

Thrusting: Spleen 4 **Yin Wei:** Pericardium 6

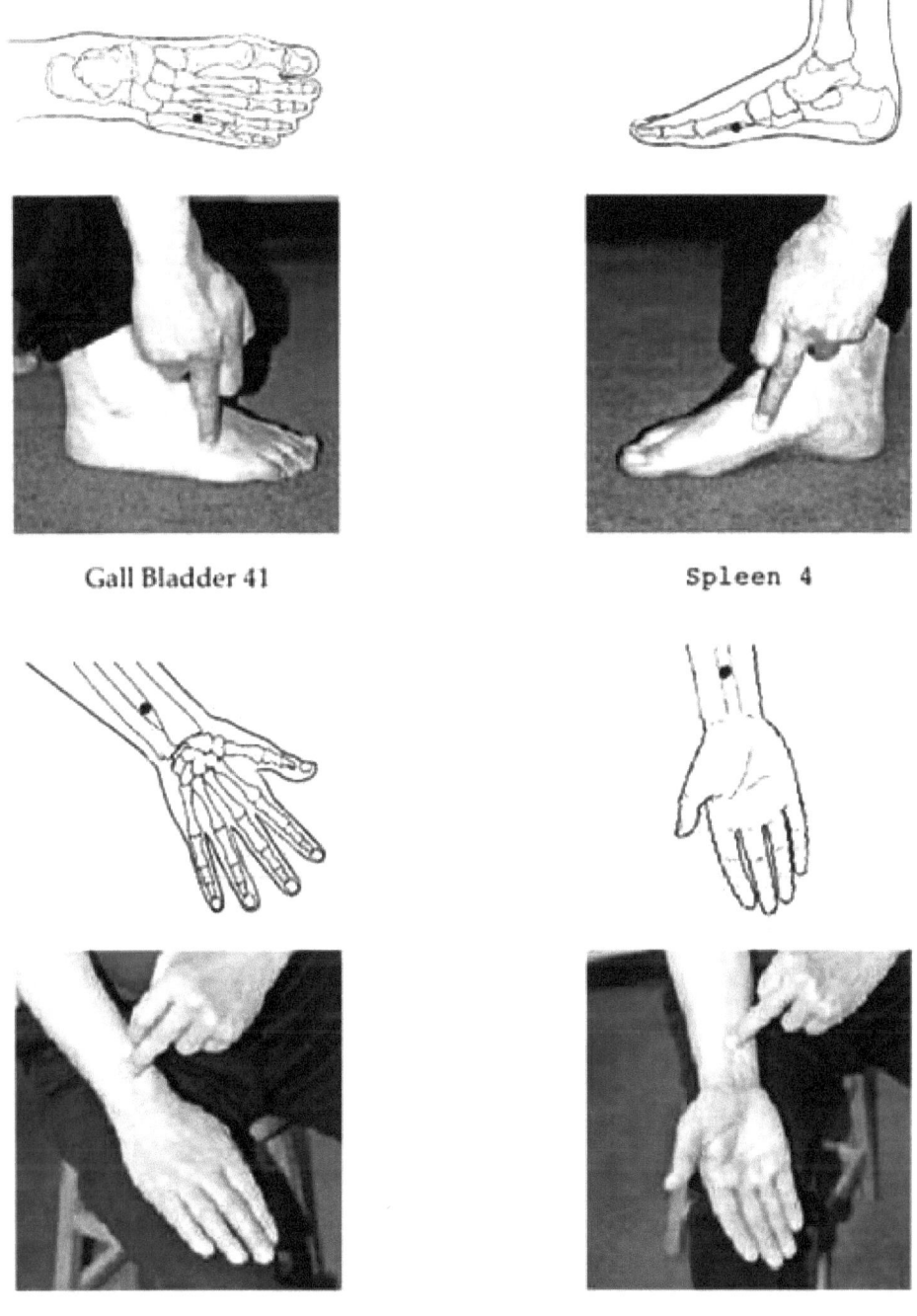

A Diamond in the Rough

Chinese culture contains a variety of spiritual traditions. Each tradition includes insights that are the basis of its teachings and practices. One insight is that each person has a *Yuan Shen* (Original Spirit). Part of this insight is that the creator and creation are one, individual whole. By experiencing one's *Yuan Shen*, the unity of life is realized; the inseparable nature of life is realized; the clarity of one's true nature is realized. By directly experiencing one's Yuan Shen, it becomes clear what *Yuan Shen* is not. This insight is essential to self-realization, health, happiness and transformation. Acupuncture (and Qigong) can have a profound influence on releasing attachments and imprints that prevent an individual from realizing *Yuan Shen*. And it can guide one's focus or attention on self-realization.

"A diamond in the rough" is an image that illustrates how the process of self-realization can occur. Each person has a diamond. The diamond is the *Yuan Shen*. The rough includes the stresses, conditioning, imprints, patterns, emotions, and unfavorable influences that exist in our life. We all have a diamond shining within, and we all have rough edges. The level and types of rough vary among people. Acupuncture can assist in releasing, clearing, and removing the rough. Acupuncture (and Qigong) can clear away the rough, allowing insight and alignment with the diamond, which can be life changing. This insight can provide the inspiration and motivation to change a life, to live in a way that allows synchronization with *shen*, to be a living expression of *shen*. This is a way acupuncture (and Qigong) can influence one's spirit. The knowledge of the channels, points, and energy centers allows the practitioner to develop customized treatments to treat the unique roughness of each person.

The *shen* relate to the five Yin organs – Heart, Spleen, Lungs, Kidneys, and Liver – and their spirit correspondences – *shen, yi, po, zhi*, and *hun*. Each *shen* has specific psychological qualities, and are used to match their corresponding organ and channel. They provide a way to identify which organ and channel system is imbalanced and should be treated. Nei Dan and Qigong traditions offer many insights into the five *shen* .

When these emotions – hate, worry, sadness, fear, and anger – are imbalanced, match the emotion to the *shen* virtues – love, openness, courage, gentleness, kindness – and organ, and treat their corresponding channels. In the model of the diamond in the rough, imbalances of these emotions are the rough. Acupuncture (and Qigong) can assist in clearing the roughness, revealing the shining light of the diamond, the *Yuan Shen*. The *Eight Extraordinary Channels* provide a way to support the clearing of the roughness, releasing chronic and old patterns of roughness and redirecting a person to their diamond. Union with *Yuan Shen* can inspire, motivate, and provide the impetus for change and transformation.

- Excerpts from David Twicken's book: **Eight Extraordinary Channels – Qi Jing Ba Mai**

What is Sheng Zhen?

Passages in the book "Sheng Zhen Wuji Yuan Gong" answer the question What is Sheng Zhen?

"Within the depths of the human heart lies a paradise waiting to be experienced. It is the experience of Sheng Zhen – the experience of unconditional love. Sheng Zhen is pure, taintless, and totally free, depending on nothing for its existence. It is what every human being yearns for in his search for pleasure, happiness. Peace, and contentment. It is man's ultimate quest. The human being can truly rest only when he has experienced the fullness of unconditional love in his heart. Often hoping to find answers to life's questions, he looks everywhere outside of himself to satisfy his needs. It is ironic that the very thing he is searching for is found resting in his heart.

Sheng Zhen is found in the heart of every human being as a seed waiting to be watered and nourished. Once Sheng Zhen is experienced in the heart, it is seen everywhere. There is nowhere that it does not exist, for the very fabric of existence is Sheng Zhen.

A glimpse of Sheng Zhen can shed light on the mystery of man's existence and his relationship with his fellowmen and the universe. A natural understanding of life and the order of the universe develops. Coming in touch with Sheng Zhen affects and colors the way one sees and tastes life. In that love, the destructive power of differences and seeming inequalities is conquered; one's view of the world expands to embrace all. This is the power of unconditional love. It dissolves all conflicts and makes the light of truth shine; all differences melt in its luminosity and clarity. Sheng Zhen is the highest most sacred truth.

The experience of Sheng Zhen is the gift of the practice of Wuji Yuan Gong. Through the practice, the heart is opened; the experience of unconditional love becomes tangible and accessible. As the Qi flows through the body in the practice, it brings about an experience of inner delight. This can only be described as being in a state of love. With time, one can even feel this blissful inner sensation while going through an ordinary day in one's life. Slowly and naturally, balance, harmony, wisdom, compassion, joy, and divine inspiration characterize one's existence.

To an individual whose being is permeated with Sheng Zhen, there is no such thing as a spiritual or materialistic life. There is only life and the beautiful poetry of existence in this realm. Such is the gift of Sheng Zhen."

- Master Li Jung Feng from Sheng Zhen Wuji Yuan Gong book

Sheng Zhen Gong Forms and Functional Names:

Kuan Yin Sitting Gong – Heaven Earth Gong

Kuan Yin Standing Gong – Heaven Nature Gong

Jesus Sitting Gong – Heart Spirit as One Gong / Jesus Standing Gong – Heart Mind as One Gong

Mohammed Sitting Gong – Listening to the Heart Gong

Mohammed Standing Gong – Releasing the Heart Gong

Return to Spring Gong – Return to Nature Gong

Hanuman Qigong – Origin of the Heart Gong

Awakening the Soul Gong and Sheng Zhen Healing Qigong (1, 2, & 3) with Nine Turns Gong

Union of Three Hearts (*Zhongtian Yiqi Gong*) is a non-moving Qigong that trains the mind. As this practice quiets the mind one is able to connect with Heaven, Earth and humanity through the central channel – *chong mo*. Breathing lightly helps the body relax and frees the mind of all worries and thoughts. Then one can go back to the beginning of time and see the world with renewed understanding. Union of Three Hearts Meditation opens the three main energy centers of the body and connects one to the Earth, Sky and Heart.

From a place of relaxation and focus, one guides the Qi along the *chong mo*, the central channel between the dantian (in the abdomen) and the ni-wuan (in the center of the head). As one progresses, the act of guiding one's Qi slowly transforms into the Qi guiding the mind. This is a calming and nourishing experience that brings one a sense of peace and connection.

Diaphragmatic abdominal breathing - 2 inhalations when guiding Qi upwards and 1 exhalation when guiding Qi downwards - (**XiXi Hu**) with tip of tongue in the roof of mouth is important.

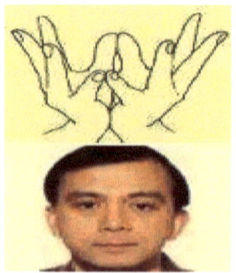

Awakening the Soul

Benefits of Sheng Zhen Gong Practice

The sacred truth – Sheng Zhen or unconditional love – can only be known by experience, not by thoughts or beliefs. Oneness or Qigong state characterized as a harmony between heaven, earth and man is experienced as a final outcome when the unhealthy Qi is completely dispelled with a Yin and Yang balance and when the Jing and Qi are plentiful in the body, and the Shen or Spirit within one's own heart opens that naturally radiate unconditional love reconnecting one's heart to the unconditional love of the universe.

According to Master Li Jun Feng's article Essence of Life, "Everyone now needs qigong. To explain what qigong is: Qi is the essence of life. It is the origin of life. With qi, everything grows. Without qi, everything dies. We believe that life comes from qi. The quality of qi affects our life. Through the practice of Real Qigong, it is good for both physical and emotional health. It stimulates the qi to flow, improving the qi exchange between the individual and nature. Through this qi flow, unhealthy qi is replaced with pure qi. When qi flows smoothly, it generates more energy in the body. Blood circulation becomes better. We believe that qi is the commander of blood – qi leads the blood to flow. When the blood flows smoothly, there is less stagnation, and the body becomes healthier.

Qigong is good for emotional health because, with the movements and understanding of the philosophy of the Real Qigong, like Sheng Zhen Wuji Yuan Gong, people understand the meaning of life better. This can remove worries and stress from their minds and bodies. Qigong changes your life to become a happy and healthy life.

Happiness and health are the essence of life. On a higher level, the main purpose of life is to learn what unconditional love is – to give more love to the world. Life comes from qi. Qi comes from the power of love. Qi and love are never separate. Each person can affect the environment, and the environment can affect the person. Each individual can positively affect the universe as a whole by sending unconditional love everywhere and to all beings. We hope unconditional love goes everywhere and to everyone. In our world, full of love, this world will become like paradise." Chant *Namo Kuan Shi Yin Pu Sa* to cultivate the same compassion embodied by Kuan Yin Bodhisattva. See *Da Bei Zhou*, pages 108 - 109

The Three Treasures: Essence (Jing), Breath (Qi), and Spirit (Shen) affect one another. When they follow the course, they form the human being; when they invert the course, they form the Elixir. See Union of Three Hearts (Zhongtian Yiqi Gong), page 80

What is the meaning of "following the course" (shun)? "The One generates the Two, the Two generate the Three, the Three generate the ten thousand things." Therefore Emptiness transmutes itself into Spirit, Spirit transmutes itself into Breath, Breath transmutes itself into Essence, Essence transmutes itself into form, and form becomes the human being.
What is the meaning of "inverting the course" (ni)? The ten thousand things hold the Three, the Three return to the Two, the Two return to the One. Those who know this Way look after their Spirit and guard their corporeal form. They nourish the corporeal form to refine the Essence, accumulate the Essence to transmute it into Breath, refine the Breath to merge it with Spirit, and refine the Spirit to revert to Emptiness. Then the Golden Elixir – Original Spirit - is achieved.

The Virgin and the Unicorn

Let me enlighten this book with the legend and symbol of the Unicorn as taught by my late beloved Unicorn Meditation Master Miguel Nator, "there lived a fierce, horse-like beast that roamed the earth. Its savage spirit could only be tamed by the touch of a virgin. Once touched, the beast is transformed into a noble white steed marked by a long, singular horn at the center of its forehead. In its spiritual ascent, a pair of wings appear to free the Unicorn from its earthly bondage forever.

The Unicorn is likened to Man – part animal, part divine. Its fierceness and savagery represent and signify the animal nature. Its whiteness represents purity and signifies the divine nature. The taming of the Unicorn by the touch of the virgin signifies the taming of the animal nature in man by the awakening influence of his higher self, or soul, symbolized by the virgin. The long horn symbolizes the achievement of right fusion or the integration of man's lower and higher self.

Until man awakens to the touch of his own soul who virtually tames and controls him to return to the center of his being, he remains veiled. Because of this, the acronym UNICORN is a fit symbol of the program of regeneration and of the self transforming man. The colors that surround him represent the key activities involved towards achieving transformation. Violet for Meditation, Green for Service, and Blue for study." See Yuan Shen (Soul) below and in page 130

According to Taoist Cosmology, physical alignment with Polaris is believed to be found in your Pineal gland. Your Pineal Gland opens up your Crown Celestial Chakra and is the "Doorway to Heaven". Polaris is said to be a ladder to the Universe. The Wu Chi, or Universal Tao, gives birth to the Tai Chi, or Yin and Yang. This then gives birth to the Three Pure Ones: Shen, Qi and Jing. The Three Pure Ones gives birth to the five stars of the Big Dipper upon which Polaris is doorway through your Crown Chakra!

Taoist astrologers believe the Big Dipper to come from a grouping of Violet Stars. The infrared light from Ursa Major "Big Dipper" combined with the Violet light of Polaris is cosmic nutrition for your Crown Chakra. This is a great time for Pineal gland activation through Violet Light meditation. Visualize the Big Dipper as a Ladle or Drinking Gourd and imagine Violet light pouring from this Great Ladle into your Crown Chakra into your Pineal gland. Do this visualization once a day throughout the lunar cycle. The opening of the Agya Chakra (Pineal Gland) awakens our ability to truly receive Lalitha's grace, dance with Shiva (as Shakti), unite Ida, Pingala, and Sushumna, be guided by Tarini (the inner Star) and open the doorway to access our superconscious mind beyond the Sahasrara. The Agya sits like a crystal inside your Brahma's Cave and conducts Jiva into the heart center. It is the lens through which we receive the bliss of that union of Shiva and Shakti in the heart. By activating our third eye we become intuitive, develop siddhis or powers, be more creative, visionary and develop the ability to not only direct bliss to our hearts but also manifest whatever we visualize and send healing Prana to every part of our body as well as to others. You can become a Skywalker - one who walks with Siddha yogis - via Sri Vidya upasana and grace of Lalitha Tripura Sundari. **See Kundalini awakening, pages 12, 138; Maha Vidyas, p. 120; Sri Vidya, p. 140**

The Great Invocation

From the point of Light within the Mind of God Let light stream forth into the minds of men.

Let Light descend on Earth.

From the point of Love within the Heart of God Let love stream forth into the hearts of men.

May Christ return to Earth.

From the center where the Will of God is known Let purpose guide the little wills of men.

The purpose which the Masters know and serve.

From the center which we call the race of men Let the Plan of Love and Light work out

And may it seal the door where evil dwells. Let Light, Love and Power restore the Plan on Earth.

People of goodwill throughout the world are using this invocation daily in their own language. Join them in using the Great Invocation every day – with righteous intent, thought and dedication. Use the Triangles Work with the Great Invocation by Holy Master Djwhal Khul and encourage others to use it. No particular group or organisation is sponsored. It belongs to all humanity. The "descent of light" results in each person's alignment with his or her Higher Self. "May Christ return to Earth" invokes the opening of each of us to the Unity Band, or Christ Consciousness. When your will is aligned with Divine Will, you become a Divine Instrument. "Sealing the door where evil dwells" refers to the dissolution of the veil of separation, and the plan will work out. Master Djwhal Khul says, "The Great Invocation is best used with the Triangles Work and Meditation on Three Hearts."

The Golden Elixir of Immortality is the goal, the target, the intent, the prize, and the gift of the highest forms of "cultivation."

Golden Elixir is another name for one's fundamental nature... There is no other Golden Elixir outside one's fundamental nature. All human beings have this Golden Elixir complete in themselves: it is entirely realized in everybody. It is neither more in a sage, nor less in an ordinary person. It is the seed of the Immortals and the Buddhas, the root of the worthies and the sages. Ancient immortals used the term Golden Elixir as a metaphor of the essence of true consciousness, which is fundamentally complete and illumined. – Liu Yiming (1734•1821)

From the Secret of the Golden Flower: "Consciousness IS light. Turn the light around to focus within. Experience that which is the most real."

The Golden Elixir is Yuan Shen (Original Spirit). See **Atma (Soul) Yoga of Immortality**, page 103

A Short Autobiography of a Saint

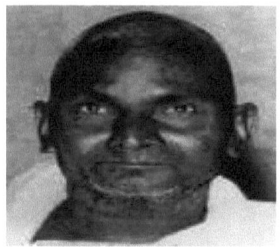

Bhagawan Nityananda

"Bhagawan Nityananda was the incarnation of Lord Krishna, therefore, Bhagawan Nityananda and Lord Krishna are one." – Acharya Ricardo B Serrano

"The heart is the hub of all sacred places, go there and roam."

"One must seek the shortest way and the fastest means to get back home – to turn the spark within into a blaze, to be merged in and to identify with that greater fire which ignited the spark."

"Happy is he who has overcome his ego." – Buddha

A man asked Lord Buddha, "I want happiness."

Lord said: First remove "I" that's ego. Then remove "want" that's desire. See now you are left with only "happiness."

"Ego is nothing but identification of oneself with their body instead of their Soul." – Acharya Ricardo B Serrano

"To feel the love of one's soul is the goal of yoga, according to the Bhagavad Gita." – Acharya Ricardo B Serrano, See page 100

Hare Krishna mantra is a prayer to God's energy (Shakti) for taking away all the sorrows, pains and shortcomings of the chanter and provide him bliss, joy, peace and oneness with Higher Self.

It is an Atma (Soul) Yoga mantra together with OM Namah Shivaya for attaining oneness with Higher Self.

Hare Krishna Hare Krishna Krishna Krishna Hare Hare

Hare Rama Hare Rama Rama Rama Hare Hare

OM TAT PURUSHAYA VIDMAHE

MAHA DEVAYA DHIMAHE

TANNO RUDRA PRACHODAYAT

Om you the Ideal Purusha (Universal Being)

I meditate on you Maha Deva (Great Lord)

Bless me Rudra (Living Shiva) with Inner Light.

Bhagawan Nityananda was born just before the beginning of the twentieth century (about 1896) and lived until 1961. He was a Sat Purush, or Antarjnani, an enlightened being who was always in the Atmic state, even as a child. He was found as an infant in a jungle in India by a woman collecting firewood who was attracted to a heavily wooded area by the loud cawing of crows. She had her own family, so she took up the infant and gave him to her friend who had a barren daughter. The daughter was a servant in the home of a high caste Brahman lawyer, Ishwar Iyer. She named the baby Ram (a synonym for God).

As an infant, Nityananda was troubled by a serious ailment and was miraculously cured in a very strange manner. His adopted mother took the sick child for a walk and soon saw a dark skinned foreigner carrying a large bag slung over his shoulder. Thinking maybe he could help she explained the problem and as if the mysterious stranger had been waiting for just this moment, he took out a packet from his bag and told her to mix the contents with the flesh of a freshly killed crow that had been fried in ghee (clarified butter). She was also to rub the blood of the crow all over Ram's skin. Just then a plantation worker whom she had never seen before appeared with a dead crow which he gave over to the mother. The mother was overjoyed but when she tried to thank the two strangers they had disappeared. She carefully followed the instructions and within days the ailing child regained full health. However the skin of Ram which at birth had been a light tan, was turned permanently a dark bluish brown by the crow's blood. This same color is comparable to the color often ascribed to Krishna who is said to have been the color of a thunder cloud. In later years, if any devotee pressed Nityananda for details of his birth or childhood, he only said cryptically that a crow came and a crow left.

As the young Ram grew into childhood, Mr Iyer, the lawyer for whom the mother worked grew very attached to him. The foster mother died when Ram was six, and Mr Iyer adopted him into the family. The devout Mr Iyer felt a spiritual attraction to Ram and took him on his pilgrimages to the Krishna temple. On these trips Ram would often explain abstruse metaphysical points to the amazed elder Iyer. A well-known astrologer told him that, as shown in Mr. Iyer's chart, the boy was an incarnate personality and thus it was a great blessing for him to be in Ram's company.

When Ram was ten years old, Mr Iyer took him to the holy city of Benares. There Ram asserted that he was leaving the household. Though Mr Iyer pleaded tearfully with him he would not change his mind. Before going though he conferred on Mr. Iyer a divine vision and promised they would meet again. Ram wandered widely around the North of India and the Himalayas for six years. Several sources indicate that he was known in the Himalayas as a great Kundalini Yogi. The Kundalini is the Serpent Power of the Mother aspect coiled up in the Muladhar chakra situated at the base of the spine in each person. In a spiritually advanced individual the awakened Kundalini energy rises up along the spinal column piercing the chakras and conferring new powers and states of consciousness as it rises until full Samadhi is attained on its reaching the highest chakra at the crown of the head.

Meanwhile Mr. Iyer had returned sadly back to his home and resumed his life without the spiritual young Ram. As he grew older and approached the close of his life he thought constantly of the boy. At this time, quite unexpectedly, Ram turned up at his house, knowing Mr. Iyer's end was near and thus keeping a promise to see him once again.

Mr. Iyer was ecstatic and kept repeating "Nityananda! Nityananda!" (endless bliss). After this incident Ram became known as Nityananda. The young Nityananda (then 16) took Mr Iyer to the city of Udipi for *the* darshan of Krishna and the Ananteshwar temple. Later Nityananda remarked that he had been present at the construction of the temple of Ananteshwar approximately 400 years earlier.

Shortly afterwards, Mr Iyer became gravely ill. As he lay with his head on Nityananda's lap he expressed a desire to have a vision of the Sun God Bharga which he had worshiped his entire life. Bharga is the divinity whose outward expression is the sun of our solar system. Nityananda granted his request and Mr. Iyer merged into the ocean of spirit.

"One must seek the shortest way and the fastest means to get back home – to turn the spark within into a blaze, to be merged in and to identify with that greater fire which ignited the spark."

After this Nityananda wandered far and wide and is said to have been in Ceylon, Rangoon, Singapore, and Burma before returning to spend time in the south of India. During World War I he was forcibly drafted into the army. He later laughed as he told of being examined for his physical. The doctor could not hear any heartbeat nor find any pulse and so rejected the hearty Nityananda as unfit.

During this time period he is known to have gone to Palani. After the morning worship, the priest of the Palani shrine was locking the doors and going down the steps when Nityananda accosted him and asked him to re-open the doors so that he could wave lights before the deity (Arathi ceremony). The priest was astonished that the young vagrant would ask a person of his stature to perform such a favor and refused the request. Nityananda proceeded as if he had not heard the refusal and somehow opened the locked doors and entered the temple. Shortly afterwards the priest heard the temple bell ringing and he looked up to see Nityananda in place of the deity with invisible hands waving arathi lights before him. Then Nityananda came down from the temple and stood on one leg looking upward in a yogic asana (posture). As he stood motionless a lot of money was poured at his feet and Nityananda gave it to the leader of the local sanyasis to establish a meal center for the visiting pilgrims. Later it came out that the local sanyasis had been praying to the Lord at Palani to be provided with at least a daily meal during their stay there.

Again when he stayed at Mangalore, visiting devotees would often leave money at his feet. He would ask that the money be collected and after a few days when there was enough he would order a feast for the poor. He would allow only the finest quality foods to be purchased and would himself help in preparing and distributing the food. He would ladle out huge portions to each person even when it appeared that there was not enough food to go around, but many people who had been present at these feedings attested that the food never ran out before everyone had enough. Later when he had established a permanent ashram at Ganeshpuri, he instituted a daily feeding of the poor children in the area which continues even today.

In the early days of feeding the poor many people would help pay for the feedings although others around them thought they were being manipulated by the young Nityananda. One such was a youth from a well to do family who would occasionally bring sums of money and give them over to Nityananda. The father of the boy thought he was being influenced unduly by what he considered to be an eccentric drifter and hired assassins to have Nityananda removed from the scene. Nityananda was with some devotees one day when he suddenly got up and walked away from them with a smile on his face. They followed to see why he had left so unexpectedly and came upon him being held by one of the hired men while the other had a knife which he held above his head with his arm extended upward. The devotees grabbed the men and took the knife away from the one would be assassin. He was in great pain and shouting to have his arm restored to normal. It was frozen in the upright position and nobody could bring it back down to a normal position. Finally Nityananda touched the man's arm and it went back to normal. Afterwards the police had the would be assassins locked up but Nityananda wanted them to be freed. The police did not agree and so Nityananda determined to stay outside the jail until they agreed. After three days without food or water his devotees finally convinced the officials to let the men go free. The two later became devotees and the local officials gained a deeper appreciation of the young eccentric sadhu.

Particularly holy people attract both good and evil and young Nityananda was once attacked by some young roughs who wrapped a kerosene soaked rag around his hand and set in on fire. Nityananda characteristically stood there stoically as his hand burned, outwardly unfazed, but he transferred the actual pain to the person who had lit the rag on fire. The perpetrator ran about screaming in pain and apologizing for his behavior. Nityananda extinguished the fire and simultaneously the pain felt by the young man.

On another occasion a man wanted some leaves for his mother who was seriously ill with a lump in her leg. Medicines had been tried but to no avail. Nityananda responded, "This one knows and is there" but did not offer any leaves. The man did not understand and returned and brought his mother to the tree where Nityananda was but the young master was no longer there so he left. When he returned home with his mother he was surprised to see Nityananda descending the stairs of his home from the attic. Nityananda rubbed the affected area for a few minutes and the mother soon recovered. After many such incidents the reputation of the strange young ascetic as a healer spread far and wide.

A peculiar characteristic of the young Nityananda was that he would not take food or water for himself. Occasionally a devotee would give him something to eat or some water to drink and he would signal when he had enough. If no one offered anything he would go days without food or water. He also seemed to be oblivious to heat or cold and he often stayed on the hot sands of the Ganga under the hot Indian sun for days at a time. Some days he would spend the entire day just sitting there looking directly into the sun. Some people tried to approach to visit him but they could not cross the burning sands until evening.

In 1918 he was in the city of Udipi at the Krishna temple there. Two of the local men, Dr Kombarbail and his friend Mr. Bhat used to daily walk to the temple and one day were attracted by the lean, bright looking Nityananda standing among the usual collection of ascetics at the temple. They tried to talk to him but he turned away from them declining to be recognized. A few weeks later they saw him again alone at the Ananteshwar temple. The doctor seized his hands so he could not retreat and addressed him rapidly in three different languages (Hindi, Kanarese, and English), not knowing which Indian dialect he might speak. The young ascetic appeared to be having trouble speaking and repeated several times "Nityananda, Nityananda" alluding to the fact that his blissful state made the formulation of speech difficult. When he finally responded to the two gentlemen, the unschooled Nityananda replied to them fluently also in three different languages – two of which they had used in questioning him (English and Hindi), and a third, Konkani, which was their own native language which they had given no indication of knowing.

During this period of his life, Nityananda traveled to many different villages and cities in the area. His presence was unpredictable and he had an uncanny knack of turning up unexpectedly somewhere whenever people in the area would gather and express the desire to see him. Often he would disappear in one place and appear up to fifty miles away and nobody could explain how he had covered the distance so quickly.

Once he was invited to Mrs. Krishnabai's house who had lovingly prepared the place for his visit. He arrived but left immediately saying he could not stay. There was a large crowd watching as Mrs Krishnabai's husband and a friend tried to restrain the young master and bring him back, but the tall thin Nityananda casually picked them both up and continued walking. Finally after about half a mile he turned back to the house saying "She stopped me"; meaning that the magnetic pull of her love and devotion had made him return while the men's physical efforts to stop him had been fruitless.

At the Krishna temple some of the local delinquents took a disliking to him and would throw rocks at Nityananda to keep him away. Whenever a rock would hit him, it would scintillate but then fall to the ground again as an ordinary rock. After one such incident, a large number of these stones were later inexplicably found at the feet of the Krishna statue. Recognizing the true status of Nityananda, the elderly Swami of the local monastery let it be known that Nityananda was no ordinary sadhu and was to be treated with the respect he was due.

One day Nityananda picked up a coconut and offered it to Mrs. Sitabai, a young married woman. Normally it is very auspicious to receive a coconut from a holy person and a married woman would receive it gratefully as a benediction warding off widowhood. However this woman was filled with doubts because she was from a high-caste family and she didn't know if it was proper for her to receive a gift from the casteless Nityananda. Nityananda held it for several minutes waiting for her to accept it. She refused. Three months later she was a widow.

"There are various tests to which a devotee is subjected: they could be of the mind, or the intellect, of the body, and so on. A number of such tests are there. In fact, God is conducting tests all the time; every occurrence in life is a test. Every thought that crops up in the mind is in itself a test to see what one's reaction will be. Hence one must be always alert and aloof, conducting oneself with a spirit of detachment, viewing everything as an opportunity afforded to gain experience, to improve oneself and go on to a higher stage."

Nityananda was fond of riding the trains. Since many of the railroad personnel knew him, they would often let him ride in the engine car or in the train, even without a ticket. Once a new official had him forcibly removed from the train because he was without a ticket. Nityananda remained passive even though he had been handled roughly, but when it was time for the train to depart, the train simply would not move. Some of the passengers approached the official, explained that Nityananda, who was not an ordinary sanyasi, should not have been handled so roughly. They then escorted Nityananda back onto the train and the train was able to start as soon as he boarded.

In 1925, Nityananda settled briefly in the Kanhangad area and began construction of the Sunrise – Sunset caves. This project entailed building a road up to the area and clearing the surrounding jungle. The sudden activity in the area was noticed and some of the local officials asked him with what authority he was taking these actions. He told them that someday there would be government offices at the site and that he was clearing the area for them. This answer seemed to satisfy them and they left him alone. Subsequently, in later years this came true. After the preliminary clearing and road work was over, Nityananda began carving the caves from the rock hills of the area. Forty caves in all were dug with six entrances, three facing East and three facing West so that there was always light within the caves no matter what time of day it was. Many of the locals were hired to assist with the digging of the caves and the manner in which they were paid was most unusual. Nityananda would sometimes direct the foreman to a certain tree where he would find just the right amount of money lying on the ground at the foot of the tree. At other times the workers would line up and walk past Nityananda and as each man went by, Nityananda would open and close his empty fist and down would drop the exact daily wages for each man.

After a while Nityananda told one of the jailers that he had to urinate. He was given a container to use, but it soon filled up and started overflowing. They brought him another and it too was quickly filled. Next they brought a large water pot and he soon filled that as well. The police concluded that he was indeed as reported by the devotees an extraordinary individual and should not be locked up. The authorities soon released him and he returned back to the construction site in time to disperse the afternoon wages.

After the caves were completed around 1933, Nityananda spent several years traveling about once again. Once three Muslims came to him and stood reverentially before him. They had just returned from a pilgrimage to Mecca and they told him so. He asked them what they saw there and they replied, "We saw you there, Swamiji, and hence we are here to pay our homage". Nityananda averted his face but not before a smile was seen on his lips.

In his travels he carried out a number of construction tasks. He repaired the hot spring tanks at Akroli and also built a charity hospital opposite the Vajreshwari temple. He repaired the Nath Mandir near the temple, and also supervised construction of a large well which is the main source of water for the temple.

At about that time it is reported that an earnest seeker came to him and asked to have his Kundalini energy awakened. Nityananda touched his spinal cord and the man went into the samadhi state.

By this time, Nityananda had a very large following of devotees and people whose lives he had touched in some way. In 1936 he moved to the Ganeshpuri area outside Bombay. He stayed near the Bhimeshwar temple and for the most part his travels were behind him. At that time the city of Ganeshpuri was surrounded by jungles and thickly wooded areas filled with wild animals including dangerous ones such as tigers and cobras. At the temple there was a massive old pipal tree in which many snakes lived. In some mysterious manner, Nityananda ordered the snakes to leave the area, which they did. He then performed a ritual at the site of the sacred pipal tree and had it cut down.

As word spread of his presence in the area, many devotees gathered there and began to construct a shelter. Nityananda began clearing the jungle around the area and constructing a road up to the ashram. There were many hot springs in the area and these were fashioned into suitable pools used for ritual bathing. Many of the local poor stopped by daily and Nityananda would share food with them. This was the beginning of an Ashram and Nityananda was to remain there until leaving the body in 1961.

As time went on, many facilities for lodging were built by devotees and simple furnishings were provided for comfort and preparation of food. It should be noted that the Master never was known to consider anything as "his". He would say "There are so many things in this Ashram. If this one goes elsewhere, none of these things would be taken". Being established in the Atmic consciousness he never referred to himself as "I" but would say "this one" or "from here".

As the years passed the number of visitors to the Ashram increased. Swami Chetanananda, tells of going on a visit to the Ganeshpuri Ashram in a taxi in 1973, 12 years after the Master's passing. The taxi driver who was taking him told of going to the same ashram as a young man. He had heard of a great saint living at Ganeshpuri and had gone there to get his blessings. He arrived to find a very long line of people waiting to file past Nityananda for his darshan.
As he got closer he observed that as each person's turn came they would say something to Nityananda or offer a gift and he would respond very simply with a nod, a gesture, or just a sound. Therefore he was very surprised when his turn came and Nityananda said to him, "Go and bring your brother here." His brother had been blind since birth and the next week, he

returned to the Ashram and was told by Nityananda to leave the brother and come back for him in three days. When he returned, his brother could see.

Once a family came to the Ashram bringing their severely sick infant. The child had been sick with pneumonia for three days and had not opened its eyes during that time. The family held the baby up to Nityananda and asked that the child's eyes be opened. He passed his hand in front of the baby's face and the eyes opened but as he brought his hand down again the eyes closed once more. He told them to perform the last rites as the child had died.

Later a close devotee ventured to remark that it was unfortunate that the child died at the ashram. If it had to die, it would have been better if had happened elsewhere. Nityananda rebuked him saying "What do you know or understand about these matters? This is the fourth time the same child has come out of the same mother's womb and it has been seeking mukti (liberation). It has been wanting freedom but karmic law has been dragging it down again and again for manifestation in the same family. Its intense desire has been fulfilled now and it won't have to come again." The devotee later talked with the family and learned that there had indeed been three previous children that had all died shortly after birth.

Around 1942 a businessman came to the Ashram. He at one time had a profitable business but had since lost everything. He came to the Ashram seeking Nityananda's blessing. On the day of his visit, the Master kept repeating the word raddi (waste material) over and over. The word planted itself in the man's mind and he kept thinking of the word that day and the day after even though he had left the Ashram. The next day he was walking through the city and he came across an auction in progress. A quantity of raddi was being auctioned and he purchased it immediately and was able to resell it at a profit. He continued buying and selling the manure and soon was making back some of the money he had lost earlier. He became a regular devotee and was thereafter known as Radiwalla (he who is in charge of manure).

Another visitor was a man who had consulted a well-known astrologer to examine his wife's horoscope. The astrologer did so and informed the man that his wife would soon die due to a bad affliction of the planet Saturn. The man was greatly upset as he had also two young children who would have been left motherless. He went to see Nityananda and seek his aid in the matter. He arrived at the Ashram at a time when there were only a few people present. He quietly sat down and Nityananda immediately said to him, "Saturn is there, but God is also there." He then gave the man a series of complicated instructions to carry out. The man carefully followed out the instructions to the letter and when the day came for the predicted event, it came and went without incident.

At the nearby Krishna temple there was a box in which donations were collected. One night Nityananda asked his devotees to go and check to see how much money there was in the collection box. He was told it was nearly full, and he told them to empty it but to leave one-fourth of the money in it. The next morning the devotees found that the box had been broken into and all the money was gone. They ran to tell Nityananda but of course he already knew of it. That is why he had asked that most of the money be removed. He explained that among the visitors the previous day was a very poor man who had sat there and prayed silently to be allowed to break into the collection box as he was near starvation. The master had approved but said the amount left for him was adequate to meet his current needs.

One night at the Ashram, a group of visiting devotees was staying in a room and Nityananda came and sat with them. He remained silent most of the time. One of the ladies spoke to another of his silence and the second woman replied that it was sunset, a good time to meditate, thus implying that the Master was probably deep in meditation. Nityananda heard the conversation that was going on in his presence and said to them, "All that was over in the mother's womb".

Once a long time devotee asked Nityananda if he could see God. He replied "More clearly than you can be seen". Another time a Swami came to the ashram to ask Nityananda some questions. He said, "Why do they call you God?" and Nityananda replied, "Everyone is a God here including yourself and all the ones who are seated here." His devotees often experienced his awareness of whatever was transpiring in their lives. He told them, "Whenever devotees meet and talk (about him), this one is there." A similar statement he made is also very enlightening:

Once one is established in infinite consciousness, one becomes silent, and though knowing everything, goes about as if he does not know anything. Though he might be doing a lot of things in several places, to all outward appearance, he will remain as if he does nothing.

Around that time period, several famous Indian Swamis had gone West to bring the Vedantic knowledge to America, including Vivekananda and Yogananda. A devotee asked Nityananda if he too would be going. He answered, "One has to go abroad only if one cannot see places from here or deal with people there."

The Master made a similar statement towards the end of his life. It appears that there were many signs of his impending passing but his devotees were mostly unaware of them. One woman devotee properly interpreted some of the signs and was distraught to learn of his plans to depart. He said to her, "Why are you crying? Don't cry. More is possible on the subtle than on the gross."

Although the number of people coming to the Ashram increased greatly towards the end of his life, many of them came merely to secure material benefit, such as a better house, more money, a car, etc. Often these wishes were granted through his blessings but instead of being satisfied, the people would just return to ask for more. Nityananda appeared to have been sad that so few were interested in what he had truly come to give them – spiritual enlightenment.

Late in the evening of August 7, 1961 Nityananda was alone with one devotee and he told him that he would be leaving the body the next day. The devotee was in tears and asked him to change his mind or at least postpone the Mahasamadhi. He replied: "It is possible only if a few devotees come forward and make a request; not any devotees but those imbued with desireless devotion, bhava (feeling) and prema (love) …. Even one such is enough and the samadhi will be canceled. When such a devotee is present, even God cannot take leave without his permission, or be able to disengage himself from the bond of his pure love."

However though there were dozens of close devotees and hundreds and even thousands who came to him, there were none advanced enough to be able to say they were completely without desire. The next day towards noon he took a few deep breaths and then one very deep breath so that his chest was fully expanded. He straightened his legs, put his hands over the abdomen, and then was not seen to move anymore.

Though he had shed the body and the point of contact on the physical plane was no more, his devotees continue to have experiences that he is still looking out for them. Even on the day of his Mahasamadhi, his devotee, Dr. Pandlaskar, received his grace in a strange form. The Doctor's young son (then nine years old) arose earlier than usual and in a very uncharacteristic manner said to the mother and father, "What are you doing here? Go to Ganeshpuri. He will be going today. There is a call for him from the assembly of sages for help he alone can render in connection with the forthcoming ashtagraha conjunction (in February 1962, eight planets lined up in the sign of Capricorn) which portends great evil to the world in general and to India in particular." The son knew nothing about astrology and certainly had no way of knowing about the passing of the Master on that day.

During his life Nityananda never held forth views or any dogma to be followed. He never required any certain beliefs or practices of his devotees. He preferred that they not even discuss their own paths or experiences with one another. "People come here with different predilections", he once explained. Once some devotees of Shirdi Sai Baba came for his darshan. Before they could all enter he shouted to them, "Go to Shirdi. Is the Old Man sitting there different than here?"

The devotees received his darshan in silence for the most part but they knew that he was always aware of whatever was transpiring in their lives and was actively involved in looking out for their spiritual unfoldment. A devotee once asked what mental state should be cultivated and Nityananda said: "It (the state of mind) should be like a lotus leaf, which though in water, with its stem in the mud and flower above, is yet untouched by both. Similarly, the mind should be kept untainted by the mud of desires and the water of distractions, even though engaged in worldly activities."

During his life he always set an example by rendering service to others through his feeding of the poor and other activities. His devotees knew that he placed a high value on serving others. Once one of them asked him what would be the result of performing seva (service) for Satpurushes such as himself. In an angry tone Nityananda said to him, "Who wants seva? Does the God asked to be worshipped? It is the man who does so, to get something out of him. Go back and do your duty without desire for fruit (ie reward for your actions) and without sacrificing efficiency. That is the highest seva that you can render. As for spiritual progress, the essential thing is vairagya (detachment from worldliness). Without that there can be no progress."

*As a form of seva (selfless service) to Acharya Ricardo's spiritual grandfather, Bhagawan Nityananda, the above short autobiography of Sadguru Bhagawan Nityananda was taken from popular websites in the internet to inspire aspirants in their spiritual journey toward enlightenment by remembering him, the Shakti, the energy of our lineage, doing our spiritual practices, and honoring the teachings of the great beings of all traditions, to realize the Self within.

In the Shiva Sutras 2.6 of Kashmir Shaivism, the basic scriptural context for Siddha Yoga, states: "The Guru is God's grace-bestowing power."

> "He is the teacher universal who is devoid of mind.
> One who has left all desire is the teacher of all."
> Verse: Chidakash Gita (Nityananda's sacred teachings)

With thanks and acknowledgement to the websites the Chidaksha Gita and this short autobiography of Bhagawan Nityananda were taken.

With thanks and acknowledgement also goes to the late Shri M. D. Suvarna for Nityananda's pictures. "It is only when the scriptural knowledge, instructions of a preceptor (guru) and true discipleship come together that self-knowledge is attained." – Yoga Vashista

Before chanting the *Hare Krishna Mantra* it is beneficial to chant the Pancha-tattva mantra before beginning your japa meditation. Many people like to chant it before each round. This is a prayer to Krishna's most merciful avatar, Lord Chaitanya and His associates, to help us become ecstatic and avoid offenses while chanting. See Hare Krishna Mantra, page 123

sri-krishna-chaitanya prabhu-nityananda

sri-advaita gadadhara

srivasadi-gaura-bhakta-vrinda

"I offer my obeisances to Sri Krishna Chaitanya, Prabhu Nityananda, Sri Advaita, Gadadhara, Srivasa and all others in the line of devotion."

Acharya Ricardo B Serrano is just like a Self-Realized yogi, a Siddha teacher/ guide (preceptor) or meditation Master, who acts as a clear channel for the grace of God, and the disciple's worthiness draws that grace from him. He can awaken the disciple's dormant spiritual energy, kundalini, through Shaktipat (transmission of divine energy).

> "An ideal Guru should be capable of bestowing grace through Shaktipat... It is very rare to find such a Guru." – Kularnava Tantra

Sri Devi Khadgamala Stotram

Sri Devi Khadga Mala Stotram is a very special composition of praying to the Goddess Shakti, the Divine Mother in a unique and complete way. Unique in the sense each of the names uttered is for a significant cause, with meaning description and encapsulated with divine energy and utmost devotion. Word 'Khadga' means Sword, 'Mala' means Garland, Stotram means a hymn or song of praise. So the Khadgamala Stotram is a hymn sung in the praise of Divine Mother, which is said to bestow a protective garland of mystical weapons from the Devi from all sorts of Calamities upon those who recite it. The Devi Khadga Mala Stotram takes us mentally through the Sri Chakra; i.e. the mystical geometric representation of the Supreme Goddess and our being, describing the significance and meaning for each form given. See **Kundalini Awakening, p 12; Mahavidyas, p. 120**

Om Aim Hrim Srim Aim Klim Souh - OM (in the name of God), may you grant us benediction of knowledge, power and grace.

- Om Namah Tripura Sundari
- Hridayadevi - Compassionate heart
- Sirodevi - princely diadem
- Sikhadevi - Long flowing hair
- Kavacha Devi - protective hands
- Netra Devi - graceful look
- Astra Devi - protective weapons
- Kameswari - Controller of lust
- Bhagamalini - Garland of Suns
- Nityaklinne - Oozing wet
- Bherunde - Terrific
- Vahnivasini - Residing in fire
- Mahavajreswari - Jewel in lotus
- Sivaduti - Llarbinger of joy
- Twarite - Speed
- Kulasundari - beautiful lotus on a lake
- Nitya - Eternal
- Nilapatake - Blue flag with red tip
- Vijaye - Dominat
- Sarvamangale - All auspicious
- Jvalamalini - Flames
- Chitre - Kaleidoscope
- Mahanitye - Eternal Truth
- Paramesvara - Goddess of God
- Parameswari - Friendly
- Mitresamayi - Sexy
- Sasthisamayi - Erect
- Uddisamayi - Stroking
- Charyanathamayi – Happiness

Below given are the Names of the Saints who have worshipped the Divine Mother and thus attained liberation.

- Lopamudramayi - Lopamudra - She offered herself for worship
- Agastyamayi - Agastya - he drank the water of the oceans, drying them up
- Kalatapanamayi - Kalatana - he set time on fire
- Dharmacharyamayi - Dharmacharya - he preached the nature of good and evil
- Muktakesisvaramayi - Muktakaleisvara - not worrying about his appearace he let the hair flow loose
- Dipakalanathamayi - Depakalanada - he gazed on eternal light
- Visnudevamayi - Vishnudeva - he expanded himself, took up the whole of space
- Prabhakara devamayi - Prabhaharadeva - he became a star called the sun
- Tejodevamayi - Tejodeva - he became the light witch was speeding over all space creating space itself
- Manojadevamayi - Manojadeva - he was desire
- Kalyanadevamayi - Kalyanadeva - he was ever auspicious
- Vasudevamayi - Vasudeva - the world grew out of his memory
- Ratnadevamayi - Ratnadeva - concentrated like jewels
- Sri Ramanandamayi - Sri Ramananda - he enjoyed the Goddess Sri Rama Blissfully

1. Following are the Gods of the nine enclosures of Sri Chakra / the first enclosure.

Anima Siddhe, Laghima Siddhe, Garima Siddhe, Mahima Siddhe, Isitva Siddhe, Vasitva Siddhe, Prakamya Siddhe, Bhukti Siddhe, Iccha Siddhe, Prapti Siddhe, Sarvakama Siddhe, Brahmi, Mahesvari, Koumari, Vaisnavi, Varahi, Mahendri, Chamunde, Mahalaksmi, Sarva Samksobhini, Sarva Vidravini, Sarva karsini, Sarva Vasamkari, Sarvonmadini, Sarva Mahankuse, Sarva Khecari, Sarva Bije, Sarva Yone, Sarva Trikhande. Trilokya mohana chakra swamini Prakata yogini

The passions called : lust, anger, possessiveness, obsession, pride, jealousy, good, and evil. The procedure to control these passions and obtain the powers of: agitating all(Negativities), liquefying all (orgasmic ally), attracting all, controlling all, maddening all, directing all, moving in all space, be the information of all, be the source of all (womb), be tri-fold division of all (the known, the knowing, and the will know). The wheel of the three worlds of waking, dreaming and sleeping, expressing Herself openly without inhibitions.

2. Following are the sixteen attractive powers identified with the sixteen days of the lunar calendar:

According to the Hindu art of love, the erotic zone moves up from feet to head in the bright half of the lunar month and comes down to the dark half of the lunar month; the expression of the love through the various power of the mind described bellow: - the Gods of the second enclosure.

- Kamakarshini - Attractive powers of lust
- Buddhyakarshini - Attractive powers of discrimination
- Ahamkarakarshini - Attractive powers of ego
- Sabdhakarshini - Attractive powers of sound
- Sparsakarshini - Attractive powers of touch
- Rupakarhsini - Attractive powers of form
- Rasakarshini - Attractive powers of taste
- Gandhakarshini - Attractive powers of odor
- Chittakarshini - Attractive powers of mind
- Dharyakarshini - Attractive powers of valor
- Smrityikarshini - Attractive powers of memory
- Namakarshini - Attractive powers of name
- Bijakarshini - Attractive powers of semen
- Atmakarshini - Attractive powers of self
- Amrtakarshini - Attractive powers of immortality
- Sarirakarshini - Attractive powers of morality
- Sarvasa paripuraka chakra swamini Gupta Yogini - The wheel which fulfills all directions and all desires, the secret Yogini.

3. Following are the eight forms of erotic sentiments: - the third enclosure.

- Ananga Kusume - The sentiment of flowering
- Ananga Mekhale - The sentiment of girdling

- Ananga Madane - The sentiment of love
- Ananga Madananture - The sentiment of lust
- Ananga Redhe - The sentiment of outlining
- Ananga Vegini - The sentiment of the desire of sex
- Ananga Kusume - The sentiment of the insistence on sex
- Ananga Malini - The sentiment of orgy
- Sarva sanksoghana sadhaka chakra swamini
- Gupta tara Yogini - The wheel that agitates everyone, the esoteric yogini.

4. Following are the descriptions of the fourteen worlds of the fourth enclosure.

- Sarva Samksobhini - Agitating all
- Sarva Vidravini - Liquefying all
- Sarva Karshini - Attracting all
- Sarva Hladini - Pleasing all
- Sarva Sammohini - Deluding all
- Sarva Stambhini - Obstructing all
- Sarva Jrumbhini - Expanding all
- Sarva Vasamkari - Controlling all
- Sarva Ranjani - Enjoying all
- Sarvonmadini - Maddening all
- Sarvarthasadhini - all prosperous
- Sarva Sampattipurani - All full filling riches
- Sarva Mantra Mayi - All mantras
- Sarva Dvandva Ksayamkari - Eliminating all dualities
- Sarva Soubhagya Dayaka Cakra Swamini
- Sampradaya Yogini - The wheel of all kinds of union, traditional Yogini.

5. Following are the Gods of the fifth Chakra.

- Sarva Siddhiprade - Giver of all achievements
- Sarva Sampatprade - Giver of all wealth
- Sarva Priyamkari - Giver of all that one like to have
- Sarva Mangalakarini - Harbinger of all auspiciousness
- Sarva Kamaprade - Fulfiller of all desires
- Sarva Duhkha Vimochani - Eliminator of all misery
- Sarva Mrityu Prasamani - Eliminator of all accidental deaths
- Sarva Vighna Nivarini - Eliminator of all obstacles
- Sarvanga Sundari - Beautiful in every part of Her body
- Sarva Soubhagya Dayini Sarvartha Sadhaka Chakra Swamini Kulottirna
- Yogini - The wheel which turns you on to the right path, gives you all wealth, full fills all desirers, and makes liberation possible, the Yogini that has graduated out if all classifications.

6. Following are the Gods of the sixth Enclosure.

- Sarvaghne - Omniscient
- Sarva Sakte - Omnipotent
- Sarvaisvarya pradayini - Omni expressive
- Sarva Jnanamayi - Providing the bliss of omniscience
- Sarva Vyadhivinasini - Eliminating all maladies
- Sarvadharasvarupe - The support of all
- Sarva Papahare - The eliminator of notions of all sins.
- Sarva Anandamayi - All happiness Sarva Raksa Swaroopini - All protecting
- Sarvepsita Phalaprade - Provider of all desired fruits (Boons).
- Sarva Raksakara Chakra Swamini, Nigarbha Yogini - The wheel of all protection, the Yogini protecting the child in the Womb.

7. Following are the eight forms of Saraswati, Goddess of knowledge, Gods of the seventh Enclosure.:

- Vasini - Existing
- Kameshwari - Expression
- Modini - Pleasure
- Vimale - Pure
- Arune - Passion
- Jayini - Victory
- Sarvesvari - Owner
- Kaulini - Enjoying all
- Sarvarogahara Chakra Swamini Rahasya Yogini - The wheel which eliminates disease, the secret Yogini.

8. Following are the powerful weapons of the Divine Mother

- Baanini - The five flowered arrows of Manmatha (God of love, Kaamdev) representing the five senses of sound (music), touch (feel), form (beauty), taste (sweetness), smell (fragrance).
- Chapini - The sugar cane bow (the mind which likes sweet things of life).
- Pasini - The attractive power of love.
- Ankusini - The repulsive power to controling evil.
- Maha Kameshwari - The thrust of God expressing the desire to see Himself in many forms
- Maha Vajreshwari - The ability to obtain the cosmos in seed form
- Maha Bhagamalini - The ability to express the cosmos out of the seed
- Sarva Siddhiprada Chakra Swamini Ati Rahasya Yogini - The wheel of realizations, the most secret Yogini.

9.1 Following is the central hub of the wheel of Sri Devi, the Supreme Goddess: - in ninth enclosure.

- Sri Sri Maha Bhattarike, Sarvananda Maya Chakra Swamini
- Paratpara Rahasya Yogini - The Goddess Sri Devi is present in the whole cosmos. The wheel of all bliss, the transcendental secret Yogini.

9.2 Following are the nine Goddesses controlling the nine wheels above.

- Tripure - Three states of Waking, Dreaming and Sleeping.
- Tripureshi - The controller of these three states
- Tripurasundari - The beautiful one among all these three states
- Tripura Vasini - The one who lives in all these three states
- Tripura Sriyah - The riches of all these three states
- Tripuramalini - The sequences of all these states experienced by all people
- Tripura Siddhe - The achievements possible in all these three states
- Tripurambe - The experience of the cosmos in Her three states unifying all the experiences of all life
- Maha Maheswari - The great cosmic controller
- Maha Maha Raghni - The great cosmic empress
- Maha Maha Shakte - The great cosmic power
- Maha Maha Gupte - The great cosmic secret
- Maha Maha Jnapte - The great cosmic memory
- Maha Mahannande - The great cosmic bliss
- Maha Maha Skandhe - The great cosmic support
- Maha Mahasaye - The great cosmic expression
- Maha Maha Sri Chakra Nagara Samraghni - The great transcendental conscious empress of the wheel of Sri Chakra. Namaste Namaste Namaste Namah - We bow to You, we bow to You, We bow to You in the three states of waking, dreaming, and sleeping states O Divine Mother! Divine Mother's presence is palpable through the Maha Meru Sri Yantra. See **Sri Yantra photo, page 128**

Acharya Ricardo's powerful inner blissful transformative experiences with Sadguru Nityananda's Grace while performing the tantric and Siddha spiritual practices during his three months vacation, from November, 2009 till February 2010, in the Philippines, which drove him to write about it, have convinced him that he has become just like a Siddha or an Acharya with the ability to do Shaktipat. These experiences include dreams where he met face to face his late mother and Siddhas in Siddhaloka, and Self-Realization experiences such as overwhelming God's love and universal oneness, inner peace and quiet mind he hasn't felt before. The most powerful and unforgettable experience while practicing Shaktipat was being in the flow of a powerful loving Shakti (Qi) opening his heart greatly to God's (Shiva's) unconditional love and expansion of his consciousness uniting with the universal or Cosmic consciousness. He has to ground himself, connecting with Mother Earth, with Qigong to enable his physical body to handle this powerful expansion of consciousness and overwhelming Qi flow. This liberating and enlightening experience through the Grace of Bhagawan Sadguru Nityananda and kundalini teacher Raja Choudhury would be similar to a pond of water (you) reuniting and becoming one with the vastness of the ocean (God) through a river path (Siddha).

Without God's grace through a Siddha, represented by his energy or spirit ("Shakti"), there can be no fulfillment or realization (enlightenment, liberation).
The Guru is like a boat that takes us across the ocean of worldliness toward oneness with God. Sadgurunath Maharaj Ki Jay (Hail the true Guru).

"Our entire system is one vast cosmos of energy centres that are navigated through nodes we call Goddesses or Devis who live along our spine and throughout our whole body. To open your third eye you need to unlock each of the major centres and each has its own key, code, vision, sound and most importantly application of breath. Once released, the energy coiled up at the base of your spine rises up like a serpent climbing through these centres and eventually opens your third eye and links you to a super conscious mind state. Allowing this sacred feminine energy into your life will open up not only the doors of perception to other cosmic realities but unleash a dormant energy that will transform every aspect of your consciousness and life and transform you forever." ~ Raja Choudhury

Master Choa Kok Sui describes this universal or Cosmic consciousness as the Buddhic consciousness which is an understanding of a subject matter not through a long period of study nor through inductive or deductive reasoning but through "direct comprehension or perception." Another term for Buddhic consciousness is Christ consciousness or Krishna consciousness. This state of being manifests as a person feels oneness with all, oneness with the Creator. This is the state of feeling Loving-Kindness for all.

Mahashivaratri and Cannabis

Ganja, Sanskrit word for cannabis, is associated with the Hindu God Shiva. Kundalini is also directly associated with the Hindu God Shiva. Every year in Nepal, one of the most holy events, the Shivaratri, is the celebration of Shiva through prayer, meditation and cannabis. The God Shiva consumed cannabis as a blessing according to interpretations of ancient Hindu text. Holy men and women of Shaivism are dedicated to achieving moksa (liberation) via yoga, meditation, and a devotional ritual of smoking cannabis. They find cannabis to be a catalyst for kundalini awakening, self-realization and mystical experiences.

"The subtler attainments come with birth or are attained through herbs (cannabis), mantra, austerities or concentration."

Cannabis use allows for a quieting of the outside world, and the ability to focus more totally on the interior process of meditation." - Patanjali Yoga Sutras 4.1

Theologian, Ariel Glucklich, PhD, Georgetown University states, "Marijuana is used in rituals for Shiva in order to attain higher levels of consciousness, visions, loss of individuality, identity with God. A whole range of psychic and spiritual phenomenon that are produced by cannabis are the goals of allowing and encouraging it's utilization."

Cannabis is not only used by yogis of every tradition for spiritual awakening but also used for healing chronic diseases due to its homeostatic balancing effect on inflammatory diseases by the endocannabinoid system of the body activated by cannabis.

It is a fact that Chinese medicine has used cannabis (Ma Fen) as a healing herb for millennia according to The Divine Farmer's Materia Medica (Shen Nung Ben Cao Jing). However, Traditional Chinese medicine physicians are dedicated Qigong, herbal and acupuncture practitioners so they have the skills to harness the transformative healing potential of cannabis, and neutralize its mild side-effects. Self-medicating with cannabis without the Chinese medicine knowledge and therapies, and Qigong training can make existing symptoms worse or create other imbalances.

Western research has confirmed that cannabis, Qigong and acupuncture work with the endocannabinoid system of the body, and a specific type of acupuncture can heal pain, anxiety, depression, addiction and deliver that great stoned feeling similar to cannabis. Therefore, medical cannabis can revolutionize the practice of TCM because the body's endocannabinoid system is activated to heal diseases. Additionally, Qigong and acupuncture are definitely needed to balance Qi in the body when cannabis is taken.

Cannabis does not affect disease as much as it affects the endocannabinoid system (ECS) that regulates the processes affecting said inflammatory related diseases. Proper activation of the ECS helps to homeostatically regulate the inflammation in the body that is associated with many diseases such as neurological diseases, diabetes, cancer, cardiovascular, Alzheimer's disease, pulmonary diseases, arthritis and autoimmune diseases.

For more information on the endocannabinoid system and the use of diet, herbs, medical cannabis and Qigong for healing chronic diseases, read Ricardo B Serrano's book "The Cure & Cause of Cancer."

Cannabis is regarded as the "food of Kundalini", the female subtle creative energy that transforms sexual energy into spiritual experience. See Jesus and Cannabis, page 136

As a Chinese medicine and Qigong practitioner, I find that Cannabis is both an herbal medicine and an entheogenic substance used for healing and awakening our inner divinity via meditation/ Qigong. – Ricardo B Serrano, R.Ac.

"I am truly that supreme Brahman, which is eternal, stainless, and free; which is one, indivisible, and nondual; and which is of the nature of bliss, truth, knowledge, and infinity." – Shankaracharya, Atmabodha, v.36

"The Self is the knower of the modifications of the mind." – Shankaracharya, Viveka Chudamani, v.133

"That by which one perceives both dream state and waking state, having known That as the great, omnipresent Self, the wise man does not grieve." – Katha Upanishad, 2.1.4

"That by which one perceives form, taste, smell, sounds, and touches of love, by that alone one perceives. What is there which remains unknown to it? This, verily, is That." – Yoga Vasishtha.

"That shines through all our senses, yet is without senses. It supports the senses, yet remains apart from them. It experiences all the qualities of nature, yet remains detached from them." – Bhagavad Gita, 13.14

"When Chiti, universal Consciousness, descends from its lofty state as pure Consciousness, it becomes chitta, the mind." – Pratyabhijnahridayam, sutra 5

"When one acquires the strength of Kundalini, one is able to assimilate the entire universe into oneself." – Ibid., sutra 15

"By this path of the Guru, knowledge of one's Self rises." – Guru Gita, v.110

After the awakening yoga experience because of Shaktipat initiation that re-created and recognized God within his consciousness, Ricardo has now been made aware that man is a living being, a living material expression, and a living soul "God gave in nostrils of man the breath of life and man became a living soul."

"Always remember, Self. And that the material body of man is but a container, a shell for the soul (inner Self) within as explained by the ontological law (Gen.2:7): "God breathed into the the Shakti, the energy of our lineage, comes from Bhagawan Nityananda." – Baba Muktananda

"A person receives Shaktipat from the Guru according to his attitude." – Baba Muktananda

"Shaktipat is the secret initiation of the greatest sages, and it has been passed on from Guru to disciple since primordial times. It is not the monopoly of the Indian tradition. Great beings of every religious tradition had their own inner energy awakened and could awaken it in others; some spoke of it specifically, while others did not. If Jesus moved his hand over someone, that person would be transformed, and great love and happiness would arise in him. That was nothing else but Shaktipat. Saint Francis also had this power. And it was through Shaktipat that Ramakrishna Paramahamsa gave his disciple Swami Vivekananda an instantaneous experience of the Absolute." – Baba Muktananda

"When the Kundalini is awakened, She unites with the pranas and moves through the body, purifying all the nadis and making our system strong and fit for spiritual sadhana. This process of purification is very important. Physical diseases, as well as such negative qualities as anger, lethargy, envy, and greed, are caused by impurities blocking the flow of prana in the nadis. Once the nadis are purified and the prana can run smoothly through the body, the body is rejuvenated and the mind becomes pure." – Baba Muktananda

Shaktipat from a Guru of an authentic Shakti-based lineage is not only necessary to become a true enlightened being, but also a must to become a true Guru yourself. – Ricardo B Serrano

"A Guru is one who has saturated himself with the divine power of grace and has become just like the divine. He also has the power of transmitting grace into others, and enables them to become just like himself... A Guru is one who has power of Shaktipat, and who can pierce all the spiritual centers of a seeker, and who can stabilize his mind in his sahasrara. A Guru is videhi, he is above body-consciousness, and he is totally serene. He removes all the blockages, and he transmits knowledge as thoroughly outlined in all the scriptures." – Baba Muktananda

According to Swami Shankarananda in Nityananda: the Living Tradition, "The specialty of Bhagavan's yoga is shaktipat, the awakening of the kundalini energy that lies dormant in every person. The gurus of this lineage awaken the kundalini energy by look, touch, word or thought. Once this energy is awakened by one of the Siddha gurus and the grace of Bhagavan Nityananda, a seeker evolves rapidly, ultimately attaining permanent repose in the Self.

Bhagavan died physically in 1961, but for his devotees and the Ganeshpuri villagers, his spiritual power is completely present and available even now. Indeed, his samadhi shrine, his place of burial, is a perpetual dynamo, a cauldron of Shakti...

This lineage produced enlightened beings in earlier generations, and it continues to produce them today. Though each person's realisation is uniquely their own, the realisers of the Nityananda tradition have a quality that is characteristic of the great Shakti-based lineages. Their enlightenment is based on the recognition of the Self within, and on the freedom that arises from being centred beyond the mind. But it is also centred in love, seeing the Divine in others. Its core is the transmission of Shakti, and while it may make a devotional affirmation of the world, it is ultimately non-dual. The realisers of the Nityananda tradition blend love, wisdom and Shakti in a matchless dynamic. Our lineage makes a great and unique contribution. It brings the Divine within reach of everyone. The gurus of our lineage have awakened the kundalini shakti of thousands of seekers. They have offered us a direct path to God, and also given us the experience of the Self."

"Ignorance is the root cause of all suffering. It is also the forgetfulness of one's own Self." – Shankaracharya, Aparokshanubhuti, 17

"Moksa or liberation is nothing else but the awareness of one's true nature." – Abhinavagupta, Tantra I, p. 192

"Neither reject anything, nor accept, abide in your essential Self which is an Eternal presence." Abhinavagupta, Anuttarastika, 2

"Why do you look for Him only in churches or mosques? Do you not see His creation? Where does He not abide? The whole universe made by Him recites His tale." – Sarmad

"He is the real Guru Who can reveal the form of the formless before your eyes; who teaches the simple path, without rites or ceremonies; Who does not make you close your doors, and hold your breath, and renounce the world; Who makes you perceive the Supreme Spirit whenever the mind attaches itself; Who teaches you to be still in the midst of all your activities. Fearless, always immersed in bliss, he keeps the spirit of yoga in the midst of enjoyments." – Kabir

"Like oil in sesame seeds, butter in cream, water in the river bed, fire in tinder, the Self dwells within. Realize that Self through meditation." – Shvetashvatara Upanishad

"Just by repeating the Name, that which cannot be understood will be understood. Just by repeating the Name, that which cannot be seen will be seen." – Jnaneshwar Maharaj

"Contemplate Kundalini, Who is supreme Consciousness, who plays from the base of the spine to the crown of the head, Who shines like a flash of lightning, Who is fine as the fiber of the lotus stalk, Who has the brilliant radiance of countless suns, Who is a shaft of light as cool as hundreds of nectarian moonbeams." – Shri Vidya Antar Yaga

"Yoga is the stilling of the vrittis [modifications] of the mind." – Patanjali Yoga Sutras, I, 2

In Taoism Qigong theory, there are 2 kinds of shen (spirit): yuan shen and shi shen. Yuan Shen (original mind) is the shen of stillness. The mind of no mind. It is the intuition mind. Oneness is attained by meditating on the space between the breaths where yuan shen is. See page 60.

Shi shen (knowledge mind) is the shen of action. It is called the logical mind. The key is to start Qigong with shi shen (doing) and eventually reach the stage of yuan shen (non-doing).

"To feel the love of one's soul is the goal of yoga, according to the Bhagavad Gita." – Acharya Ricardo B Serrano

Quotations from Bhagavad Gita: The Beloved Lord's Secret Love Song

"Hear still further the greatest secret of all, my supreme message: "You are so much loved by me!" Therefore I shall speak for your well-being." - BG 18.64

This secret of divine secrets is now revealed: "You are so much loved by me!" The simple message here is that the divinity passionately loves souls, as indicated by the use of the Sanskrit word istah, meaning "desired" or "ardently loved," and the use of the adverbial intensive so much. These few words constitute the very essence of the song or "Gita" of the Beloved Lord. Every verse in the Bhagavad Gita thus revolves around these words. Krishna understands this declaration of divine love by calling it his "supreme message," and further emphasizes the message with the use of the Sanskrit equivalent of quotation marks. This ultimate statement establishes the tone of the entire text, the inner intention of the author, and the controlling principle for understanding the text. No other statement in the Gita receives such attention.

Krishna builds up to the revelation of this greatest secret, as we have seen, with a dramatic summary of his teachings in the first sixty-three verses of chapter 18, thus positioning the greatest of all as the climax of the work. In verse 65, following this greatest secret, Krishna urges souls to love him, and promises that they will come to him since they are "dearly loved" by him:

"Be mindful of me with love offered to me; sacrificing for me, act out of reverence for me. Truly you shall come to me - this I promise you for you are dearly loved by me." - BG 18.65

This verse reveals the best possible response of souls to Krishna's greatest of all secrets is bhakti, the love offered by the soul to the supreme divinity. Bhakti, therefore, is not merely a means to reach the divine, but is itself the perfection of all other means for attaining an intimate connection with the divinity in yoga.

According to the Gita, yoga is not a reclusive meditation in some distant mountain hermitage; rather, the hermitage is found within one's heart, and in the hearts of others. The ultimate yoga for souls is to attain a state of full-heartedness - a heart that offers itself in unremitting, unconditional love in response to the divine yearning. This yearning, the greatest secret of all, is pronounced as "You are dearly loved by me."

The Bhagavad Gita is truly the Beloved Lord's "secret love song." This ever-beckoning song urges souls to embrace divinity just as divinity forever embraces souls. The Gita begins with a question that speaks to everyone of us: "How are we to act in this world of conflict and suffering?" The Gita's answer is simply to act out of love. This hidden song of the divinity calls souls to act out of love in all that they do, in all that they think, feel and will. The Gita insists that human life is meant for hearing this innermost song of the heart. It behooves souls to search for this song, and upon hearing it, to listen to the divine love song as it resonates in everything, everywhere, and at every moment - to hear it through the hearts of all beings and in all life. Once heard, this secret love song is celebrated as the most blessed gift of divinity to humankind.

Excerpts from pages 276-278 of Bhavagad Gita: The Beloved Lord's Secret Love Song by Schweig

The supreme message of the Gita is revealed gradually in the text, as Krishna discusses the ways in which the hearts of souls can either move toward him, which is the essence of yoga, or away from him, which could be understood as vi-yoga ("that which moves one away [vi-] from yoga"). The soul that follows the path of vi-yoga leads a life of ego-centeredness (ahankara) and selfishness (mamatva); whereas the soul that practices some form of yoga focused on divinity leads a life without selfishness and ego-centeredness. In the former, the self, disconnected from the inner world of self, becomes entangled in a precarious existence within the outer world of conflict and suffering. In the latter, the self, connected in any number of ways with some dimension of the divine, experiences the inner world of transcendence in which it finds Brahman, "the supreme Spirit," or Purushottama, "the supreme Self." The soul may even see the innermost world of the heart in which it discovers the heart of divinity, as the ultimate human achievement. This concept of the soul moving toward or away from yoga is behind every practice and philosophical discussion presented in the Gita...

When the soul is bound to this world, it is subject to the powerful conditioning of the qualities of nature. Furthermore, when a soul is reborn, the life of that soul is largely determined by the positive and negative effects arising from the activities of one's previous births. The worldview of the Gita, however, blends conceptions of free will with this deterministic view. Free will is a necessary ingredient in love; that love cannot be coerced or controlled is axiomatic for the Gita. This subtle but critical theme shows that souls are given the power of choice, without which there is no possibility of love.

The love call of God, found within his sacred teachings, awakens free will, enabling the soul either to accept the cycle of endless birth and rebirth that binds the soul to this world, or to choose a path leading to the eternal world that frees the soul from the cycle of suffering. This mortal world, the Gita implies, exists so that souls can exercise choice, without which, again, there is no possibility of love. The implication is that there can be no true love in the divine world without an alternate world. Thus, this world, ultimately designed to facilitate love, is brought into being by the divinity to give souls the freedom to love. - Excerpts from pages 249-250 of Bhavagad Gita: The Beloved Lord's Secret Love Song by Schweig

Let go our Ego

"Ego is nothing but identification of oneself with their body instead of their Soul."

Ego is nothing but to feel oneself more important than others, to feel different and superior to others. Such a feeling of finding oneself different from others is nothing but ignorance and such an illusion is called ego. We all are part and parcel of the Omnipresent Soul and that one same soul is present in all of us. So if we are able to realize that soul within all of us then we cannot find ourselves different from others.

Under the influence of ego a human being forgets the truth about God and thinks his/her identity to be different than others. Once a person knows this knowledge of God, then the delusion of "Maya" disappears and that person shed his / her ego to become one with God again.

Human beings generally crave for Name, Fame, Pleasures of life etc. which satisfies one's ego and these are the Idols in one's life which a person adores very much. But these Idols do not do any good to one self as it obscures one's real 'Soul nature', which is divine with unlimited powers and is always blissful. Such craving for Name, Fame and Sense pleasures drowns one's self-respect and obscures the divine being from our sight. These worthless temptations destroy one's reputation and always give delusion by which a person is not able to know his Divine Self.

Below is Bhagavad Gita 16. 18 which tells how an egoistic person behaves:

"Sri Krishna said: O Arjuna, Bewildered by false ego, strength, pride, lust and anger, these egoistic people become envious of the Supreme Lord, who is situated in their own bodies and in the bodies of others, and blaspheme against the real religion."

Below is Bhagavad Gita 18. 62 which tells how surrendering one's ego one can achieve God:

"Sri Krishna said: O Arjuna, surrender your ego fully unto the God. By His grace you will attain transcendental peace and the supreme and eternal abode."

As a rope that is burnt retains its shape intact, but has become all ashes, so that nothing can be bound with it; similarly, the person who feels one with everyone and is devoted to God, retains only the form of his egoism, but not have any idea of vanity (Ahamkâra).

So let's shed our ego and not be egoistic, as it shall not do any good to one self. Let's surrender our ego in the Divine feet of God and adore Him only so that He can give us a blissful life. --- With thanks to Sanjay Chopra for his above article "Let's shed our ego," Bhagwat Gita Blog

Hare Krishna mantra is a prayer to God's energy (Shakti) for taking away all the sorrows, pains and shortcomings of the chanter and provide him bliss, joy, peace and oneness with Higher Self.

Atma (Soul) Yoga of Immortality

Atma (Soul) Yoga of Immortality, also called Soham Yoga, founded by Acharya Ricardo B Serrano, is about becoming a *numinous* Self-realized soul by attaining oneness with the Higher Self (Soul) via the advanced meditation and Qigong practices based on his seven books and 2 DVDs used in the curriculum of the Integral Studies of Inner Sciences at http://atmayoga.info. See What is Kundalini Awakening?, page 9; How to Conquer Death Now, page 49; Wei Qi field in Medical Qigong, page 63; So'ham, page 118; Yuan Shen, page 130

The Atma (Soul) Yoga of Immortality is an advanced combination of meditation and Qigong forms for healing and attaining oneness with Higher Self or Self-realization – to become a *numinous* Self-realized being (Zhenren) or Srivatsa symbolized by Swastika or Yuan Shen (Original Spirit). "Heal the soul first; then healing of the mind and body will follow." – Dr. Master Sha

"If there is light in the soul, there is beauty in the person, if there is beauty in the person, there will be harmony in the house, if there is harmony in the house, there will be order in the nation, if there is order in the nation, there will be peace in the world."
"The healing compassion of Kuan Yin Bodhisattva is palpable by regularly chanting her small and great compassion mantras." – Acharya Ricardo B Serrano

The above Zen quotation refers to oneness – realignment - with the light of the soul which is the Higher Self, Light of God or Atma, Yuan Shen (Original Spirit) – the Golden Elixir via *So'ham* or *Namo Kuan Shi Yin Pu Sa* mantra. See *Da Bei Zhou*, p. 109

The heart is connected to the Original Spirit through the soul. The practice of true meditation or Qigong opens the heart and clarifies the soul. Consequently, the Original Spirit can shine through the clarified soul and flourish as true love in the heart. The key to awakening the soul is the opening of the heart. Ultimately, union with Spirit means to be in harmony in the universe. See Union of Three Hearts, p. 80; Meditation on Three Hearts, p. 140

The reality of this whole universe is God consciousness. It is filled with God consciousness. This world is nothing but the blissful energy (shakti) of the all-pervading consciousness of God. God and the individual are one, to realize this is the essence and goal of meditation and Qigong. See Mahashivaratri and Cannabis, p. 96; Jesus and Cannabis, p. 136

The central teaching of the Upanishads is that the Self of a human being is the same as Brahman, the Absolute. The goal of life is the realization of that Truth. I am Spirit Soul. Aham Brahmasmi. See *Who am I?*, p. 40; *Da Bei Zhou*, p. 109; *So'ham*, p. 118

YOUR OWN SOUL IS YOUR GURU, QUIET THE MIND AND LISTEN TO YOUR HIGHER SELF.

"Atma Namaste" This phrase addresses the "higher" soul of the person: "To the higher Soul", I honor the place within you where the universe resides. I honor the place within you of love, light, and truth. When you are in that place and I am in that place we are One. This practice starts with you placing your hands in the prayer position on your heart. Gaze above the head of another person, 6 to 8 inches, and say Atma, Namaste. Then, look into their eyes (you may also look into your own eyes in a mirror). Really look, and wait. See what comes back to you. Do you feel the love? This is an intense practice; do not reserve it for a few.
Atma Namaste! "Atma" means Soul in Sanskrit. "Namaste" – I Salute the Divinity in you, I Salute the Atma in you, I Salute the "I Am" Presence within you! Make it happen often, and with many. May you enjoy this practice, another blessing from our Beloved Gurus to you.

Acknowledgements:

With thanks and acknowledgements to my Sri Vidya Guru Sri Amritananda Natha Saraswati, Sadguru Nityananda's grace and to Swami Lakshmanjoo's Shiva Sutras and my Siddha Guru teacher Baba Muktananda for the excerpts from his books which are dedicated to my meditation and Qigong students who are interested in the Siddha path to Self-realization.

With thanks and acknowledgements to Master Victor Shim and Pranic Healing teachers Master Choa Kok Sui, Master Nona Castro, Mang Mike Nator, Taoist Master Michael Winn for his 8 Extraordinary Vessels Qigong, Master James MacRitchie for his Drawing in Heaven and Earth practice and extraordinary meridians photos, David Twicken for his Eight Extraordinary Channels book, Master Alton Kamadon for his Merkaba teachings, Zhan Zhuang Qigong Master Richard Mooney, Qi Dao Master Lama Tantrapa, Sri Vidya teacher Raja Choudhury, Wing Chun Kung Fu Sifu Samuel Kwok, Dr. Master Zhi Gang Sha of the Great Compassion Mantra (Da Bei Zhou) and my Sheng Zhen Gong teacher Master Li Jun Feng for his Sheng Zhen Gong forms especially Hanuman Qigong which, I believe, is the perfect Qigong to balance, ground, and toned down the powerful Siddha meditation practices.

Book References:

Does Death Really Exist? and Mystery of the Mind by Swami Muktananda, 1981.

Kundalini: the Secret of Life, Getting Rid of What You Haven't God by Muktananda, 1978.

Secrets of Eternal Life: Tao Teh Ching by Tai Chi Grand Master Victor Shim, 1985.

The Perfect Relationship and Secrets of the Siddhas by Swami Muktananda, 1980.

Play of Consciousness (1978) and I Have Become Alive by Swami Muktananda, 1985.

Practical Psychic Self-Defense for Home and Office by Master Choa Kok Sui, 2005.

Hanuman Qigong, Origin of the Heart by Master Li Junfeng, 2011.

Sheng Zhen Wuji Yuan Gong by Master Li Junfeng, 2000.

Meditations for Soul Realization by Master Choa Kok Sui, 2000.

Shiva Sutras by Swami Lakshmanjoo, 2000;

I AM THAT: the,Science of Hamsa by Swami Muktananda,1978.

The Eight Extraordinary Meridians Qigong by James MacRitchie, 2008.

Eight Extraordinary Channels – Qi Jing Ba Mai by David Twicken, OMD, Lac, 2013.

Bhagavad Gita: The Beloved Lord's Secret Love Song by Graham M. Schweig, 2010.

Six healing Qigong sounds by Acharya Ricardo B Serrano, 2021

Young Nityananda

Sadguru Nityananda

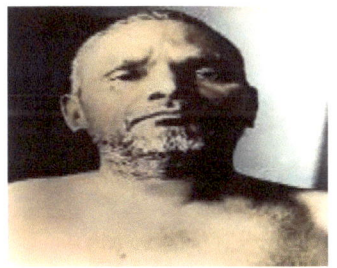

Sadguru Nityananda

Sadguru Nityananda

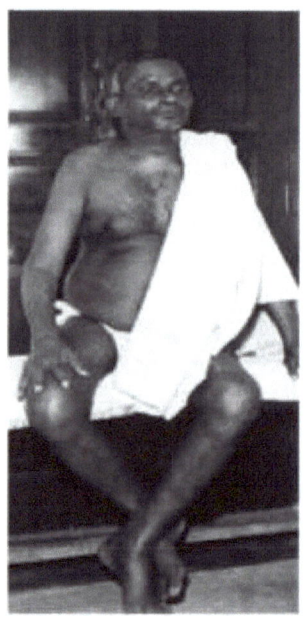

Baha'ullah

Nityananda Samadhi Shrine

Nityananda Bhunt Bhavan

Baba Muktananda

Swami Lakshmanjoo

Mang Mike and Master Choa Kok Sui

Ricardo and Master Li Jun Feng   Dr. Master Zhi Gang Sha

Da Bei Zhou (Great Compassion Mantra) and Namo Kuan Shi Yin Pu Sa (Small Compassion Mantra)

The *Da Bei Zhou mantra* on page 109 is usually used to remove the negative karma, for energetic protection and to purify the soul of the practitioner conducive to progress toward complete spiritual enlightenment. One who recites and holds this sacred mantra can heal all the 84000 different types of diseases of the world, without exception.

Namo Kuan Shi Yin Pu Sa – *Kuan Yin* small compassion mantra. Reciting this mantra daily brings peace and safety to the family, prosperity and wealth, healing and peace of mind, during difficult times. It cultivates your mind and heart, eventually quiets the mind and stills all other vibrations or thoughts.

Chant *Namo Kuan Shi Yin Pu Sa* to cultivate the same compassion embodied by Kuan Yin Bodhisattva. – Dr. Sha

Read *Swastika*, p. 19; *Atma (Soul) Yoga of Immortality*, p. 103; *Yuan Shen*, p.130; *Meditation on Three Hearts*, p. 139

DA BEI ZHOU (Great Compassion Mantra of Kuan Yin)

Qian Shou Qian Yan Wu Ai Da Bei Xin Tuo Luo Ni (3x)

1. Nan Mo He La Da Nu Do La Ye Ye
2. Nan Mo Wo Lie Ye
3. Bo Lo Jie Di So Ben La Ye
4. Pu Ti Sa Duo Po Ye
5. Mo Hu Sa Duo Po Ye
6. Mo Hu Jia Lu Ni Jia Ye
7. An
8. Sa Ben La Fa Yi
9. Su Da Nu Da Xia
10. Nan Mo Xi Jie Li Do Yi Meng Wo Lie Ye
11. Bo Lo Jie Di Shi Fo La Leng To Po
12. Nan Mo Nu La Jin Chi
13. Xi Li Mo Hu Ben Do Sa Mi
14. Sa Po Wo To Dou Shu Peng
15. Wo Shi Yun
16. Sa Po Sa Duo Nan Mo Po Sa Duo Nan Mo Po Qie
17. Mo Fa Te Dou
18. Da Zhi To
19. An Wo Po Lu Xi
20. Lu Jia Di
21. Jia Lo Di
22. Yi Xi Li
23. Mo Hu Pu Ti Sa Duo
24. Sa Po Sa Po
25. Mo La Mo La
26. Mo Xi Mo Xi Li To Yun
27. Ju Lu Ju Lu Jie Meng
28. Du Lu Du Lu Fa She Ye Di
29. Mo Hu Fa She Ye Di
30. Tuo Lo Tuo Lo
31. Sai Li Ni
32. Shi Fo La Ye
33. Zhe La Zhe La
34. Mo Mo Fa Mo La
35. Mu Di Li
36. Yi Xi Yi Xi
37. Shi Nu Shi Nu
38. Wo La Sheng Fo La She Li
39. Fa Sha Fa Sheng
40. Fo La She Ye
41. Hu Lu Hu Lu Mo La
42. Hu Lu Hu Lu Xi Li
43. So La So La
44. Xi Li Xi Li
45. Su Lu Su Lu
46. Pu Ti Ye Pu Ti Ye
47. Pu To Ye Pu To Ye
48. Mi Di Li Ye
49. Nu La Jin Chi
50. Sai Li Se Ni Nu
51. Po Ye Mo Nu
52. So Po Hu
53. Xi Tuo Ye
54. So Po Hu
55. Mo Hu Xi Tuo Ye
56. So Po Hu
57. Xi Tuo Yu Yi
58. So Ben La Ye
59. So Po Hu
60. Nu La Jin Chi
61. So Po Hu
62. Mo La Nu La
63. So Po Hu
64. Xi La Seng Wo Mu Qie Ye
65. So Po Hu
66. So Po Mo Hu Wo Xi Tuo Ye
67. So Po Hu
68. Zhe Ji La Wo Xi Tuo Ye
69. So Po Hu
70. Bo To Mo Jie Xi Tuo Ye
71. So Po Hu
72. Nu La Jin Chi Ben Qie La Ye
73. So Po Hu
74. Mo Po Li Sheng Ji La Ye
75. So Po Hu
76. Nan Mo He La Da Nu Do La Ye Ye
77. Nan Mo Wo Lie Ye
78. Bo Lo Jie Di
79. So Ben La Ye
80. So Po Hu
81. An Xi Dian Du
82. Man Duo La
83. Ben To Ye
84. So Po Hu
85. Jin Gang Sheng Zhuang Yan So Po Hu
86. Sheng Wen Sheng Zhuang Yan So Po Hu
87. Mo Jie Sheng Zhuang Yan So Po Hu
88. An Bo Zhe La Xi Lie Xie So Po Hu

Fanatical Attachment

"Among individuals, as among nations, respect for the rights of others is peace." – Benito Juarez

An extreme example of fanatical attachment is about China's claim and historical belief that it owns the whole South China Sea as shown in the following:

"A fanatic is one who can't change his mind and won't change the subject." – Sir W. Churchill

I believe that as long as CCP's fanatical attachment to the historical belief that it owns 90 percent of South China Sea with its disrespect to the sovereign rights of its ASEAN neighbors are not changed or let go by the CCP officials despite the international support by its small neighbors in disputed isles, war is inevitable.

"Fanaticism obliterates the feelings of humanity." – Edward Gibbon

The beginning to letting go of fanaticism is love and respect for self and others. To let go of the most extreme form of fanaticism requires an ability to question the beliefs (Communism, religion, politics, cult, philosophy, medicine, relationship, materialism (greed) or diet) or agreements that are tied to it. The act of questioning produces a moment of clarity that allows us to see our truth. A moment of doubt or skepticism in a belief can be the crack that will begin to expand our perception.

"Doubt is to me the handmaiden to faith, its cop, the one that keeps faith straight. To doubt is an indication of freedom and a guard against fanaticism." – Nora Gallagher

Skepticism makes it possible to reassess and make a decision to hold on to it by saying yes or no. Do I really believe this? Why do I believe this? Does this belief serve me? Re-evaluating our beliefs introduces the option to continue to believe or to change. Letting go of fanaticism is to allow ourselves to listen to what we perceive and reassess our willingness to say yes or no to it with awareness. The best way to let go of illusion is to say yes to the truth when it is presented to us just as it is.

Another way to cleanse the beliefs, the five levels of attachments: authentic Self, preference, identity, internalization and fanaticism, and karmic residues from past lives is to practice the Eight Extraordinary Meridians Qigong and Sri Vidya kundalini meditation.

With awareness (the Authentic Self), you will know the truth and the truth will set you free.

The key to all forms of transformation is awareness (the Authentic Self) with love, sincerity, honesty and respect for

self and others. Read "*How to Quiet the Mind*" on p. 20; *Da Bei Zhou*, p. 109; *Awakening your Kundalini*, p. 138.

Divine Mother (Source) manifests as blissful reunion of Shiva and Shakti in us. - Acharya Ricardo B Serrano

See Sri Devi Stotram, p. 92; Lalitha Tripura Sundari, p. 112, 119; Inner Soma, p. 122; Sri Yantra, p. 128; Awakening Kundalini, p. 138

Shiva Sutras & So'ham

"Shiva Consciousness is the Self." – Shiva Sutra 1.1

The mantra So'ham is the awareness "I am That," the awareness of the identity between the individual soul and the supreme.

"The limitation of your ego is the only thing standing between you and God, the only thing that prevents you from attaining liberation or God-realization. The only reason to take a Guru is to destroy the limitation of the ego." See page 113

"My unforgettable experience seeing auras of the clairvoyance participants and seeing Master Choa Kok Sui's spiritual heart and crown chakras brought tears in my eyes realizing that we are spiritual beings. We are the Self." – Acharya Ricardo

Chapter 4

Tao in Its Original Essence (Form) is everywhere and Within ourselves. In order to tap It, one must still the rational mind. In order to feel It, one must be completely relaxed. In order to use It, one must use the "Will" of Tao as our own.

Rotate the Magic Wheel of life along the Microcosmic orbit daily. Only when the microcosmic channels are cleared or cleansed of Grossness, Sins or negativity;

Then and only then will Tao appear within inside Yourself as Yourself. When you have seen Tao appearing inside yourself as Yourself, You would exclaim:

"There He is. Born before the birth of Heaven and Earth. Unborn, He is older than God!"

Quotations from The Secrets of Eternal Life: Tao Teh Chieng by Victor Shim, 1985.

"When a man is in perfect-union with his True Self through Yoga, Tai Chi, Chi Kung or Nei Kung meditation, he experiences the highest form of Bliss, peace, happiness and harmony unknown to the materialistic people. There is no form of happiness on Earth that can equal Divine Consciousness or Cosmic Consciousness. The gross experiences of human senses and pleasures can never be compared and matched in one tone with Cosmic Realization."

– Tai Chi Grand Master Victor Shim

Divine Mother (Source) manifests as blissful reunion of Shiva and Shakti in us. – Acharya Ricardo B Serrano

The ringstone symbol was designed by `Abdu'l-Bahá, Bahá'u'lláh's son/ successor, and as its name implies, is the most common symbol found on rings worn by Bahá'ís, but it is also used on necklaces, book covers, paintings. It consists of two stars (haykal) interspersed with a stylized Bahá'. The lower line is said to represent humanity and the world of creation, the upper line the world of God, and the middle line represents the special station of Manifestation of God and the world of revelation; the vertical line is the Primal Will or Holy Spirit proceeding from God through the Manifestations to humanity. The position of Manifestation of God in this symbol is said to be the linking point to God. The two stars or haykals represent Bahá'u'lláh and the Báb. It symbolizes "Allah'u'abha", means "God is most glorious."

Baha'ullah (Glory of God) is the Manifestation of God and the Holy Spirit referred to is the same as the Yuan Shen or the Higher Self (Atma), see page 130. See Baha'i faith and Baha'ullah in Dedication, page 3

May your heart merge into the heart of the Divine via Baha'ullah, divine teacher of Ricardo B Serrano.

Reference: Baha'ullah and the New Era, An Introduction to the Baha'i Faith by Dr. J.E.Esslemont, 2006

The predominant sign of such a yogi is joy-filled amazement. - Shiva Sutra 1.12

This yogi is filled with joy and amazement. The Sanskrit word vismaya means "amazement completely filled with joy." Just as a person seeing some wonderful object is amazed, in the same way, this yogi is filled with amazement who, in the objective world of senses, experiences entry in his own self filled with consciousness, which is unique, intense, always fresh and uncommonly charming, and by which entry all his varieties of organs are filled with blooming, ever smiling, one-pointed joy.

What kind of amazement is this? This yogi, upon entering into that limitless state of bliss (ananda), is never satiated with the experience. On the contrary, he feels bathed with the amazement of joy. This is the predominant state of yoga of a yogi who has become one with the supreme Lord, the supreme tattva, Siva tattva. And by this, you can surmise that he has ascended to the state of Siva.

"He should be considered as the real Sadguru who makes the disciple experience perfect calmness of mind by making him realize his own Self. For no other reason should one person be considered as the Sadguru of another." - Eknath Maharaj

May all who read these words be uplifted and filled with God's Grace and the All-Pervasive Love of the Endless One, Bhagawan Nityananda (everlasting bliss) of Ganeshpuri.

May your heart merge into the heart of the Divine. The heart is the hub of all sacred places, go there and roam.

Sri Devi by Guruji Amritananda Natha

Hindus call her Gayatri, Christians call her the Virgin Mary, Buddhists call her the Compassion, Sufis call her the Movement; other ancient religions simply call her Mother Earth. She is our source, our sustenance and our end. She is Kundalini, the power moving us toward the unity of all life.

She combines in Herself the tenderness of all mothers and the passion of all lovers, wisdom and insanity, childishness and experience, cruelty and faithfulness. She is maya; dissolution of maya leads to mahasamadhi from which there is no return. This is the reason why it is insisted that you treat Devi as your mother; then the thought of enjoying Her does not arise that easily in the head, preserving your life. But think! what better way to die than in the hands of mother, to become Shiva, a death like corpse? If you are Her child, She feeds you with milk from Her ever full breasts; and the milk of life is sweet indeed. But in the total recognition there is no second - one does indeed become Shiva and Shakti in union; then there is no manifest world, except the continuous unending bliss. And one who has once tasted the sweetness of it, does not want to come back, except as a sacrifice of freedom brought about willfully! **See Lalitha Tripura Sundari, p. 119; Inner Soma, p. 122; Awakening Kundalini, p. 138**

Bhagawan Nityananda says, "The heart is the hub of all sacred places, go there and roam." In order to accomplish this, your heart needs to be purified of all the false impressions and dirt deposited there by the impure ego. For this you need a Guru.

According to Acharya Kedar, "I am often asked why a Guru is necessary. Some people who come to our programs have expressed concerns about the fact that there are pictures of my Gurudev and the other Siddhas of my lineage hanging on the walls of our Meditation Hall. People want to know why I worship Gurudev and why we encourage worship of the Siddhas. There are those who believe that one should only worship the formless God. So, we have this question. "Why?" And it is a very good question which the Disciple must ask.

To be clear, the limitation of your ego is the only thing standing between you and God, the only thing that prevents you from attaining liberation or God-realization.

The only reason to take a Guru is to destroy the limitation of the ego. This ego cannot be destroyed by attempting to worship that which you cannot see or experience through your senses since, in order for the ego to be purified, the senses must also be purified.

Since the function of your senses is to attach themselves to objects of form (people, places, and things) the senses and the ego can only be purified by becoming attached to that which will destroy their limitation in the fire of Yoga. This must be an object with agency, an object with the power to bestow God's Grace. That object is the Guru who is a Siddha.

If you constantly remember that the Guru is not the physical body, but the Grace-bestowing power of God that is being transmitted through the Acharya; and if you worship the Master, remembering this, taking the form of the Guru inside your being in meditation, or meditating on the Acharya's Guru or any of the saints of the Guru's lineage, you will begin to experience a wonderful and powerful purification and opening of the heart.

This leads to a burning devotion to and love for the Guru, which leads to surrender of the impure ego. Once this surrender is complete, you still have an ego, but it is purified ego which proclaims, "I am Shiva, I am Shakti, I am the Absolute, I am Pure, I am Worthy, I am Perfect." You begin to bask in your own natural, free state of divine unconditional love.

That Love has the power to perform miracles and it will transform your entire being and also, over time, heal all your latent illnesses. This Love comes from the Grace-bestowing power of the Guru and your own Self-effort at daily spiritual practice. It is your own Grace, known as Disciple's Grace, that is the foundation for this relationship between Acharya and Disciple. Your Grace is the most important element. Without it, the Master cannot do his work."

Shiva Rock (Shankaropal), where fifteen hundred years ago, the Shiva Sutras were revealed to the Sage Vasugupta

The joy of his samadhi is bliss for the whole universe. - Shiva Sutra 1.18

Whatever joy he feels while he is in samadhi is said to be the insertion of bliss for the whole universe. This yogi doesn't have to do anything. He only has to remain in samadhi and he will carry the whole universe into that supreme bliss.

According to Kashmir Shaivism teachings found in the Vijnana Bhairava, when a yogi resides with full awareness in the state of subjectivity, with the full joy of experiencing his own nature (camatkara), this is said to be the joy of his samadhi (mystical rapture).

There is another explanation of this sutra given by masters and that is, "Whenever this yogi, who is always residing in his own self (svatmarama), is introverted and established in his own self, then he naturally enjoys the bliss of samadhi. Anyone who sees this and thinks that this yogi is enjoying the bliss of samadhi will, at that very moment, also enter into samadhi. This is just like seeing a cobra not from distance, but face to face.

When you see a cobra and it bites you, you will be filled with the poison of that cobra. In the same way, when you observe a yogi who is established in the joy of samadhi and you understand that he is experiencing the joy of this samadhi, you will at once also relish the joy of samadhi. This reveals how this bliss is bestowed on the whole world.

"The supreme Shakti, whose nature is to create, constantly expressed herself upward in the form of exhalation, and downward in the form of inhalation. By steadily fixing the mind on either of the two spaces between the breaths, one experiences the state of fullness of Bhairava." - Vijnana Bhairava (v. 24)

You can practice *Hamsa* whether you are walking or sitting, eating or sleeping. Brahmananda said, "As you contemplate this mantra, you attain the supreme state." Namdev, another great saint, said, "Just keep repeating *So'ham, So'ham* all the time, and you yourself will become God." This mantra has the power to transform you completely.

Swamiji Lakshmanjoo said, "When, by the grace of Lord Siva or the grace of his master, this limited being comes to the real understanding of his nature, then he knows that he is one with Paramasiva. At that point there is no difference between him and Paramasiva. Your consciousness becomes filled and adjusted with the reality and truth that this whole universe is only God. Nothing is experienced as being outside of God. This is the unification of your individual God Consciousness with Universal God Consciousness."

"He becomes just like Siva." - Shiva Sutra 3.25

According to Swamiji Lakshmanjoo, "He becomes like Lord Siva. Why is it said that he becomes like Lord Siva? Why not say that he becomes one with Siva? It cannot be said he becomes one with Siva because he has a body, a physical frame. As long as his physical frame is existing, he is just like Siva, he is not one with Siva. His having a physical frame will divert him toward inferior states. For instance, he may cough, have headaches, experience muscle pain, stomach aches, ulcers, or fever. Siva does not have these ailments or suffer these physical discomforts. So, as long as the yogi possesses a body, he can only be like Siva, not one with Siva. When he casts off this physical frame composed of the five elements, then he becomes one with Siva.

Because his physical body is existing, even when he becomes like Siva, that action (karma) that has brought his body into existence is ended by enjoying that action, not by casting it aside. Prarabdha karma cannot be overcome unless it is enjoyed. For an embodied being, prarabdha karma is unavoidable. He may be just like Siva or he maybe an ordinary person; prarabdha karma must be overcome by being enjoyed. It cannot be cast aside or abandoned.

So, for the remainder of his life, he must continue to exist with this physical frame. He must welcome whatever comes to him, whether it be good or bad. Whatever he gets to eat, he must eat. It is not worthwhile to cast his body aside. For such a yogi, this body is to be maintained until the time of death."

"The independent state of supreme consciousness is the reality of everything." - Shiva Sutra 1.1

This first sutra, caitanyamatma, states that individual being is one with universal being. The reality of this whole universe is God consciousness. It is filled with God consciousness.

In this sutra, the state of complete independence is indicated and accomplished through the use of the word caitanya... It is only this one aspect, svatantrya, that is revealed by the word caitanya. This indicates that the word caitanya means "the independent state of consciousness."

The independent state of consciousness is the self. It is the self of everything, because whatever exists in the world is the state of Lord Shiva. So Lord Shiva is found everywhere.

"Let Shiva, who is my Self, let Shiva do pranam (bow down) to his real nature – to Universal Shiva, by his own Shakti, for removing the bondage and limitation, which is Shiva." - 1st verse, Shiva Dhristi

Here, Shiva bows to himself, for the removal of obstacles, which are also Shiva, through his own energy (shakti) which is one with Shiva, and in the end He resides in the state of universal Shiva. That is the state of Para (Supreme) Bhairava!

> "God and the individual are one.
>
> To realize this is the essence of Shaivism."
>
> - Swami Lakshmanjoo

"Trika philosophy is situated in the heart of that supreme energy of God consciousness. It teaches you to realize that this whole objective world, which is already in front of you, is not separate from God consciousness. You do not have to realize God situated in some seventh heaven. God and the individual are one, to realize this is the essence of Shaivism."

Swamiji Lakshmanjoo tells us,"freedom from all our miseries, as Abhinavagupta boldly declares, can neither be obtained through the renunciation of the world, nor by hatred towards this world, but by experiencing the presence of God everywhere."

NOTE: Kashmir Shaivism is not a religion. It is a philosophy open to those who have the desire to understand it; hence, for its study there are no restrictions of caste, creed, color or gender.

"Kundalini shakti is the concealing and revealing energy of Lord Shiva. Para (supreme) kundalini is the heart and existence of Shiva, in fact it is the life and glory of Shiva, it is Shiva himself." - Kashmir Shaivism, the Secret Supreme

"Kashmir Shaivism proclaims that there are three means (upayas) for entering into the state of Universal God consciousness, i.e. shambhavopaya (supreme), shaktopaya (medium), and anavopaya (inferior). The difference is, in anavopaya you take the support of everything as an aid to strengthening awareness. In shaktopaya you begin in the center and become established there. In shambhavopaya no support is needed, you reside at your own point, the rest is automatic. It is important to realize that although these means are different, they all lead to the state of one transcendental consciousness."

"Creating, protecting, destroying, concealing and revealing are the five great acts of Lord Shiva. The individual soul also accomplishes these five acts and feels he is acting according to his own will, but, in reality his actions are dependent to the will of God, Lord Shiva. Still, as long as he has ego and feels that he is the actor, the limited individual is responsible for his own actions.

In the kingdom of spirituality Lord Shiva creates masters and disciples through his act of revealing, also known as grace or shaktipata. There are three types of grace, intense (tivra-tivra), medium (tivra) and inferior (madhya). Within each of these there are three levels which means Lord Shiva bestows grace and creates masters and disciples in nine different ways. The greatness of Lord Shiva is that no matter what intensity of his grace is with you, it will carry you to his nature in the end."

"Kundalini shakti is the concealing and revealing energy of Lord Shiva. Para (supreme) kundalini is the heart and existence of Shiva, in fact it is the life and glory of Shiva, it is Shiva himself.

When para kundalini creates the universe Shiva conceals his real nature and becomes the universe. Cit kundalini is experienced by great yogin's, who through maintenance of awareness, enter the junction and experience the rise of the seven states of turya. Prana kundalini is experienced by those yogin's who are attached to spirituality and worldly pleasure side by side."

"There are seven variations in the rise or penetration (vedha) of prana kundalini. These are determined by the inherent desires of the individual aspirant. For example, to achieve recognition of supreme I (aham), to uplift others, to have peace of mind, to become strong and maintain perfect physical condition, to experience kundalini in the form of a serpent (cobra), and to give initiation secretly. The type of rise is however, out of the hands of the individual, as it is automatically determined by ones deepest desires and longings."

"Kashmir Shaivism is known as the pure Trika system, which means "the three-fold science of man and his world." It is a system meant for any human being without restriction of cast, creed, color or gender. The four sub-systems of Trika philosophy – known as Pratyabhijana, Kula, Krama and Spanda, form the one thought of Trika. They all accept and are based on the ninety-two scriptures (agamas or tantras) of Shaivism."

The mantra *So'ham* is the awareness "I am That," the awareness of the identity between the individual soul and the supreme.

"The connection of pure consciousness with prana is natural." – Shiva Sutra 3.43

Shaivism explains that when the divine consciousness begins to descend into manifestation, it first transforms itself into prana, the universal life force. The two main forms it assumes in the individual are the inhalation and exhalation. That is why the easiest way to attain union with the divine is by taking the help of prana, the essence of all living beings. It leads us to the awareness of our own Self. "Matrika, the power of sound inherent in the alphabet, is the source of limited knowledge." - Shiva Sutra 1.4

It is because you do not understand the true nature of the letters that you are bound by them. When you understand their true nature, they no longer have the power to bind you. To understand these two syllables, *ham* and *sa*, as they really are is liberation. *Ham*, the sound which comes in with the inhalation, is *Shiva*, the pure "I" consciousness, the inner Self. *Sa*, which goes out with the exhalation, is *Shakti*, God's creative energy. The *Spanda Karikas* say that the first throb, the first movement of Shakti, is called *sa*. Inhalation and exhalation are the dance of Shiva and Shakti, of God and His creative energy. As the supreme energy comes in, it makes the sound *ham*. As it goes out, it makes the sound *sa*. In this way, it creates and dissolves infinite worlds. If you perceive this with true understanding, you realize the truth immediately. By understanding the mystery of *Hamsa*, you come to know the Self.

The poet Sunderdas said, "The Self is God, the Self is consciousness, and the Self is always repeating its own mantra, *So'ham*, *So'ham*." The mantra *Hamsa* is the source of all knowledge. Therefore, to obtain knowledge, you should repeat it. The poet Kalidas, who knew the mystery of words, said that whether in mundane or spiritual, we cannot understand anything without using words. Without words, we cannot carry on any of our activities. Even mute people use sign language to communicate with one another. We can describe an object only when it has a name, only when letters are combined into words and have a meaning. In mundane life, the word conveys knowledge of an object and therefore is one with that object. In the same way, knowledge of God is contained in these two syllables, *ham* and *sa*.

However, if you want this mantra to bear fruit for you, you must understand it in the right way. Everyone in the world repeats Hamsa, but most people do not gain its fruit. This is because no one has the right understanding about it. Shaivism says, "If the mantra is kept separate from the repeater of the mantra and its goal, one cannot attain the fruit of the mantra." There should not be any feeling of duality between the mantra and the repeater of the mantra. In the practice of *Hamsa*, the mantra takes place on its own, and the goal of the mantra is the Self. It is That which repeats it, it is That which is its goal, and it is That which is attained by repeating it. When the mantra, the repeater of the mantra, and the goal of the mantra become one and the same for you, you attain the fruit of the mantra. This is the method of practicing the mantra. Ekanath Maharaj used to say, "I am God, I am devotee, and I am the articles of worship." In the same way, when you practice *Hamsa* mantra, you should remember that you are the mantra and the goal of the mantra. You should always remember that you are Paramahamsa, you are Shiva, you are the Lord Himself.

When the breath comes in with the sound *ham* and merges inside, there is a fraction of a moment which is completely still and free of thought. This is the *madhyadasha*, the space between the breaths. This is where you have to focus in meditation. To focus on that space is the highest meditation and the highest knowledge. That still space between breaths, that space where no thoughts exist, is the true goal of the mantra. It is a miraculous space. It is *aham vimarsha*, the inner pulsation of consciousness. It is from this space that all words arise and subside. It is this space without form which pulls the *apana* inside and which pushes the *prana* out. This space where *ham* merges inside, before *sa* has arisen, is the space of God, of supreme Consciousness, of the Self. The place where *sa* merges outside is equally the place of God. So realize that moment of merging of the two syllables. If you come to know that moment, if you become established in it, you experience the truth.

This is *hamsa vidya*, the science of *Hamsa*. Not only is it natural mantra repetition; it is natural pranayama... So *Hamsa* is natural meditation.

The Guru Gita says: "Ham is the seed." In the seed of the Self the entire universe is contained. In the same way, *Hamsa* mantra is the seed of all spiritual practices. Just as a huge banyan tree springs from a tiny seed and contains branches, roots, leaves, flowers, fruit, and thousands of other seeds, the seed of *Hamsa* contains yoga, meditation, japa, austerities, and all powers.

Natural Kundalini Awakening

As you keep repeating the mantra, as through the Guru's grace you become aware that it is going on within, the inner Kundalini energy, which has been dormant, awakens automatically.

The Upanishads say, "The Kundalini Shakti operates through the power of *Hamsa*, which is not different from the Self. *Hamsa* flows with the prana, and the prana flows through the nadis (subtle channels for the flow of prana). One who strives for liberation without knowing the science of *Hamsa* is like one who tries to satisfy his hunger by eating the sky." When, through the practice of *Hamsa,* the inhalation exhalation becomes balanced, and the breath is retained in spontaneous kumbhaka, the breath, which has been going in and out through the ida and pingala nadis, moves into the sushumna, the central channel. The inner Kundalini, which has been dormant, becomes active and begins to unfold. Then a self-born yoga, the yoga of the Siddhas, takes place within you.

The awakening of Kundalini brings about the completion of the spiritual journey. Until Kundalini awakens, you practice yoga by your own efforts and according to your own whim. But after Kundalini has awakened naturally, yoga takes place according to the inspiration of God. It goes on in a spontaneous manner, while you go about your daily life...

It was after seeing that blue pearl light that the great ecstatic being Mansur Mastana said, "I am God." After seeing that, Shankaracharya said, "I am Brahman, I am the absolute." With the awareness of that, Jesus said, "The kingdom of God is within." God's kingdom does not lie only with Jesus or within these other great beings. It is inside you and inside me and inside everyone.

One day, in meditation, the tiny blue light, the light of the Self, expands to fill the universe, and then you experience your all-pervasiveness. You attain the state of the supreme truth, the state beyond all pain and pleasure. You experience true bliss of consciousness. You know without any doubt, "I am God, and God is me." From then on, you live in constant awareness of the Self, in the state of perfect fearlessness and freedom.

This is liberation. This is what you attain through the practice and understanding of *Hamsa.* This is the secret of a Siddha's sadhana. This is the practice of perfected beings. This is the wisdom of the greatest saints. Practice it with great reverence. There is no other mantra than *Hamsa*, no greater worship than meditation, no greater diety than the Self. Always remember this. It is the final instruction of the Guru, the command of Shiva.

Sit very quietly. Become aware of the breath coming and going out repeating *Hamsa, Hamsa*. Understand that *ham* is the perfect "I," the pure consciousness. Understand that *sa* is the universal energy. Focus subtly on the place where these syllables arise and subside, and you will know the Self. This is the true state of God. You are That.

Illusion vanishes totally when the mind gets fully absorbed in *So'ham, So'ham*.

By constant meditation on *So'ham*, the ego and the awareness caused by the three gunas vanish.

When you become the deity of meditation within your own self, the meditator, meditation, and the object of meditation become one.

Swami says: "Then all that remains is the effortless enjoyment of your own bliss." - Svarupananda

O mind, fill yourself with the universal name. Recognize the eternal name of God.

In this way, do japa continuously. Day and night, you will be awake.

Namdev says: "The mind becomes the embodiment of God by ceaselessly repeating *So'ham, So'ham*." - Namdev

Source: I AM THAT: the Science of Hamsa by Swami Muktananda, 1978.

Why are Krishna, Rama, Shiva and Hanuman shown blue symbolically? This is connected with the blue pearl (light of the inner Self) that is connected to your Higher Soul. By meditating on the blue pearl, you can achieve a higher degree of oneness with your higher soul and achieve illumination.

The Sadguru or higher soul may sometimes appear as a blue person. That is why when Swami Muktananda was doing his sadhana, he would sometimes see the blue pearl and would then see a small blue person. Read Play of Consciousness by Baba Muktananda, pages 168-174

Why is Krishna dancing on a serpent? By meditating on the blue pearl, you can bring "Krishna energy" or divine energy down and conquer the kundalini so it can rise up. But Krishna is always on top of the serpent because Krishna or divine energy controls the kundalini energy. That is why, symbolically speaking, Krishna is standing on top of the cobra. You have to invoke for Lord Krishna through the *Hare Krishna mantra* to dive into the river so he can conquer the snake and bring it up to the crown from where it can circulate to the whole body's eight psychic channels.

More Notes on Kundalini Syndrome

Many people experience *Kundalini Syndrome* without ever knowing it, especially practitioners of meditation. When Kundalini energy starts to flow abundantly in a person who has not developed or maintained a clean energy system, then it can cause certain physical, emotional and mental problems. Common physical effects would be overheating, discomfort, exhaustion or hyperactivity. Emotional problems might be heightened temper, depression or manic states. Mental problems might be lack of concentration or oversensitivity to surroundings. When one starts experiencing *Kundalini Syndrome*, one should temporarily stop or reduce the meditation practices, and concentrate on purifications of the energy bodies. Salt baths and following a vegetarian diet will help to cleanse the energy bodies. From my personal experience, alkaline vegetarian diet, herbs, Qigong and exercise alone are not enough to purify the body and subtle energy bodies, and has to be supplemented with drinking alkaline water which is a God send to totally cleanse the acidic wastes of most people suffering from *kundalini syndromes*, and restore the body's pH balance or alkaline (yin) and acid (yang) balance.

Grounding and rooting to mother earth through the practice of Enlightenment Qigong forms especially Hanuman Qigong, Eight Extraordinary Meridians Qigong, and Meditation on Three Hearts are added to Siddha spiritual practices to balance the Shakti Qi flow in the body and avoid post-kundalini syndromes often seen in yoga practitioners.

Quotes on Lalitha Tripura Sundari by Guruji Amritananda Natha

In Hindu culture, Goddess Lalitha occupies the top most place. She is the embodiment of power, grace, beauty and voluptuousness. She is the archetype of "free woman", the empress of the world, the mother of the Trinity Brahma, Vishnu and Shiva. She rides on Siva the male principle, and a lion, the king of beasts. She gives abundant pleasure, procreating children and so is revered as the goddess of fertility.

Even more important, Lalitha is the Goddess preventing the cycle of births and deaths giving moksha. If you are born, you must die. If you are not born, you can't die. It is as simple as that. In this role, she is the Goddess of birth control, the preventer of birth to overcome death, offering the human seed into the fire of navel chakra (through mudras and bandhas, processes of yoga) or into an external vedic/tantric fire in purna-ahuti meaning full offering of self (seed of self which causes rebirth). Even Lalitha is both light and shade, day and night, sun and moon, and also the middle zone of twilight.

During day, she is revered as Gayatri, the power of life streaming from the Sun. During night, She is revered as the healing power of Moon called kama-kala, the art of love. Love and love-making are both healing. Kamakala also means yoga. During twilight transitions, she is worshipped as Fire of creation. In this role, she is promoting pleasure, offering human seeds for creating a world that we want.

Her energies are encoded secretly into Sri Chakra; which is both an abstract geometry of stunning geometrical beauty as well the physical union of 9 to 108 adept couples in a Chakra formation seeking control over the grip of time and overcoming causality creating samsara, the cycle of birth and death. She is the very definition of quantum model; which says that the objective world we see is our own creation. This power of creating the world of perceptions is called Maya.

Thus Hindu culture adores every woman- a little girl(kumari), budding teen(baala/shodasi), adult woman(sundari/suvasini), or an old crone(wisdom goddess) all equally for being a female and a mother. She has given us life. Nothing has any value, if life is not there. Life is the highest gift of the mother. In Her womb, we have been made, we sucked life giving fluids from her breasts, she sang lullabies of love extolling us as Gods. As an adult woman, she gives us sensual enjoyment and our children we bond to. She is liberated, she directs our life, and is on top of male in procreation, deciding whether to beget a child or not. She is a patriarchal male as well as tantric female. She celebrates life; she is life, she is consciousness itself. Life looks like a man when in a male body and a woman in a female body. Life itself is genderless. Like light creates light, life creates life; Life is the light of lights. Hindus are called Bhaaratis, Bhaa=light, Rati=Love; Bhaarati= lovers of light. Light of life is Goddess Lalitha. Her opposite, darkness of death is Kali. Time is cycles of Light and darkness. Lalitha is time and its energies that change things. Let us celebrate life. See **Kundalini Awakening, p. 12; Sri Devi Stotram, p. 92; Inner Soma, p. 122; Sri Yantra, p. 128; Sri Vidya Upasana, p. 140**

Sri Vidya Mantra Chanting stimulates the vagus nerve

With continued practice, toning, chanting and humming will literally "tone" the vagus nerve which can help to regulate the nervous system by slowing the heart rate and lowering blood pressure.

A higher vagal tone index is linked to physical and psychological well-being. A low vagal tone index is linked to inflammation, negative moods, loneliness, and heart attacks. — Psychology Today

Prayer is conversation with God. God is the great compassionate physician who alone gives true healing.

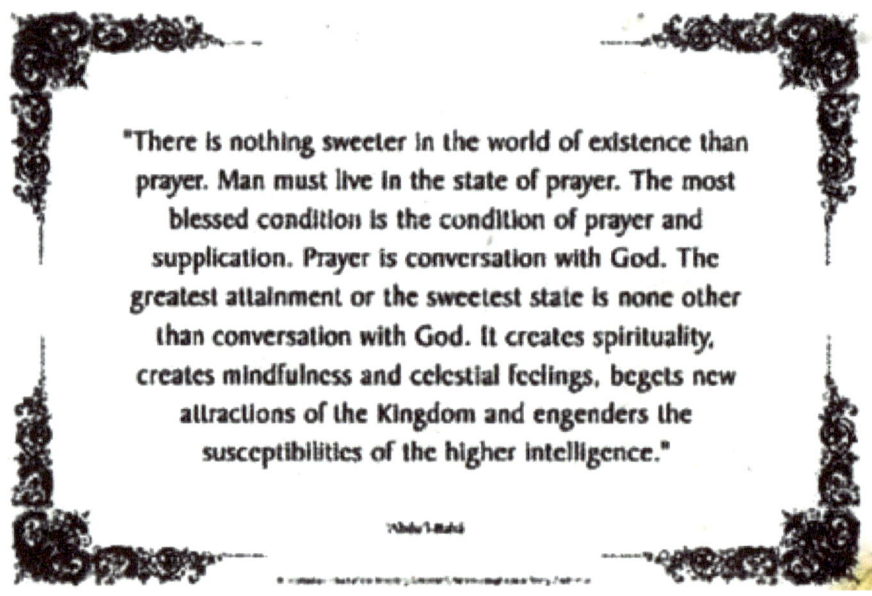

Prayer and meditation is like food for the soul or spirit. Praying with prayer beads amplify its effects.

See Kundalini Awakening, p. 12; Sri Yantra, p. 92, 125, 128; Awakening your Kundalini, p. 138

Dasa (10) Mahavidya and Mantras (Remover of Obstacles)

In Tantra, worship of Devi-Shakti is referred to as a Vidya. Of the hundreds of tantrik practices, the worship of the ten major Devis is called the Dasa Mahavidya. These major forms of the goddess are described in the Todala Tantra. They are Kali, Tara, Maha Tripura Sundari (or Shodasi-Sri Vidya), Bhuvaneshvari, Chinnamasta, Bhairavi, Dhumavati, Bagalamukhi, Matangi, and Kamala. These ten aspects of Shakti are the epitome of the entire creation.

1. **Kali Vidya**: Kali. Seated on a corpse, greatly terrifying, laughing loudly, with fearful fangs, four arms holding a cleaver, a skull, and giving the mudras bestowing boons and dispelling fear, wearing a garland of skulls, her tongue rolling wildly, completely naked (digambara - clad in the directions), thus one should meditate on Kali, dwelling in the centre of the cremation ground. The Kali Mantra as given in the Mantra Mahodadhi is: "Kreem Kreem Kreem Hum Hum Hreem Hreem Dakshine Kaalika Kreem Kreem Kreem Hum Hum Hreem Hreem Swaha" It bestows the eight supernatural powers.
2. **Tara Vidya**: Tara is described as seated in the pratyalidha asana, on the heart of a corpse, supreme, laughing horribly, holding cleaver, blue lotus, dagger and bowl, uttering the mantra Hum, coloured blue, her hair braided with serpents, the Ugratara. She is the bestows all supernatural powers. Her mantra is given in Mantra Mahodadhi as: Om Hreem Streem Hum Phat
3. **Sri Chakra (Sri Yantra) Pooja**: "Om Aeem Hreem Shreem Sri Lalita Tripurasundari Padukam Poojayami Namah" Or better still with the Panchadasakshari Mantra, which is one of the greatest mantras of Devi and next only to the Shodasi Mantra: "Ka E i La Hreem - Ha Sa Ka Ha La Hreem - Sa Ka La Hreem" **See What is Kundalini Awakening?, p. 12; Sri Devi Khadgamala Stotram, p. 92; Awakening your Kundalini, p. 138**
4. **Bhuvaneshwari** - Means the Queen of the Universe, Maya, power of love, peace within, as void. She is like the red rays of the rising sun, with the moon as her diadem, and with three eyes, a smiling face, bestowing boons, holding a goad, a noose and dispelling fears. On the right side of Bhuvaneshvari, who in the heavens, on earth, and in the underworlds is known as the Adya, worship Tryambaka. The mantra is: Om Hreem Bhubaneswaraye Hreem Namah
5. **Chinnamast** - Her left foot forward in battle, she holds her severed head and a knife. Naked, she drinks voluptuously the stream of the blood nectar flowing from her beheaded body. The jewel on her forehead is tied with a serpent. She has three eyes. Her breasts are adorned with lotuses. Inclined towards lust, she sits erect above the god of love, who shows signs of lustfulness. She looks like the red China rose. - Chinnamasta Tantra Her mantra as per Mantra Mahodadhi is: Om Shreem Hreem Hreem Aim Vajra Vairochaniye Shreem Hreem Hreem Phat Svaha It yields all desired benefits quickly.
6. **Tripura Bhairavi is** Supreme Energy, Supreme Goddess of speech, as Tapas, as woman warrior. Her head garlanded with flowers, she resembling the red rays of 1,000 rising suns, smeared with red, holding milk, book, dispelling fears and giving boons with her four hands, large three eyes, beautiful face with a slow smile, wearing white gems. The mantra is: Om Bhairavi Saham
7. **Dhoomavati** - Matangi. Dhumavati. The colour of smoke, wearing smoky clothes, holding a winnowing basket, dishevelled clothes, deceitful, always trembling, with slant eyes, inspiring fear, terrifying. The Dhumavati Mantra as per Mantra Mahaodadhi: "Dhum Dhum Dhumavati Swaha"
8. **Bagala or Bagalamukhi** is the eighth Mahavidya in the famous series of the 10 Mahavidyas. She is identified with the second night of courage and is the power or Shakti of cruelty. The Bagalamukhi Mantra as per Mantra Mahodadhi: "Om Hleem Sarva Dusthaanaam Vaacham Mukham Paadam stambhaya jihvyamkilaya buddhim vinaashaya Hleem Om Swaha"
9. **Matangi**. Dusky, beautiful browed, her three eyes like lotuses, seated on a jewelled lion throne, surrounded by gods and others serving her, holding in her four lotus-like hands a noose and a sword, a shield and a goad, thus I remember Matangi, the giver of results, the Modini. The Matangi Mantra as per Mantra Mahaodadhi: "Om Hreem Aeem Shreem Namo Bhagavati Ucchisthachandali Sri Matangeswari Sarvagyanavashamkari Swaha"
10. **Kamala**: With a smiling face, her beautiful lily-white hands hold two lotuses, and show the mudras of giving and dispelling fear. She is bathed in nectar by four white elephants and stands upon a beautiful lotus. The Dhumavati Mantra as per Mantra Mahaodadhi: "Hasauh Jagatprayutai Swaha" **The tantrik worship of these most powerful Vidyas must be practiced only under the guidence of a siddha Guru.**

Healthy Fats for Healthy Brain Cells

I believe that the high carb low fat vegetarian diet followed by yoga practitioners is causing the physical, mental and emotional problems such as exhaustion, depression, brain fog, nervousness, anxiety, etc. which are symptoms of kundalini syndrome. All these symptoms can also be caused by the vegetarian diet which is deficient in healthy fats such as avocados, butter, eggs, coconut oil, fish oil, raw nuts with over consumption of starchy and sugary refined foods. I personally follow a high fat low carb coconut ketogenic diet which is beneficial to my physical, mental and emotional health, and is a diet that is a source of high octane metabolic energy fuel for my brain, thyroid, endocrine hormones and body cells.

Of all the organs in your body, your brain especially needs healthy dietary fat. It's largely made of fat — 60% by volume. Your brain cell membrane integrity largely depends on the quality of the fats you eat. You may have heard that coconut oil can increase your cholesterol. And that's a good thing for your brain! Your brain specifically needs cholesterol. The brain has higher cholesterol content than any other organ with about 25% of the body's cholesterol found in the brain. Low cholesterol increases the risk of suicide, depression, and dementia. The risk of dementia is reduced by 70% in those with high cholesterol.

Any process relating to the role of fats in the body is complicated. The mechanism by which coconut oil uniquely feeds the brain is no exception. Here's a condensed version: Most vegetable oils such as corn oil and canola oil are long-chain triglycerides. These are larger molecules that are harder to break down and are more easily stored as fat. Coconut oil uniquely consists of medium-chain triglycerides which are smaller and can be used as a backup source of energy. There are only two significant sources of medium-chain triglycerides (MCTs) — human breast milk and coconut oil.

Your brain is a hungry little organ. At just three pounds, it uses 20% of your daily energy input. Your brain's main fuel is glucose. Your brain cells can't store energy and can live for only a few minutes without it. If your brain cells don't get the energy they need, they soon start to die. Fortunately, there's a back-up energy system for times when you can't get enough energy from carbohydrates. Your liver can produce ketones that can be used as a substitute fuel during times of starvation. But you don't have to starve to access ketones as a source of brain fuel. The MCTs in coconut oil can do the job. They're broken down into ketones by the liver, and readily cross the blood-brain barrier to provide instant energy to brain cells.

Regular exercise, meditation and Qigong, lifestyle change, avoidance of alcohol and drugs, taking 1-2 tablespoons of virgin coconut oil before meals 3x a day and cooking with virgin coconut oil instead of hydrogenated vegetable oils together with low carbohydrate high fat coconut ketogenic diet with healthy meats, nuts, fruits, vegetables, herbs and alkaline water and avoiding refined carbohydrates such as starchy and refined sugary foods and drinks will not only prevent kundalini syndrome but also strengthen the immune system, prevent and heal diseases such as obesity, dementia, Alzheimer, neurological problems, diabetes, allergies, cancer, fungal and bacterial infections, skin problems and heart diseases such as high blood pressure, high blood cholesterol, atherosclerosis, and other diseases.

Excellent Book references: Coconut Oil Miracle and Coconut Ketogenic Diet by Dr. Bruce Fife

Connect with the inner Soma by Guruji Amritananda Natha

The Goddess Lalitha's force releases the Soma, the eternal nectar of immortality. She prepares our sacred vessel to receive Shiva's beatitude as the healing balm of meditative stillness. Shakti initiates an inner inebriation, a subtle intoxication beyond the limitations of our dualistic thoughts and emotions. Her overwhelming state is one of passion, enthusiasm, peace, sheer delight and rejuvenation, beyond any body or personhood. The Goddess replaces the intoxication of samsara, our absorption in transient worldly pleasures, with the greater intoxicated state of nirvana, a complete immersion in eternal bliss.

The Yoga Shakti does not carry the ordinary Soma or the beauty of a full Moon, but rather the mystic Soma of the dark Moon, which our hearts absorb, granting us a mysterious inner light. Her Soma is the secret light of darkness which reveals a deeper truth, the inner Sun that disperses the outer world of duality and opens us up to the inner world of unity, contentment and happiness.When this flow becomes steadfast, it manifests as dhyana, the state of meditative bliss. Resting in this beatific state, the Yogini's mind beckons Shiva to come to her. The power and passion of her call draws Shiva into her life – how can He not hearken to the cry of a Tantrika's heart? That she may not always see Him or sense His presence is another samsaric saga. Being caught up in the whirlpool of mundane existence revolving in our creaturely consciousness, we fail to see the divine that is ever around us. But Shiva will continue to play with the heart of the Yogini, enticing her into His cosmic play in His own time.

To connect with this inner Soma, we can follow a simple mantra meditation. Silently repeat the mantra OM during a deep inhalation to draw the flow of Soma from the outer universe into the heart. Then silently repeat the mantra Hrim on exhalation to energize the Soma to revitalize the heart. Ending exhalation with a quick silent repetition of the mantra Hum adds zest to the fire in hastening its mystical alchemy – Om Hrim Hum! Mantras carry the potency of Soma in their vibratory fields, honing the subtle nuances of our intuitive voice. In trusting our profound insight, perception and sensitivity we connect with our higher selves. Communing with this sacred voice we are guided to the ultimate truth of the soul's reality. Being present and aware within our own bodies is cultivating the art of divining our inner essence. In consecrating our being through yogic practices, our bodily energies open up to their subtle essences and lead us to our deeper self where we access the revered wisdom deep within ourselves.

The spiritual practice of turning within oneself, being calmly aware of our senses, thoughts and triggered reactions, allows us to connect with our deeper realities. Looking within ourselves with compassion allows us to address our internal struggles, passions and conflict with empathy. Empathizing with ourselves we bring the flow of loving kindness to our inner beings, reflecting a benevolent approach to our personal misgivings, making us tolerant to all worldly situations. **See Kundalini Awakening, p. 12; Sri Devi Stotram, p. 92; Lalitha, p. 119; Sri Yantra, p. 128; Awakening your Kundalini, p. 138; Sri Vidya Upasana, p. 140**

Hare Krishna Mantra

"This transcendental vibration by chanting of Hare Krishna, Hare Krishna, Krishna Krishna, Hare Hare/ Hare Rama, Hare Rama, Rama Rama, Hare Hare, is the sublime method for reviving our Krishna consciousness. As living spiritual soul, we are all originally Krishna conscious entities, but due to our association with matter from time immemorial, our consciousness is now polluted by material atmosphere. In this polluted concept of life we are all trying to exploit the resources of material nature, but actually we are becoming more and more entangled in our complexities. This illusion is called maya, or hard struggle for existence, for winning over the stringent laws of material nature. This illusory struggle against material nature can at once be stopped by revival of our Krishna consciousness.

Krishna consciousness is not an artificial imposition on the mind. This consciousness is the original energy of the living entity. When we hear the transcendental vibration, this consciousness is revived, and the process is recommended by authorities for this age. By practical experience also, we can perceive that by chanting this Maha-mantra, or the Great Chanting for Deliverance, one can at once feel transcendental ecstasy from the spiritual stratum. When one is factually on the plane of spiritual understanding, surpassing the stages of sense, mind and intelligence, one is situated on the transcendental plane. This chanting of Hare Krishna, Hare Krishna, Krishna Krishna, Hare Hare/ Hare Rama, Hare Rama, Rama Rama, Hare Hare is directly enacted from the spiritual platform, surpassing all lower stratus of consciousness — namely sensual, mental and intellectual. There is no need of understanding the language of the mantra, nor there is any need for mental speculation nor any intellectual adjustment for chanting this Maha-mantra. It springs automatically from the spiritual platform, and as such, anyone can take part in this transcendental sound vibration without any previous qualification and dance in ecstasy. We have seen it practically. Even a child can take part in the chanting, or even a dog can take part in it. The chanting should be heard from the lips of a pure devotee of the Lord, so that immediate effect can be achieved. As far as possible, chanting from the lips of non-devotee should be avoided as much as milk touched by the lips of a serpent causes poisonous effect. The word Hara is the form of addressing the energy of the Lord. Both Krishna and Rama are form of addressing directly the Lord and They mean the highest pleasure, eternal. Hara is the supreme pleasure potency of the Lord. This potency when addressed as Hare helps us in reaching the Supreme Lord. The material energy, called as maya, is also one of the multi-potencies of the Lord as much as we are also marginal potency of the Lord. The living entities are described as superior energy than matter. When the superior energy is in contact with the inferior energy, it becomes an incompatible situation but when the supreme marginal potency is in contact with spiritual potency, Hara, it becomes the happy, normal condition of living entity.

The three words, namely Hara, Krishna and Rama, are transcendental seeds of the maha-mantra and the chanting is spiritual call for the Lord and His internal energy, Hara, for giving protection to the conditioned soul. The chanting is exactly like genuine cry by the child for mother. Mother Hara helps in achieving the grace of the Supreme Father, Hari, or Krishna, and the Lord reveals Himself to such sincere devotee. No other means therefore of spiritual realization is as effective in this age as chanting the Maha-mantra: Hare Krishna, Hare Krishna, Krishna Krishna, Hare Hare/ Hare Rama, Hare Rama, Rama Rama, Hare Hare." - A.C. Bhaktivedanta Swami Srila Prabhupada

Glossary

Abhinavagupta (993-1015): commentator and exponent of Kashmir Shaivism: of the lineage of Vasugupta and Somananda.

Acharya: Sanskrit word for teacher, spiritual teacher or meditation master.

Ananda: absolute bliss.

Anava Mala: in Kashmir Shaivism, one of the impurities or limitations which brings about bondage of the universal Self and reduces it to a limited, individual being; the individual's innate ignorance of his true nature.

Benares (or Varanasi, Kashi): a holy city sacred to Shiva located in North on the banks of the Ganges River.

Bhagavad Gita: the most popular of Hindu scriptures; a portion of the Mahabharata in which Lord Krishna instructs Arjuna about the path to liberation.

Bhakti: divine love, devotion.

Bhartrihari (5th century A.D.): a king who renounced his kingdom in order to become a yogi; author of many spiritual poems.

Blue Pearl: A tiny, shimmering light seen in meditation, and occasionally with open eyes, by people whose inner meditative energy has been awakened. The scriptures and saints call it the light of the inner Self.

Buddha Palm: Blessing by an enlightened master used for shaktipat, Qi-healing, and physical or psychic protection, empowered by Amitabha, Padmasambhava, Kuan Yin, and other masters.

Brahman: Vedantic term for the Absolute Reality, or God.

Chakra: literally, "wheel."

Chidvilas: literally, "the Play of Consciousness."

Chit or Chiti: divine conscious energy; the creative aspect of God, portrayed as the Universal Mother.

Chitshakti: (1) the power of self-revelation by which the Supreme shines by itself; (2) universal Consciousness.

Consciousness: the intelligent, supremely autonomous energy that manifests, pervades, and supports everything in the cosmos.

Dharana: centering technique. See also Vijnana Bhairava.

Dharma: duty, the law of righteousness. See *Da Bei Zhou* (Great Compassion Mantra of Kuan Yin Bodhisattva), page 109

Ganges: the most sacred river in India, which flows from the Himalayas through North India.

Guru: a spiritual Master who has attained oneness with God and who initiates others into the spiritual path and guides them to liberation.

Guru Gita: literally, "song of the Guru." A scripture in the form of a dialogue between Shiva and Parvati, which explains the identity of the Guru with the Absolute and describes the nature of the Guru, the Guru/disciple relationship, and meditation on the Guru.

Guruseva: See Seva.

Hanuman Qigong: Origin of the Heart Gong. The basic idea for this qigong is to integrate qi with Heaven, to integrate the heart with the spirit in dance-like movements. The spirit we refer to here means both the human being's soul and also the soul of the Universe. This qigong is beneficial to health when the practitioner reaches a state of integrating himself and heaven.

Hatha Yoga: one of the eight classical yogas, by which the Samadhi state is attained by uniting the ingoing and outgoing breath. Various bodily and mental exercises are practiced for the purpose of bringing about the even flow of the breath, thus stilling the mind.

Japa: the repetition of a mantra, usually in silence.

Jnana Yoga: the path of knowledge; the yoga of attaining supreme wisdom through intellectual inquiry.

Jnaneshwar: (1275-1296): a highly revered poet-saint of Maharashtra whose commentaty on the Bhagavad Gita – Jnaneshwari – is regarded as one of the world's most important spiritual books.

Kabir (1440-1518): a renowned Indian poet-saint who was a weaver in Benares. His followers were both Hindu and Muslim, and his influence was a powerful one in overcoming religious factionalism.

Karma: physical, mental, or verbal action; the results of such action.

Kashmir Shaivism: a nondual philosophy that recognizes the entire universe as a manifestation of Chiti, or divine conscious energy.

Kirtan: a devotional chant consisting of the names of God.

Koan: a question or statement contemplated in Zen Buddhism for the purpose of achieving a moment of revelation or enlightenment.

Kriya: a gross (physical) or subtle (mental, emotional) purificatory movement of the awakened kundalini Shakti. Kriyas purify the body and nervous system to allow a seeker to sustain the energy of higher states of consciousness.

Kularnava Tantra: treatise on yoga; a basic work of the Kaula school of North Indian tantrism.

Kundalini: literally, "coiled one." The primordial Shakti, or cosmic energy, that lies coiled in the muladhara chakra of every individual. When awakened, kundalini begins to move upward within the sushumna, the subtle central channel, piercing the chakras and initiating various yogic processes which bring about total purification and rejuvenation of the entire being. When kundalini merges in the sahasrara, the spiritual center in the crown of the head, the individual self merges in the universal Self and one attains the state of Self-realization

Kundalini Yoga: one of the eight classical yogas, whereby the aspirant awakens the Kundalini Shakti and directs it upward through the chakras of the subtle body.

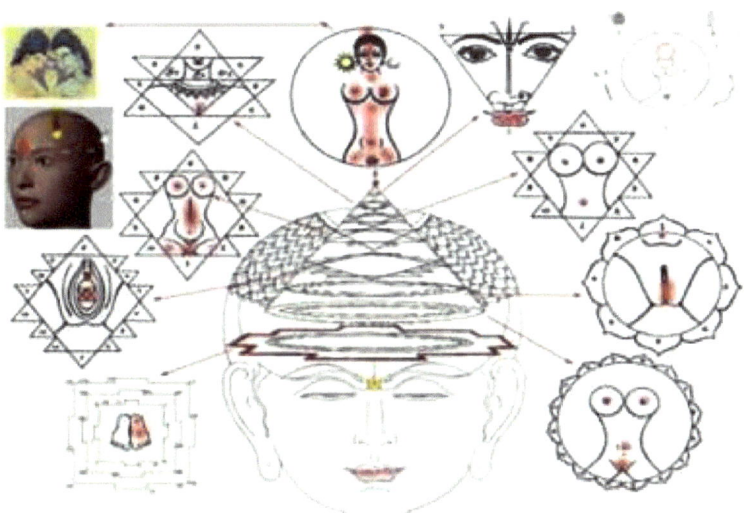

Summary: Placement of enclosures on the body, from Ajna to Sahasrara, See Sri Yantra, page 128

Chakras with Petal letters and Bija letters

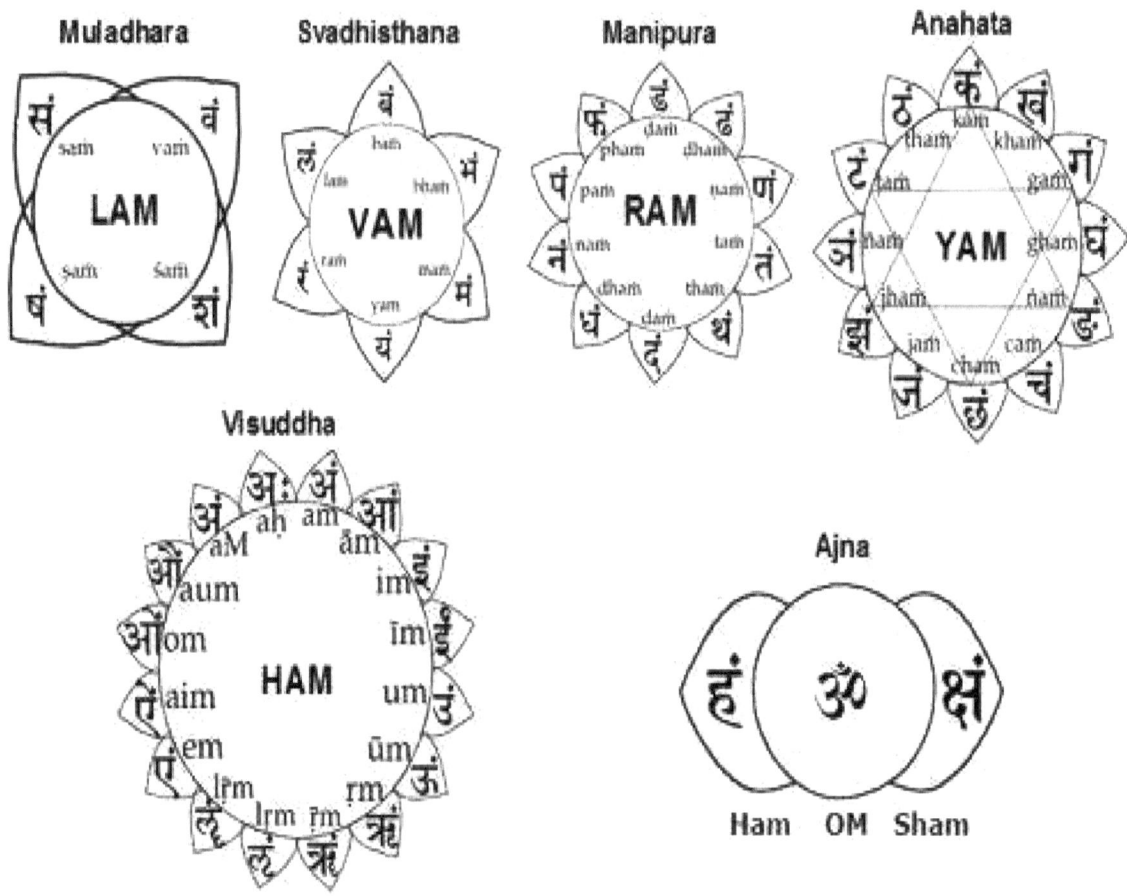

Laya Yoga: the yoga by which Samadhi is attained through the absorption of the mind in inner lights or inner sounds

Lila: divine play. Creation is often explained in the yogic scriptures as lila, or play, of God.

Mahabharata: an epic composed by the sage Vyasa delineating the struggles of two families over a kingdom. The rich and varied story of the epic contains the definitive teaching on right action (Dharma).

Mahapurusha: literally, "great person." A saint or holy being.

Maharaj: king

Mahayoga: literally, "the great yoga" because it contains the eight classical yogas. Another name for Siddha Path.

Mantra: a sacred word invested with the power to transform and protect one who repeats it.

Mantra-Virya: the perfect "I" consciousness, which is the fountainhead of all the powers of potencies behind the mantra; Shiva consciousness.

Matrika: letter or sound syllable which is the basis of all words and hence of all knowledge.

Maya: the force that shows the unreal as real and presents that which is temporary and short-lived as permanent and everlasting; the power of illusion.

Mudra: literally, "to give joy." Hatha yoga postures of the hands and arms.

Muladhara chakra: spiritual center at the base of the spine where the kundalini lies dormant.

Nada: the unstruck sound experienced in meditation.

Narada: a divine rishi, or seer, who was a great devotee and servant of God. He appears in the Puranas and is the author of the Narada Bhakti Sutras, the authorative text on bhakti yoga.

OM: the primal sound or vibration from which the entire universe emanates. It is the inner essence of all mantras.

OM NAMAH SHIVAYA: a mantra meaning "Salutations to Shiva." Shiva denotes the inner Self. It is known as the great redeeming mantra because it has the power to grant worldly fulfillment as well as spiritual realization.

Paramahamsa: literally, "supreme swan." An honorific title given to a Self-realized Master.

Patanjali: a great sage and author of the Yoga Sutras.

Pitruloka: the world of ancestors.

Prana: vital life force.

Pranayama: breathing exercises that lead to the control of the prana.

Prasad: (1) a blessed or divine gift; (2) food that has been blessed by being offered to God.

Pratyabhijnahrdayam: literally, "the heart of the doctrine of recognition." A text of twenty sutras on Kashmir Shaivism with commentaries by Kshemaraja.

Puja: worship.

Raja Yoga: the yoga of the eight steps, or limbs, directed toward the purification and control of the mind, through which the Self is realized.

Rudram: a powerful Vedic chant in honor of Rudra (Shiva).

Sadguru: a true Guru; divine Master, See also Guru.

Sahaja Samadhi: the spontaneous state of Samadhi that remains continuous and unbroken throughout the waking, dream, and deep-sleep states.

Sahasrara: thousand-petaled spiritual center at the crown of the head where one experiences the highest states of consciousness.

Samadhi: state of meditative union with the Absolute.

Samsara: the cycle of birth and death; worldy illusion.

Samskara: an impression of a past thought or action embedded in the subconscious.

Satchitananda: the nature of the Supreme Reality. Sat is truth or being, that which exists in all times, in all places, and in all things; chit is consciousness, that which illumines all places, times, and things; ananda is absolute bliss.

Satsang: literally, "the company of the Truth." A meeting of devotees for the purpose of listening to scriptural readings, chanting, or sitting in the presence of a holy being; the company of saints and devotees.

Self: the source of joy, being and Consciousness, the Witness of the other three states, the inner Knower, the One who illuminates our mind and understanding, the One who watches all our thoughts and deeds. Satchitananda. We are the Self.

Seva: selfless service to the Guru.

Shakti (also known as Chiti, kundalini, kundalini Shakti): the divine cosmic power which projects, maintains, and dissolves the universe, and which, when awakened in a seeker, brings about a spiritual evolution.

Shaktipat: the transmission of spiritual power (Shakti) from the Guru to the disciple; spiritual awakening by grace.

Shankaracharya (788-820): one of the greatest of India's philosophers and sages, who expounded the philosophy of absolute nondualism (Advaita Vedanta). In addition to his writing and teaching, he established ashrams in the four corners of India.

Shiva: a name for the all-pervasive Supreme Reality; one of the Hindu trinity, representing God as the destroyer. In his personal form he is portrayed as a yogi wearing a tiger skin and holding a trident, with snakes coiled around his neck and arms.

Shiva Sutras: a Sanskrit text which Shiva revealed to the sage Vasuguptarcharya. It consists of seventy-seven sutras, which were found inscribed on a rock in Kashmir. It is a major scriptural authority for the philosophical school of Kashmir Shaivism.

Siddha: a perfected yogi; one who has attained the highest state and become one with the Absolute.

Sri Yantra or Shri Chakra is a yantra formed by nine interlocking triangles that surround and radiate out from the central (bindu) point, the junction point between the physical universe and its unmanifest source. It represents the goddess in her form of Shri Lalitha Or Tripura Sundari, "the beauty of the three worlds". The Maha Meru Sri Yantra is the three dimensional projection of Sri Chakra (Mother of all Mandalas) that symbolizes Tripura Sundari. OM AIM HREEM SHREEM SRI MATRE NAMAH. **See Sri Yantra photo above; Sri Devi Khadgamala Stotram, page 92**

1. **Devi's Feet** - Trailokya Mohana or Bhupara, a square of three lines with four portals - Bija - AM AAM SOUH Dram
2. **Devi's Thighs** - Sarva Aasa Paripuraka, a sixteen-petal lotus - Bija - AEEM KLEEM SAUH Dreem
3. **Devi's Muladhara** - Sarva Sankshobahana, an eight-petal lotus - Bija - HREEM KLEEM SAUH Kleem
4. **Devi's Svadisthana** - Sarva Saubhagyadayaka, fourteen small triangles - Bija - HAEEM HKLEEM HSAUH Blum
5. **Devi's Manipura** - Sarva Arthasadhaka, ten small triangles - Bija - HSAEEM HSKLEEM HSSAUH Sah
6. **Devi's Anahata** - Sarva Rakshakara, ten small triangles - Bija - HREEM KLEEM BHEM Krom
7. **Devis' Vishuddhi** - Sarva Rogahara, eight small triangles - Bija - HREEM SHREEM SOUH Hasakaphrem
8. **Devi's Ajna** - Sarva Siddhi prada, 1 small triangle - Bija - HSRAEEM HSRKLEEM HSRSOUH Hsaum
9. **Devi's Sahasrara** - Sarva Anandamaya, a point or bindu - Bija - KA E I LA HREEM - HA SA KA HA LA HREEM - SA KA LA HREEM AEEM

Meru will act like an antenna, first attracting the Supreme Power, and then retransmitting it all around your home, bringing good to all. Merus from Devipuram bring home health, wealth and joy and put galactic power in your palm, home or office. – Guruji Amritananda

The sublime geometry of the Sri Chakra is revealed wisdom. It is not of human origin. It is nothing less than the genetic code of the Cosmos. It is intelligent. As one commentator aptly explained, "Sri Chakra is the technology of the Absolute, skillfully fashioned in Divinity's own self-image."

Every yantric shape emits a very specific frequency and energy pattern. Sri Chakra is said to contain within itself the essence of all other yantras, and thus it contains the essence of all traditions. Certain powers, for example, are ascribed to the six-pointed Star of David, the Christian cross, the five-pointed star, the Egyptian and Meso-American pyramids, and so on. The Meru's particular configuration is revered in all Eastern traditions: It integrates the essence of Indian Mother Goddess worship, Mahayana Buddhism, Chinese feng shui, the Eleusinian mysteries of the Ancient Greeks, and so much more. Once received from a proper and well-intentioned Guru, the Maha Meru can bring unbounded happiness and every good thing in life. In its Maha Meru form, Sri Chakra radiates an aura of Love and Order, literally creating a sacred space around itself. Wherever it is placed, it brings order, peace, happiness, health, and wealth – in short, everything that is needed. Just keeping it in one's home will confer great blessings, because the Meru subtly connects itself to the other major yantras in the world. Its mere presence is said to cleanse the home of defects under both the vaastu and feng shui systems; to ward off and neutralize negative energies and the "evil eye"; to protect against unfavorable planetary influences; and to bring about healing, prosperity and peace of mind. People of all beliefs, religions and sects may reap the benefits of peace, healing and prosperity by installing the Maha Meru in their homes, offices, shrines and places of worship, as well as in hospitals, healing centers, prayer halls and wedding centers.

Sushumna: the central and most important of all the 72,000 nadis, located in the center of the spinal column and extending from the base of the spine to the top of the head. The six chakras are situated in the sushumna, and it is through the shushumna channel that the kundalini rises. See also: Chakras, Kundalini

Sutra: aphorism, or pithy saying.

Swadhyaya: the chanting aloud of scriptures or sacred texts.

Swastika: Swa means higher self, asti means being, and ka is a suffix. The word maybe understood as "being with higher self." It is also known as srivatsa. *It symbolizes Shakti.*

Tandra: a meditative state resembling but different from the deep-sleep state, often accompanied by spiritual visions, precognition, astral travel, and other such supranormal experiences.

Upanishads: the teachings of the ancient sages that form the knowledge or end-portion of the Vedas. The central teaching of the Upanishads is that the Self of a human being is the same as Brahman, the Absolute. The goal of life is the realization of that Truth.

Vedanta: a philosophical school founded by Badarayana that contains the philosophical teachings of the Upanishads and investigates the nature and relationship of the Absolute, the world, and the Self.

Vijnana Bhairava: an important text of Kashmir Shaiivism containing one hundred twelve dharanas (centering techniques) through which the Absolute is realized.

Vilas: literally, "play."

Vishnu: the supreme Lord; one of the Hindu trinity of gods representing God as the sustainer.

Vyasa: a great sage of ancient times, compiler of the Vedas and Puranas, and author of the Mahabharata.

Wei Qi: protective auric shield. There are many other names for the invisible auric field that surrounds the physical body in various mystical traditions such as torus, Lightbody, Electromagnetic Field (EMF), energy bubble, Merkaba or aura.

Yoga: literally, "union." The state of oneness with the Self, God; the practices leading to that state. Yogi is one who practices yoga.

Yoga Sutras: Patanjali's treatise on yoga; the authoritative text on raja yoga.

Yuan Shen: Taoists refer to Yuan Shen as our *Original Spirit*. Buddhists refer to Yuan Shen as our Higher *Buddha Nature* or *Higher Soul*. Shaivism refers to Yuan Shen as *Shiva or Krishna* in each person as *Christ* in each person in Christianity or the I AM That, the Golden Elixir of Immortality.

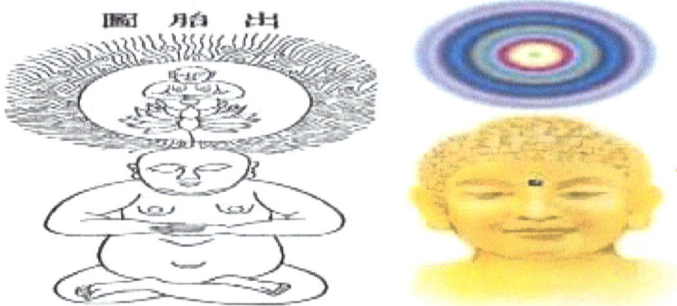

The Golden Elixir of Immortality symbolizes Self-consciousness or Self-remembering, a state of Self-awareness in which one's Higher Self (Higher Soul) - Yuan Shen (Original Spirit) is awake.

In the Taoist book "Techniques of Immortality" by Wu and Liu, there is a drawing of a Buddhist monk meditating on the 12th chakra, the *incarnated soul* or *soul star* shown as a lotus flower 12 inches above the head of the meditator. The Higher Soul and Divine Spark are above it.

Advanced spiritual techniques to develop the 12th chakra and the spiritual foetus are part of higher Taoist practices like the Eight Extraordinary Meridians Qigong.

The Eight Extraordinary channels are the links or bridges from our spirit to the external affairs of our life. This linkage is part of us and is always with us. This means you can also access your spirit at any time. A quest in our life is to reconnect or reunite with our spirit at any time through the eight extraordinary channels. They are the links between Jing and shen.

The *Thrusting Chong* channel offers the capacity to reconnect and re-align to our *Yuan Shen*, our *Original Spirit*. Chant *Namo Kuan Shi Yin Pu Sa* to cultivate the same compassion embodied by Kuan Yin Bodhisattva.

The flow of seas, rivers, streams, springs, and wells is the exterior image of the interior flows of vital substances: Jing, qi, blood, and body fluids. Proper flow of Water is essential to life and a bountiful harvest. Optimal circulation of the vital substances is a key to health and vitality. The Eight Extraordinary Meridians Qigong is a powerful way to assist in creating effective circulation of vital substances. This healthy flow clears the rough, allowing you to see and experience the diamond (*Yuan Shen or Original Spirit*) shining inside. This Qigong assists in fulfilling our life quest, achieving self-realization. See *Da Bei Zhou*, the great compassion mantra of Kuan Yin Bodhisattva, page 109

The above illustration on the left with the physical body, Energy Body and Spirit Body represents the gates of immortality when we connect with our Original Spirit. We can maintain the light of our Original Spirit with meditation and Qigong practices. In this way the higher mind, coming from the light of Wuji, rules in the hierarchy of our being. All aspects of body and mind become servants of this higher Universal Mind; we can connect with the Tao whatever we do and wherever we go.

The above Nei Jing Tu illustration on the right represents the three dantiens, and how they are involved with the transformation of *Jing* to *qi* to *shen*. It is both a body map and and a road map to enlightenment. For more information on Nei Jing Tu, please read the book "Return to Oneness with the Tao."

Descent of Holy Spirit (Pentecostal Fire) shows descent of Christ consciousness among disciples.

Each of the five *shen* has unique corresponding emotions that reflect their condition. The following are key emotions (qualities) for each of the five *shen*:

- Hastiness, impatience, arrogance, cruelty, and hatred correspond to the Heart *shen*. Joy and love are thenatural virtues.
- Worry, repetitive thinking, obsessive behavior, and jealousy correspond to the Spleen yi. Openness is the natural virtue.
- Sadness, depression, loneliness, isolation, and the inability to forgive correspond to the Lung *po*. Courage and righteousness are its natural virtue.
- Fear corresponds to the Kidney *zhi*, and gentleness is the natural virtue.
- Anger, irritability, and frustration correspond to the Liver *hun*, and kindness is the natural virtue.

OM anandamayi chaitanyamayi satyamayi parame
The Joy Permeated, the Consciousness and Truth filled Mother.
Oh Supreme Goddess!

Om - Shreem Hreem Kleem Aeem Sauh - Om Hreem Shreem

Ka E I La Hreem - Ha Sa Ka Ha La Hreem - Sa Ka La Hreem

Sauh Aeem Kleem Hreem Shreem – Namah

Om
Aeem Hreem Shreem Kleem Vadavada Vagvadini Aeem Sauh Hamsah Aam Hreem Krom Kleem Shreem Hum Swaha

Lingastakam idam punyam – Yah Pathet Shiva Sannidhau
- Shivalokam Avaapnoti – Shivena Saha Modatheh
Om – Joom – Saha – Saha – Joom - Om

Chant *Namo Kuan Shi Yin Pu Sa* to cultivate the same compassion embodied by Kuan Yin Bodhisattva. See *Da Bei Zhou*, p. 109
See Kundalini Awakening, p. 12; Garland of Letters, p. 27, 28; Sri Devi Stotram, p. 92; Chakras with Petal Letters and Bija Letters, p. 126; Sri Yantra, p. 128; Awakening your Kundalini, p. 138; Sri Vidya Upasana, p. 140

The Use of Eight Extraordinary Meridians Qigong in Psychic Self-defense

Protect yourself from psychic attacks, negative intentions, malicious entities and energetic pollution. One is constantly being bombarded and contaminated by negative and injurious energies. You are in an ocean of thought-forms and emotional energies from within and without. These ethereal inhabitants constantly exert pressure on our Wei Qi field to conform with their vibrations. If not properly protected, we could be affected spiritually, mentally, emotionally, and physically. The updated Oneness with Shiva book will not only teach you how to self-heal chronic diseases - some examples include chronic problems such as hypertension, cardiovascular disease, aging, asthma, allergies, menstrual and sexual function, neuromuscular problems, and cancer - and attain self-realization but also etheric ways of utilizing heaven and earth energies multi-dimensionally to properly protect yourself physically and psychically.

Important techniques in Eight Extraordinary Meridians Qigong:

- Strengthening of the Wei Qi field to prevent intrusions with Belt Channel (*Dai Mo*).
- Advanced psychic self-defense for laymen, healers, acupuncturists and other health professions when combined with Maitreya (Shiva) Shen Gong used with no doubt.
- Multidimensional shielding techniques for protection of the spiritual, mental, emotional, etheric and physical planes. Attacks could come in from any plane.

Qi Energy: The missing link in psychic protection - why visualization and intention alone are not sufficient - you can`t build a shield with just good intention, you need shielding Qi material.

- Use comprehensive protection from Ascended Siddha Masters and teachers.
- Scan the strength and integrity of your shields. Don`t just assume, be certain.
- Experience inner peace and calmness in the midst of a chaotic work, physical attacks (you must have some self- defense knowledge, Zhan Zhuan Gong and Wing Chun Kung Fu) or home space.
- Stop psychic vampires from draining your precious life force — it could be a cause of insomnia, anxiety, disease and unease.
- Why the traditional bubble of white light does not hold up in the real world of psychic warfare. Learn a more effective technique with Wei Qi field activation.
- Learn why improper shielding could cause a person to think he is under psychic attack by nobody else but themselves.

Learn the ultimate protection from psychic or physical attacks by using Buddha Palm - blessing with loving kindness - using Maitreya (Shiva) Shen Gong, Merkaba meditation or Meditation on Three Hearts together with grounding and rooting to mother earth via Wei Qi field activation drawing in heaven and earth essence energies, developing one's Original Breath or Yuan Qi – called Lin Kong Jing (Empty Force) by reconnecting with *Yuan Shen* thru Chong *Mo* channel.

Sri Yantra

Sri Yantra is said to ward off and neutralize negative energies and the "evil eye." It has four isosceles triangles with the apices upwards, representing Shiva or the Masculine. Five isosceles triangles with the apices downward, symbolizing female embodiment Shakti. Thus the Sri Yantra also represents the union of Masculine and Feminine Divine. Because it is composed of nine triangles, it is known as the Navayoni Chakra. "These nine triangles are of various sizes and intersect with one another. In the middle is the power point (bindu), visualizing the highest, the invisible, elusive centre from which the entire figure and the cosmos expand. The triangles are enclosed by two rows of (8 and 16) petals, representing the lotus of creation and reproductive vital force. The broken lines of the outer frame denote the figure to be a sanctuary with four openings to the regions of the universe."

Together the nine triangles are interlaced in such a way as to form 43 smaller triangles in a web symbolic of the entire cosmos or a womb symbolic of creation. Together they express Advaita or non-duality. This is surrounded by a lotus of eight petals, a lotus of sixteen petals, and an earth square resembling a temple with four doors. **See Kundalini Awakening, p. 12; Garland of Letters, p. 28 and 126; Sri Yantra, p. 128**

Enlightenment Qigong Forms

Ricardo B Serrano welcomes you to this non-denominational book that is dedicated to the spread of non-denominational integrative Enlightenment Qigong forms throughout the world for awakening our true inner selves to return to oneness by opening the heart to unconditional love.

The Enlightenment Qigong (Wuji Qigong) forms synthesized and taught by Ricardo B. Serrano, R.Ac., a Qi-healer and certified Qigong instructor, are Pan Gu Shengong, Primordial Wuji Qigong, Sheng Zhen Wuji Yuan Gong, Eight Extraordinary Meridians Qigong, and Maitreya (Shiva) Shen Gong supplemented with spontaneous Tibetan Shamanic Qigong, a formless Qigong, together with Merkaba meditation, Meditation on Three Hearts and Shaktipat Meditation to further develop the lightbody (energy bubble).

Through their ancient lineages, these five Enlightenment Qigong forms, applied individually or in combination, have been clinically tested and proven together with the formless spontaneous Tibetan Shamanic Qigong and Merkaba meditation with Shaktipat Meditation by himself and their practitioners to provide a strong basic foundation for understanding and experiencing spiritual enlightenment and healing self and others through contemplations with movements, and non-moving meditation to return to oneness by connecting oneself with heaven, earth and humanity.

May the regular practice of these five complementary Enlightenment Qigong forms together with the formless spontaneous Tibetan Shamanic Qigong and Merkaba meditation with Shaktipat meditation provide spiritual healing and enlightenment to yourself as they have provided to himself and fellow practitioners spiritual enlightenment and healing by purifying the physical body, calming the emotions, and opening the heart/ elevating the spirit, together with building the Three Treasures - Jing, Qi and Shen.

"Pan Gu Shengong, also known as the Heaven, Earth, Sun and Moon Qigong, has its fundamental philosophy and practice rooted in kindness and charity. It is designed to absorb the essence of Qi (energy) from the universe. It regulates and intensifies life force and the human immune system.

PGSG, which is a complete set of Qigong exercises, consists of a Moving Form, a Non-moving Form (meditation) and an Advanced condensed Form. The Moving Form is the basis, which only takes you 20 minutes to finish. The Non-moving Form is a meditation, focusing on the regulation of the nervous system and the spirit. The Advanced condensed Form is a condensed form which takes less time but produces more powerful effect. Qi-healing is an energy treatment offered by a Qigong Master. The energy emitted by the Master works on the patients' body, fighting the disease and improving the immune system." - Pan Gu Shen Gong Master Ou Wen Wei

Primordial Qi Gong opens the heart to the true force of unconditional love emanating from Wuji, the Supreme Unknown." - Wuji Qigong Master Michael Winn

"In the Sheng Zhen forms of qigong, opening one's heart is the primary purpose. The qi is the vehicle of unconditional love, of Sheng Zhen.

Love can transform people's hearts. Love can dissolve hate. Love can affect the environment. Unconditional love is the best medicine and the highest power." - Sheng Zhen Qigong Master Li Jun Feng

"Historically, all styles originated at one time or another from a primordial foundation of Qigong that was deeply rooted in Shamanic Medicine Dances." - Qi Dao Master Lama Tantrapa

"... tantra is the right practice for Westerners and of the utmost need in this twentieth century. After all, the Buddhas wanted us to have as much perfect pleasure as possible; he certainly didn't want us to be miserable, confused or dissatisfied. Therefore we should understand that we meditate in order to gain profound pleasure, not to beat ourselves up or to experience pain. If entering the Buddhist path brings you nothing but fear and guilt then it's certainly not worth the effort."

"Maitreya is the manifestation of the love of all the Buddhas - the supreme beings who have achieved limitless, universal love. When we practice the yoga method of Buddha Maitreya we unify with the universal love energy that is Maitreya by developing to their ultimate extent the limited qualities of love, compassion and purity that presently lie within us." - Lama Yeshe

"The hologram of love (or *Merkaba*) is the sacred geometric pattern which gave birth to the whole universe. It is based on unconditional love, so it must be the pattern of unconditional love, because everything in the universe resonates to it, no matter what it is or what dimension it's in. That means that you and I, as human beings, also have that pattern within us, so we are actually walking, talking unconditional love. We always have been, we've just never recognized it.

With the breath and thought intention, the hologram of love will obey your every command and you will transverse the angles of linear time and into the higher dimensions of no time and endless love." - Merkaba Master Alton Kamadon

"Spiritual energy is needed for expansion of consciousness and traveling in the inner worlds. Stillness and awareness are not enough. No spiritual energy, no expansion of consciousness. Spiritual empowerment or Shaktipat is the transference of tremendous spiritual energy to enable the consciousness of the disciple to be able to travel to the different levels of the inner world. This transference of tremendous spiritual energy is called spiritual initiation in modern esoteric books. Shaktipat is an Indian term for spiritual empowerment." - Master Choa Kok Sui

"One must seek the shortest way and the fastest means to get back home - to turn the spark within into a blaze, to be merged in and to identify with that greater fire which ignited the spark." - Bhagawan Nityananda

"Qi-healing, Tai Chi, Ling Kong Jing and Enlightenment Qigong forms are both meditation in motion practices to achieve spiritual oneness." - Ricardo B. Serrano, R.Ac.

"Let Love Light Your Path, Truth Guide Your Way and Joy Sing From Your Soul." - Sananda

Enlightenment is another term for Qigong state, ascension, illumination or spiritual oneness, wherein the incarnated soul is achieving a higher degree of oneness with the higher soul, and a certain degree of oneness with God and oneness with all, experienced as expansion of consciousness accompanied with blissful joy, inner peace and quiet mind.

- The Supreme Being is known by many names God, Origin, Primal Mother, Tao, Shiva, Pan Gu, Dream Being, Source at the center of all sacred space called Wu Ji, Void, Nothingness, supreme unknown, the primordial space.
- Qigong is an interexchange of Qi (universal life force) between men and the universe. As an integral system of Oriental medicine, Qigong is based on the coherence of human energy fields within the universal flow of Qi, or life force. Qi comes from the power of love, Qi and love are never separate, and

Love is the Source of All. Enlightenment Qigong is also called Wuji Qigong, meaning "skill at entering the Supreme Unknown."

The complete integrative Enlightenment Qigong Forms taught by Acharya Ricardo B. Serrano:

1. Pan Gu Shengong with foundation Yuan Qi.
2. Primordial Wuji Qigong with Tao immortals
3. Eight Extraordinary Meridians Qigong
4. Maitreya (Shiva) Shen Gong
5. Sheng Zhen Wuji Yuan Gong
    - Awakening the Soul Qigong
    - Zhongtian Yiqi Gong and Nine Turns Qigong
    - Kuan Yin and Jesus standing Qigong
    - Jesus, Kuan Yin and Mohammed sitting Qigong
    - Mohammed and Lao Tzu's Return to Spring standing Qigong
    - Sheng Zhen Healing Qigong 1, 2 & 3, *Six healing Qigong sounds, Da Bei Zhou* mantra
    - Hanuman Qigong (Origin of the Heart), Tai Chi 8 form, *Namo Kuan Shi Yin Pu Sa* mantra

* The above five Enlightenment Qigong forms are supplemented with Tai Chi, Shaktipat meditation, Meditation on Three Hearts, Merkaba meditation, *Zhan Zhuang Gong*, Toltec wisdom and spontaneous Tibetan Shamanic Qigong with Guo Lin Qigong, to spontaneously go with flow of Qi thereby master being in the flow to experience personal freedom together with *Wing Chun forms*: Siu Lim Tao, Chum Kiu, Biu Gee, Wooden dummy, and Baat Cham Dao.

Dedication and Acknowledgement: Ricardo B. Serrano, R.Ac., a registered acupuncturist, Qi-healer and certified Qigong teacher/ founder of integrative whole body Enlightenment Qigong, has dedicated this work to the present and future generations of eclectic Wu Ji Qigong practitioners and bodhisattvas who want to experience spiritual enlightenment, healing and heaven on earth by radiating light, love, peace and healing to the hearts of all humankind, and to all his Qigong teachers whose Qigong and meditation teachings have greatly contributed to his spiritual development, healing and enlightenment through opening the heart to unconditional love and service. With great thanks and acknowledgement to all his beloved ascended and living spiritual teachers.

It is in blessing that you are blessed. It is in giving that you receive. It is in going with the flow of Qi and surrendering to it that you master being in the flow. This is the law or principle - "*Where energy flows, awareness follows*" - followed by Qigong masters, and the way to become enlightened! Depending on how strong the Qi connection is to the higher soul, the 5 important keywords for Qigong practitioners and energy healers to remember when it comes to effective and safe Qi healing of self and others are replenish, activate, cleanse, energize and balance.

WARNING: The practice of Enlightenment Qigong Forms with spontaneous Tibetan Shamanic Qigong, Meditation on Three Hearts, Merkaba Meditation and Shaktipat Meditation may lead to overwhelming love, joy and happiness.

The Qigong Healing Method - a synthesis of Qi-healing, Emotional Freedom Technique (EFT therapy), Pan Gu Shengong, Primordial Qigong, Sheng Zhen Gong, Zhan Zhuang Qigong with 8 Extraordinary Meridians Qigong and Qi Dao, Guo Lin Qigong, Maitreya Shen Gong, Wing Chun Kung Fu, Merkaba activation and traditional body and ear acupuncture with nutrition, Chinese tonic herbs and alkaline water - was formulated by Qigong healer Ricardo B. Serrano, R.Ac. after two decades of research and practicum as a proven classical Chinese method for wholistic integrative healing, enlightenment (realization of Buddha Nature & Buddha Palm), and psychic self-defense.

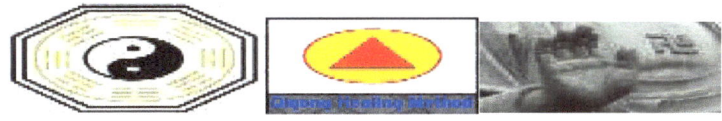

Jesus and Cannabis

Jesus was almost certainly a cannabis user and an early proponent of the medicinal properties of the drug, according to a study of scriptural texts published this month. The study suggests that Jesus and his disciples used the drug to carry out miraculous healings.

The anointing oil used by Jesus and his disciples contained an ingredient called kaneh-bosem which has since been identified as cannabis extract, according to an article by Chris Bennett in the drugs magazine, High Times, entitled Was Jesus a Stoner? The incense used by Jesus in ceremonies also contained a cannabis extract, suggests Mr Bennett, who quotes scholars to back his claims.

"There can be little doubt about a role for cannabis in Judaic religion," Carl Ruck, professor of classical mythology at Boston University said.

Referring to the existence of cannabis in anointing oils used in ceremonies, he added: "Obviously the easy availability and long-established tradition of cannabis in early Judaism would inevitably have included it in the [Christian] mixtures."

Mr Bennett suggests those anointed with the oils used by Jesus were "literally drenched in this potent mixture. Although most modern people choose to smoke or eat pot, when its active ingredients are transferred into an oil-based carrier, it can also be absorbed through the skin".

Quoting the New Testament, Mr Bennett argues that Jesus anointed his disciples with the oil and encouraged them to do the same with other followers. This could have been responsible for healing eye and skin diseases referred to in the Gospels.

"If cannabis was one of the main ingredients of the ancient anointing oil and receiving this oil is what made Jesus the Christ and his followers Christians, then persecuting those who use cannabis could be considered anti-Christ," Mr Chris Bennett concludes.

"Christ" is the Greek translation of the Hebrew "Messiah." In modern English, this term would be translated as the "anointed one." The title "Christ" was only placed upon he who had "God's unction upon him."

As Jesus and his followers began to spread the healing knowledge of cannabis around the ancient world, the singular Christ became the plural term "Christians," that is, those who had been smeared or anointed with the holy oil. As the New Testament explains: "The anointing you received from him remains in you, and you do not need anyone to teach you. But as his anointing teaches you about all things and as that anointing is real, not counterfeit — just as it has taught you, remain in him" (1 John 2:27).

The Christians, the "smeared or anointed ones," received "knowledge of all things" by this "anointing from the Holy One" (1 John 2:20). Thereafter, they needed no other teacher, and were endowed with their own spiritual knowledge. Indeed, from Jesus' own words after his initiation by John, it would appear his own spiritual power came through the anointing:

The Spirit of the Lord God is upon me, because the Lord has anointed me

to bring good tidings to the afflicted; he has sent me to bind up the broken-hearted,

to proclaim liberty to the captives, and the opening of the prison to those who are bound;

to proclaim the year of the Lord's favor, and the day of vengeance of our God; to comfort all who mourn.

"I have included this historical cannabis study because I believe that Jesus not only use cannabis for healing the sick but also as an entheogenic substance for expanding the awareness of his true followers for attaining Christ consciousness via meditation and Qigong.

The ancient healing practice where cannabis oil is integrated with external Qi-healing (Wai Qi Liao Fa) as done 2000 years ago by Jesus Christ and the Classical Chinese Medicine practitioners has been rediscovered." - Qigong master Ricardo B Serrano, R.Ac. See External Qi-healing, p. 61

See Mahashivaratri and Cannabis, page 96; Union of Three Hearts, p. 80; Meditation on Three Hearts, p. 139; Atma (Soul) Yoga, p. 103

Earth needs Love after Yolanda

By Acharya Ricardo B Serrano, R.Ac.

"Man follows Earth. Earth follows Heaven. Heaven follows the Tao. Tao follows what is natural." – Tao Te Ching

Mother earth needs Love from Heaven via humanity after Yolanda.

Mother Earth, as a living entity, more than ever, as shown in earth's upheavals such as earthquakes and typhoons with tsunamis especially in the recent super typhoon Yolanda in the Visayas region of the Philippines, urgently needs Qi and love from Heaven. Since humans are the victims of these catastrophes, we are also the means to prevent these calamities and suffering, I believe, by being channels of heavenly divine love and Qi through the practice of loving-kindness with meditation and Qigong together with practical solutions.

We do these spiritual practices not only for our personal evolution, healing and transformation but most importantly as human conduits of heavenly Qi and love for the survivors and thousands of victims of the typhoon and earthquakes and mother earth's evolution, healing and transformation. Energetically, as part of earth's energy body humans need earth not only for physical survival such as food source and other physical factors but also for its Qi and Love and electromagnetic field's grounding and rooting support to humans' physical and spiritual anatomy.

From my personal observation of the Yolanda catastrophe, heavenly essence and energies in the form of bio-photons or light particles and Qi from the sun, moon, planets, and stars unceasingly support and sustain life on earth and its inhabitants despite the climate changes and global warming caused by environmental pollution and destruction contributed by civil wars and illegal drugs, fossil fueled greenhouse gases, forest loss, mining by inconsiderate foreign companies, illegal fishing and land grabbing for oil by China's aggressive military, and everyone who are litterbugs.

Most people affected by climate change such as typhoon Yolanda, and earthquakes often wander, What can an individual do to help the planet heal itself? Three possible natural practical solutions are: adherence to the rule of law and being proactive towards peace to prevent civil wars and corruption and spread of illegal drugs, taking individual responsibility not to pollute and destroy the environment, and through the practice of loving-kindness with meditation and Qigong by large number of individual practitioners globally.

Why do all these? These practices are based on the principles of karma and oneness or interconnectedness of everyone with the Tao (nature). Eastern self-realized masters teach the divine law What you give is what you receive and God helps those who help themselves.

His Holiness The Dalai Lama writes, "Our Mother, is telling us to behave. All around, signs of nature's limitations abound. Moreover, the environmental crises currently underway, involves all of humanity, making national boundaries of secondary importance. It is important that we forgive the destruction of the past and recognize that it was produced in ignorance.

If we develop good and considerate qualities within our own minds, our activities will naturally cease to threaten the continued survival of life on Earth. By protecting the natural environment and working to forever halt the degradation of our planet we will also show respect for Earth's human descendants - our future generations - as well as for the natural right to life of all Earth's living things. If we care for nature, it can be rich, bountiful, and inexhaustibly sustainable." - Excerpt from the foreword to "Dharma Gaia", Parallax Press, Earth Day, 1990 by the Dalai Lama

*James Lovelock developed the Gaia theory that Earth is a living entity in the 1960s while working with NASA: It claims that all of the organic and inorganic components of Earth are closely integrated to form a single and self-regulating system. This living system has automatically controlled global temperature, atmospheric content, oxygen, ocean salinity, and other factors. In summary, it posits 'life maintains conditions suitable for its own survival'. He said, "If we can't 'heal the planet' directly, we may be able to help the planet heal itself."

Anyone who are interested to help the planet heal itself can practice blessing with loving-kindness - Meditation on Three Hearts, and one of the Enlightenment Qigong forms, especially the Eight Extraordinary Meridians Qigong that draws in heavenly and earth energies into men.

The earth kundalini energy is called the Serpent of Light or called the Great White Snake in other Oriental traditions. Not only is the earth's kundalini energy very similar to a human being's, but also even such massive energy fields as the merkaba field of the planet and the human merkaba field (light body) are exactly the same except for proportional size. The earth's kundalini energy connected to the center of the earth behaves like a snake as it moves, similar to the way kundalini energy moves in the human body which is the secret energy, the inner Shakti, that gives rise to the kundalini awakening of spiritual seekers everywhere on earth.

Awakening your Kundalini

A kundalini teacher essentially guides the path of kundalini through the upward journey of the seven chakras which start from muladhara chakra and eventually culminate in the sahasrara chakra along the spine that include the activation of the subtle energy system (ida, pingala and sushumna nadis) with sounds, mantras, mudras and breath. The session always include shaktipat (shakti transmission) to activate a student's three hearts (three suns). The sahasrara is activated through the thousand suns lotus above the head. The journey's goal should result in the purification of karma with the eventual experience of samadhi.

Awakening the Kundalini energy frees your spirit to transcend the body-consciousness of the ego and align with Spirit. Pressure, fear, and struggling give way to peace, love, and bliss. You'll feel more joyously and passionately alive than you ever have before, and empowered to go forth and change the world with the gifts that only your awakened self can offer.

As you awaken your Kundalini, you begin to liberate more energy not only for your spiritual life but for your career, your creativity, and your service in the world.

Would you like to discover how you can use your spiritual body to heal yourself and others — and find wellness, balance, and inner peace in your life?

My personal mantra is "Awaken your inner Guru" within yourself by kundalini awakening. I believe everyone can and should experience this awakening. Experiencing the bliss of oneness means Kundalini mastery. If you want your kundalini awakened under the guidance by Ricardo B Serrano, please **read Awakening your Kundalini in my book Return to Oneness with Shiva**.

See Kundalini Awakening, p 9; What is the Self?, p. 15; The Guru is the Means, p. 23; Nectar of the Inner Self, p. 29; Origin of the Heart, p. 53; Sri Devi Stotram, p. 92; Atma (Soul) Yoga, p. 103; Shiva Sutras & Soham, p. 111; Mahavidya, p. 120; Chakras, p. 126; Yuan Shen, p. 130

Meditation on Three Hearts awakens the kundalini because the lower dantien is grounded or connected to the center of the earth where the Serpent of Light, inner Shakti, is sourced. One may experience being enveloped by divine light, and a feeling of ecstasy, bliss and oneness with all, and becomes a channel of Divine energy when a person does Meditation on Three Hearts. *Benefits of Meditation on Three Hearts*: With bigger chakras and energy body, the practitioner becomes healthier, more intuitive and intelligent, and becomes a more powerful healer.

The Meditation on Three Hearts is a form of world service. By blessing the earth with loving-kindness, you fill the world with positive spiritual energies. The blessings can be directed to organizations, specific countries, or group of nations. The potency of the blessings is increased many times when done by a group of persons. A group of seven people meditating together is said to carry the same energy as more than one hundred individuals meditating separately. When practiced by a large number of people, the meditation can miraculously heal the entire earth; thereby making it more harmonious and peaceful.

The Three Hearts thus refer to the navel, heart and crown chakras - three dantiens. The navel chakra or lower dantien is included to ground the physical and energy body with the center of earth. The heart chakra or middle dantien is an energy center in front of a person's chest. It is the energy counterpart of the physical heart. The heart chakra is the center for compassion, joy, affection, consideration, mercy, and other refined emotions. The heart chakra is a replica, or twin of the center of the crown chakra. The crown chakra or upper dantien, is the center of illumination, or divine love, or oneness with all. Therefore, it is a powerful meditation used to achieve kundalini awakening, illumination, self-realization or cosmic consciousness. Chant *Namo Kuan Shi Yin Pu Sa* to cultivate the same compassion embodied by Kuan Yin Bodhisattva.

Those who intend to practice regularly the Meditation on Three Hearts, however, should practice self-purification or character-building through daily reflection so their positive characteristics will be magnified or activated.

Meditation on Three Hearts is now introduced by Acharya Ricardo B Serrano to the public as a powerful tool in bringing about world peace and illumination.

WARNING: The following are cautioned in the practice of Meditation on Three Hearts: those below 18 years of age; those with heart trouble, hypertension, glaucoma and severe kidney ailments; and pregnant women. People with the above conditions who insist on practicing the meditation do so at their own risks, and are encouraged to practice the Enlightenment Qigong forms to treat their conditions naturally. Qigong is necessary when meditation on three hearts is practiced to clear Qi blockages, ground, and balance the Yuan Qi in the body. Meditation on Three Hearts has no contraindications when combined with Qigong, Sri Vidya kundalini meditation. See *Da Bei Zhou*, the great compassion mantra of Kuan Yin Bodhisattva, page 109

Meditation on Three Hearts based on the trinity model refers to the three-force energy fields, three dantiens of the body with its Three Treasures: Jing, Qi, Shen, and Heaven-Human-Earth. The Tai Chi circle contains the Yang force (white color), the Yin force (black color), and the centerline or Yuan force (center curving line), also represents a three-force energy field.

"Without love of nature and Self, Self-realization (return to oneness by being in the flow of Qi) cannot be attained."– Acharya Ricardo B Serrano

Meditation on Three Hearts Procedure:

Invoke for divine blessing: *Father, I humbly invoke Thy divine blessing! For protection, guidance, help and illumination! With thanks and full faith.*

Connect mentally your lower dantien (navel) with the center of earth.

Activate the heart chakra, concentrate on it, and also activate the crown chakra, concentrate on it. Then bless with your hands the entire earth with loving-kindness simultaneously through the crown, heart and navel chakras.

From the heart of God,

Let the entire earth be blessed with loving-kindness. Let the entire earth be blessed with great joy, happiness and divine peace.

Let the entire earth be blessed with understanding, harmony, good will and will to do good. So be it!

From the heart of God,

Let the hearts of all sentient beings be filled with divine love and kindness. Let the hearts of all sentient beings be filled with great joy, happiness and divine peace.

Let the hearts of all sentient beings be filled with understanding, harmony, good will and will to do good. With thanks, so be it!

To achieve illumination, concentrate on the point of light on top of head, on the AUM, and on the gap between the two AUMs.

To release excess energy, bless the earth with light, love and peace by connecting your lower dantien (navel) with the center of earth. Give thanks! Massage the physical body, and do physical exercise for about three to five minutes.

Most qi-healers and seekers on the spiritual path who want to attain self-realization are beset with *Kundalini syndromes* due to qi blockages or congestion in the blood and meridian circulation. As a long-time Qi-healer and seeker to attain realization of Buddha nature, having personally suffered physical, mental and emotional kundalini syndromes for years, I have been personally looking for a permanent solution to kundalini syndromes. Four solutions to treat kundalini syndromes which have greatly assisted me personally are basically: Guo Lin Qi Gong, Coconut Ketogenic Diet, Sri Vidya kundalini meditation and Meditation on Three Hearts with drinking alkaline kangen water and chanting the Hare Krishna mantra with Sri Vidya mantras and *Wing Chun forms* that effectively remove the qi blockages and acidic wastes in the body's meridian and blood circulation.

Bliss comes from within. Do not seek it without.

I am Spirit Soul. Aham Brahmasmi.

-Acharya Ricardo B Serrano

Sri Vidya Upasana is the sacred secret wisdom for accessing the Divine Mother (Adi Shakti, Para, Sri Devi) to experience grace, beauty, abundance, magic, wellness, peace and bliss. The Divine Mother is the Source. The worlds come out of her, exist because of her and then return back into her. She is the stage upon which the play of the world goes on. She is wisdom, bliss and consciousness incarnate. Sri Devi is the light behind everything through which the light and the dark can be perceived. Om Anandamayi Chaitanyamayi Satyamayi Parame. See **Sri Vidya and Mantras, Return to Oneness with Shiva**

See Kundalini Awakening, p. 12; Garland of Letters, pages 27, 28 and 126; Sri Yantra, pages 40, 44, 47, 52, 92, 120, 125, 128

About the Author

Master Pranic Healer Ricardo B Serrano, R.Ac. integrates pranic healing with Enlightenment Qigong forms, acupuncture, herbs and acupressure. He is a certified Qigong teacher trained by Pan Gu Shen Gong Master Ou Wen Wei, Sheng Zhen Gong Master Li Jun Feng, Qi Dao Master Lama Tantrapa, Wuji Qigong Master Michael Winn, Zhan Zhuang Qigong Master Richard Mooney, Pranic Healing Grand Master Choa Kok Sui, Master Nona Castro, Mang Mike Nator, Raja Choudhury, Sifu Samuel Kwok, Tai Chi Master Helen Liang, Master Faye Li Yip and Dr. Master Zhi Gang Sha of Great Compassion Mantra. He is also a certified Merkabah teacher trained by Merkabah Master Alton Kamadon. He founded Atma (Soul) Yoga of Immortality and Wing Chun Qigong.

His eight books Six healing Qigong sounds, Return to Oneness with Shiva, Oneness with Shiva, Return to Oneness with the Tao, Return to Oneness with Spirit, Meditation and Qigong Mastery, Keys to Healing and Self-Mastery, and The Cure & Cause of Cancer comprise altogether his Master Pranic Healer thesis for the Integral Studies of Inner Sciences. His blogsites are: freedomhealthrecovery.com/blog, keystohealing.ca, wingchunqigong.ca and innerway.ca. His websites are: holisticwebs.com, freedomhealthrecovery.com, qigonghealer.com, qiwithoutborders.org, and qigongmastery.ca

The Qigong Healing Method was formulated by Ricardo B Serrano, R.Ac. because there is no one perfect Qigong form or therapy that is a cure-all for every known disease.

You can contact Acharya Ricardo B Serrano through his websites for Shaktipat, meditation, Wing Chun Kung Fu and Qigong workshops and for Oriental medical therapies – acupuncture, acupressure, herbal consultations, intranasal light therapy, and Qi-healing - for your addiction and chronic health conditions.
Meditate on the Self as the Self. To become aware of *So'ham*, "I am That," is to attain oneness with the Higher Self and chant *Namo Kuan Shi Yin Pu Sa, Da Bei Zhou* to cultivate the same compassion embodied by Kuan Yin Bodhisattva.

May you practice the five Enlightenment Qigong Forms through the seven books and videos with Qigong Workshops by Ricardo B Serrano, R.Ac. because you hold the keys to healing and returning to oneness through understanding the basic theories and principles behind Qigong science, and by practicing these ancient meditation and Qigong forms regularly together with Guo Lin Qigong and Six healing Qigong sounds and Tai Chi 8 form.

Guo Lin Qigong form, also known as "Walking Qi Gong", was invented by Guo Lin (1909-1984). Guo Lin was diagnosed with cancer in the 1940s and underwent extensive surgery. Using the traditional Qi Gong her grandfather had taught her and her knowledge of TCM, she developed a new form to aid in her recovery now known as Guo Lin Qi Gong. After a full recovery she began to teach to the public. Following the success enjoyed by many other patients, in 1977 she approached the National Health Department to advocate a new approach to cancer combining the strengths of western medicine, traditional Chinese medicine and Guo Lin Qi Gong. In 1982, with government support, she built a new hospital to carry her work further which has assisted thousands of cancer patients. Guo Lin died in 1984 of a sudden stroke. Guo Lin Qigong is an important modality included in the updated The Cure & Cause of Cancer book.

Mitochondrial dysfunction is the root cause of chronic diseases. For more information on intranasal light therapy, read *Meditation and Qigong Mastery*, *Return to Oneness with the Tao*, and *The Cure and Cause of Cancer*.